POPULIST RELIGION AND
LEFT-WING POLITICS
IN FRANCE, 1830-1852

POPULIST RELIGION AND LEFT-WING POLITICS IN FRANCE, 1830-1852

Edward Berenson

Princeton University Press
Princeton, New Jersey

Copyright © 1984 by Princeton University Press
Published by Princeton University Press,
41 William Street, Princeton, New Jersey 08540
In the United Kingdom: Princeton University Press,
Guildford, Surrey

ISBN 0-691-05396-0

Publication of this book has been aided by a grant from The Andrew
W. Mellon Foundation

This book has been composed in Linotron Aldus
Clothbound editions of Princeton University Press books
are printed on acid-free paper, and binding materials
are chosen for strength and durability.

Printed in the United States of America by
Princeton University Press, Princeton, New Jersey

To my parents
Norman and Claire Berenson

CONTENTS

LIST OF ILLUSTRATIONS

LIST OF TABLES

ACKNOWLEDGMENTS

Many people have helped and guided me in preparing this book. During my undergraduate years at Princeton Arno Mayer kindled my interest in history and made me think about other important things as well. Since then he has aided and influenced me even more than he may realize. At the University of Rochester I had the good fortune to study with Sanford Elwitt, Christopher Lasch, William J. McGrath, and Perez Zagorin. They gave me superb training, and I found inspiration in the quality and intellectual breadth of their work. Sanford Elwitt advised my thesis with unfailing interest, and he read it with care and critical discernment.

Ted Margadant, John Merriman, William Sewell, and Maurice Agulhon provided indispensable advice and encouragement as I began my research, and later on Arno Mayer, Jerry Seigal, and William Reddy took time out from their own work to criticize early versions of my chapters. Susanna Barrows, Herrick Chapman, Lynn Hunt, Keith Luria, Joby Margadant, and Jeffrey Sawyer all read the entire manuscript, and their comments and criticisms did much to improve it. I am especially indebted to Ted Margadant for the example of his own work and for his detailed commentary on mine. My greatest debt is to Debora Silverman, friend and colleague, who read successive drafts of the book and gave me expert help when I needed it most.

Librarians at the Bibliothèque Nationale in Paris provided generous assistance, as did archivists at Vincennes and in the departments of the Alpes de Haute-Provence, Bouches-du-Rhône, Côte-d'Or, Drôme, Hérault, Nièvre, Var, and the Yonne. In particular I want to thank Mme Viré, archivist for the Diocese of Digne.

A generous fellowship from the Social Science Research Council made my lengthy stay in France possible, and grants from UCLA's Academic Senate enabled me to complete the research for this project. I am grateful to Miriam Brokaw of Princeton University Press for her advice and encouragement; to Gretchen Oberfranc for her excellent editing; and to Jill Penny Nirlo for her rapid and efficient typing.

As I was completing revisions on the manuscript Catherine Johnson brightened everything with love and exuberance. This book is dedicated to my parents. I owe them more than I can express.

INTRODUCTION

The vast historiography of the French Second Republic, with its detailed studies of virtually every aspect of this fascinating and tumultuous period, has strangely neglected one of the most important political forces of the era: the coalition of democrats and socialists that opposed Louis Napoleon's conservative government from late 1848 to the coup d'état of 2 December 1851. In his general studies of 1848 in France, Maurice Agulhon has done much to rehabilitate the republicans, to rescue the "quarante-huitards" from scholarly indifference.[1] But there has been no full-fledged study of the democratic-socialist—alternatively called "democ-soc" or "Montagnard"—coalition that valiantly opposed Louis Napoleon's government during the three and one-half years of quasi-democracy that followed the Parisian insurrection of June 1848. By no means was this an opposition group of marginal significance. Through an elaborate network of propaganda diffusion and an ideological appeal that resonated in the popular culture of humble Frenchmen, the leaders of this coalition managed to build a constituency of peasants, artisans, and modest members of the middle class. In the electoral contest of May 1849 the democ-socs captured some 35 percent of the vote,* and they won an absolute majority in a fifth of France's departments, concentrating in the Center and the South.[2] Despite mounting political repression, the democ-socs maintained their electoral support in the important by-elections of March 1850, and in response to Louis Napoleon's coup, some 100,000 rural Frenchmen rose up in defense of the "democratic and social republic."

---

* The democ-socs garnered 2.36 million votes, while the conservative coalition of Bonapartists, Orleanists, and Legitimists won some 3.5 million. Jacques Bouillon, "Les Démocrates-socialistes aux élections de 1849," *Revue française de sciences politiques*, 6 (1956), 78.

Although this leftist alliance failed to gain the allegiance of a majority of the nation's newly enfranchised voters—universal manhood suffrage had been decreed in February 1848—it did appear to control the southern half of the country. Complementing this regional success was the democ-socs' strong showing in Paris as well as in a large number of France's provincial cities. Despite this urban support, however, the bulk of the democ-socs' strength came from the peasants and rural artisans of central and southern France.[3] How and why so many rural Frenchmen committed themselves after 1848 to an urban-based party of democratic socialists is the subject of this study.

Why another study of 1848? During the 1960s and early 1970s historians in France produced a number of weighty *thèses d'état* devoted to the social, economic, and cultural history of rural France in the nineteenth century. All of these works tended, almost inexorably, to focus on the Second Republic.[4] Since the social and economic history of rural France in the last century was almost totally uncharted, this postwar generation of scholars, impelled by the concerns of *Annales* School historiography, set out to study the state of provincial agriculture and industry and to understand the effects of the mid-century crisis. They looked at demographic growth and analyzed its effects on economy and social structure. They painted portraits of the social groups in their regions, and in some cases they sought to illuminate the mentalities and outlooks of the various groups in question. Political developments, however, were often treated in a perfunctory manner, and even when they were handled with originality and sophistication, as in the cases of Philippe Vigier and, particularly, Agulhon,[5] they tended to slight the interplay of national political organization and ideology on the one hand and local politics on the other. What is lacking in the historiography of the Second Republic is analysis of precisely this confluence of national and local politics and ideology.

It is significant that Vigier, Georges Dupeux, Agulhon, and the other students of Ernest Labrousse who each set out to work on a different region of rural France (Vigier studied the Alps; Dupeux, the Loir-et-Cher; Agulhon, Lower Provence) focused not on the single year 1848 but rather on the four-year period of the Second Republic. Older historiography—and especially that which commemorated in 1948 the centennial of the revolution—had concentrated on the short-lived "springtime of the people," the revolutionary interlude that lasted only from February to June 1848. This older historiography essentially ignored the latter three and one-half of the Second Republic's four years because its practitioners held firm to the belief that French history took place in Paris and turned on Great Events and Important Personalities. Once the June workers' uprising had been crushed, the Great Events of 1848—so these historians assumed—came to an abrupt end. The rest of the Second Republic, therefore, afforded only minor interest. That many pre–World War II academic historians were loyal republicans added to their desire to ignore the presidency of "Napoléon le petit," the infamous violator of republican legality.[6] After World War II the newly ascendant *Annales* School banished this "histoire événementielle" and shifted the scholarly spotlight toward social and economic structures and toward the lives, culture, and aspirations of ordinary people. In so doing, the *Annales* methodology, albeit inadvertently, renewed the study of 1848.

Although the revolutionary events of the springtime of the people appeared to lose importance as a result of the new questions and orientations of the 1960s, the Second Republic as a whole took on new significance. For prewar historians, 1848 had been a turning point that failed to turn. To the *Annales*-inspired scholars who observed nineteenth-century France from the perspective of the rural provinces, the period 1848-1851 seemed, on the contrary, to represent a pivotal historical juncture. During these four years the different regions of rural France revealed for the first time the political tendencies that were to last almost to our own age. The Second Republic, moreover, saw the nation's last *ancien régime*-style crisis of subsistence turn into the first contemporary-style crisis of overproduction. Under Louis Napoleon the modern French bureaucratic state consolidated its power nationwide. And, perhaps most important, this period marked the birth of mass democratic politics in France. Unlike the First Republic, when most peasants declined to exercise a newly acquired franchise,[7] after 1848 some 70 percent of eligible peasant voters went to the polls. Not only did unprecedented numbers of rural Frenchmen participate in democratic politics, but in the Center and South they shunned the *notables* who had long dominated rural France and voted massively for the nation's left-most political organization.

French historians' pathbreaking work in nineteenth-century social history stimulated American interest in the period, and in the late 1960s United States scholars began to apply the questions and methods of their own somewhat different social history to the study of France's 1848 Revolution. Inspired by the seminal work of Charles Tilly, Americans employed quantitative techniques to measure and evaluate the violence and repression that characterized France's revolutionary mid-century. Tilly argued that forms of violent protest changed as individuals' actions were shaped less by allegiance to traditional communities and increasingly by membership in formally constituted organizations. Before 1848 protest consisted mainly of sporadic community challenges to the perceived encroachment of a national government and economy. After the February Revolution protest tended to involve large-scale associations that sought not to limit state power but to conquer some or all of it for themselves.[8] Economic changes affected political behavior only in a general and indirect way. It was the growth of formal organizations that most profoundly and directly influenced political action.

In an exemplary study that grew out of Tilly's concerns, Ted W. Margadant sought to explain the massive rural insurrection of December 1851 in terms of "political modernization"—that is, the rise of associations determined to contend for power on a national level.[9] Margadant showed convincingly that economic change played only an indirect role in sparking rebellion. In his view, new political organizations called Montagnard secret societies channeled rural grievances into a movement capable of challenging the state. Beginning in the aftermath of June 1848, France's increasingly conservative government unleashed a crescendo of repression that ultimately forced the opposition underground and convinced it of the need to prepare for insurrection. Thus it was the government's systematic effort to repress all voices of opposition that moved leaders of the republican left to build an underground network of secret societies. Margadant called attention to the Second Republic's dynamic of repression and resistance, and John M. Merriman went on to devote an entire volume to the subject. Merriman analyzed the process of repression itself, and his study chronicled in fascinating detail the agonizing step-by-step destruction of the French left from mid-1848 to the Bonapartist coup.[10]

Though most recent students of 1848 consider themselves to be social historians, the works produced by French scholars have an emphasis somewhat different from those of their American colleagues. French studies of 1848 have been primarily concerned with politicization—with how ordinary people became committed to republican politics. Americans have focused on political mobilization, violence, and repression—on why Frenchmen rebelled. Despite these differences, the two groups have generally shared a social-scientific interest in phenomena that are measurable. French historians based much of their analysis on economic and electoral statistics; Americans studied the social composition of insurrectionary crowds, evaluated data on violence and repression, and analyzed aspects of the mid-century French economy. This unusually rich body of French and American historiography has provided a sophisticated picture of France's early- and mid-nineteenth-century social and economic history. And it forms a solid foundation upon which to base new studies of more elusive cultural phenomena. The cultural roots of such problems as politicization and rebellion are difficult, perhaps impossible, to measure, but cultural analysis becomes much less hazardous when it can be moored to the kinds of economic and social histories that French and American scholars have produced over the past two decades.

Maurice Agulhon was the first historian of the Second Republic to undertake a cultural analysis of peasant politicization. Why, he asked, did Mediterranean peasants abandon their conservative or apolitical heritage to embrace democratic socialism in 1848? The answer did not lie in altered economic circumstances, for Agulhon found that the economy of Mediterranean

France changed very little during the first half of the nineteenth century.[11] A native of southern France, Agulhon turned his attention to Mediterranean village culture and found that subtle changes in patterns of social interaction prepared peasants and artisans for the new democratic and egalitarian politics of 1848. In examining culture, Agulhon discovered the key to political transformation.

Among American historians of nineteenth-century France, it was William H. Sewell Jr. who pioneered the cultural analysis of political change. In his work on Marseille, Sewell argued that politicization in the 1830s and 1840s was related to cultural influences from outside the city. Those trades that recruited apprentices and journeymen mostly from the immediate families of their own workers tended to be immune to new political ideas. But trades open to workers from outside Marseille felt the influence of France's mounting political effervescence and moved toward socialist politics during Louis Philippe's July Monarchy. Though Sewell's model suggested why some groups changed their politics while others remained the same, it could not show why the content of Marseille's new politics was socialism. His later work on the language of labor endeavored to explain skilled workers' socialist commitment through an analysis of artisan culture. Sewell argued that during the first half of the nineteenth century artisans transformed the communitarian heritage of the Old Regime's guilds into a cooperatist socialism based on a moral and economic community of worker-owners.[12]

All of these works provided foundations and models for my own foray into a social history concerned with culture and ideology. Like other French and American historians, I was fascinated by the impressive peasant commitment to the extreme left that occurred during the Second Republic, and, having benefited from the work of Agulhon and Vigier, Margadant, Merriman, and Sewell, I could go on to explore the politics of 1848 in new ways. We know much about how economic and demographic developments influenced peasant political commitment, and how the interplay of repression and resistance helped to trigger open rebellion. But historians have not closely analyzed the political ideas that circulated during the Second Republic. Nor have they explicitly studied how these ideas were diffused and precisely why 1848's democratic-socialist ideology appealed to rural Frenchmen with little prior political experience. Moreover, no one has devoted an in-depth study to the democ-socs themselves, to the political group that engineered the new peasant allegiance to the left.

In order to understand the role of political ideas, historians must comprehend not only the ideas themselves but also the precise means by which they are transmitted. They must, furthermore, attempt to perceive the junctures at which the political ideas of an elite intersect with the experiences, mentalities, and everyday needs of the masses. The key, it seems to me, to understanding how mid-century rural discontent was transformed into republican commitment lies in an analysis of the interaction of popular religious beliefs, social and economic malaise, and democ-soc ideology and propaganda.

The role of democ-soc ideologues and militants, especially at the local level, is absolutely central to an understanding of the Second Republic's rural swing to the left. In the aftermath of the December 1848 presidential election—a contest in which Louis Napoleon Bonaparte won an overwhelming mandate—a newly formed coalition of socialists and left-wing republicans made an explicit decision to convert rural Frenchmen to the democ-soc cause. The members of this coalition saw in universal suffrage a limitless opportunity for social change, but unlike the republicans of the Provisional Government (February-June 1848), the democ-socs devised a clear-cut strategy for winning the support of the rural masses. In so doing, the democ-socs became the first Frenchmen to attempt to construct a national political party, the first to campaign nationwide, the first to prepare a series of national elections under universal suffrage, and the first to undertake the political education of the peasantry, to attempt to bring rural dwellers into a system of democratic politics. Though government repression prevented the Montagnards from establishing a nationwide Paris-directed political party, the democ-socs nonetheless did succeed in constructing an elaborate network of propaganda diffusion. This network carried democ-soc pamphlets, brochures, songs, news-papers, lithographs, and almanacs from France's principal pro-vincial towns to even the most remote villages of their rural hinterlands. And it was through this process of diffusion that humble peasants and artisans were exposed to the ideas and practical programs of the republican left.

Clearly, exposure is not enough to guarantee commitment. In central and southern France seething economic discontent and a religious culture based on populist conceptions of Ca-tholicism predisposed villagers to the doctrine of republican propagandists. For these propagandists had fashioned their own political views out of an unorthodox and essentially populist version of Catholicism. Thus the existence of parallel religious mentalities facilitated the democ-socs' effort to politicize the peasantry. Religion provided the bridge that enabled two such apparently diverse groups to span wide social and cultural dif-ferences in order to forge a political alliance. Historians have tended to assume that peasants had to undergo dechristianiza-tion—that is, shed their "traditional" beliefs—before they could demonstrate allegiance to progressive or "modern" politics.[13] Tradition, in this view, had to give way as a result of techno-logical or other changes before modernity could take hold. But in mid-nineteenth-century France it was precisely the remain-ing elements of "tradition"—namely, religiosity*—in both the rural community and the democ-soc politicians that enabled the latter to awaken peasants to a progressive democratic ideology. Viewing the world in terms of Christian moral principles, but committed to the institutions and methods of mass democracy, the democ-socs were able to transform the peasants' populist and pragmatic Christianity into a rudimentary, but nonetheless genuine, allegiance to democratic socialism. Far from being in-compatible with progressive democratic ideas, Catholic reli-giosity made such ideas meaningful and acceptable to millions of peasants in mid-nineteenth-century France.

* Throughout this study I follow Carlo Ginzburg in using the term "reli-giosity" to mean the set of religious beliefs, feelings, mentalities, and practices exhibited by an individual or social group. See Carlo Ginzburg, *The Cheese and the Worms* (New York: Penguin Books, 1982), pp. 17, 38.

Who, in fact, were these democ-socs, and how do they differ from what has become the standard image of the men of '48? In many ways the Montagnard coalition of the Second Republic was a diverse lot. It included those July Monarchy radical republicans who never really flirted with "utopian" socialism—men such as Ledru-Rollin, the lawyer d'Alton Shée, and journalist Charles Delescluze. And the coalition embraced long-standing socialists such as Louis Blanc and Pierre Leroux along with one-time disciples of the great conspirator Auguste Blanqui. Both Martin-Bernard, president of La Solidarité républicaine, and Alphonse Laponneraye, editor of Marseille's influential paper *La Voix du peuple*, had paid their early political dues in Blanqui's secret societies. Lamennais, the Legitimist abbé turned democratic firebrand, quickly became a prominent member of the coalition. And Victor Considérant, director of the Fourierist journal *Démocratie pacifique*, led his followers out of the desert of abstract utopian theory into the nitty-gritty world of practical politics and the democ-soc coalition. Working-class spokesmen such as Martin Nadaud and Agricol Perdiguier counted themselves among the Montagnards,[14] as did the radical doctor Raspail and romantic writers like Eugène Sue. Despite their divergent backgrounds, all these men had developed during the 1840s a belief in the need to resurrect the moral principles of early Christianity in order to provide a new foundation for the nation's political and economic life. It was this shared Christian-moral commitment that provided the intellectual basis for the entente of republicans and socialists during the Second Republic.

By the fall of 1848 this convergent collection of French radicals came to share two other fundamental convictions. The first held that universal (manhood) suffrage could produce revolutionary change if and only if it were accompanied by a massive and disciplined campaign of political education. Suffrage was not, as members of the Provisional Government seemed to believe, a political panacea that would inevitably produce the desired social transformation. The Montagnards understood that political and social change would come about not through the airy rhetoric that has rendered the '48'ers infamous but through patient organizing and realistic proposals for reform. The second conviction shared by those who formed the democ-soc coalition was the absolute need to address the social question, to achieve radical changes in the lives of France's humble classes. The democ-socs all agreed that these radical changes could be realized through the institutions of republican democracy, but they understood that such progress would not come about automatically. Thus Montagnards were united in the belief that employment for all able-bodied Frenchmen should be guaranteed by the Constitution itself and that the republican state should encourage the collectivization of industry through financial and political aid to producers' cooperatives.

To be sure, the coalition remained a coalition; its members, agreeing on fundamentals, differed over the lengths they were willing to go in the effort to transform society. Whereas all members of the alliance sought to nationalize certain key sectors of the economy, some proposed a much more extensive list of nationalizations than others. In the field of taxation, all democ-socs fought for the abolition of indirect imposts, but they differed over whether a revamped republican tax structure should be progressive or proportional. All coalition members sought to expand peasant landownership, but some wanted to limit government initiative in this realm to providing cheap state-guaranteed credit, while others—the majority—sought more widespread state intervention.

Positions within the coalition ranged from moderate to radical, but for a variety of reasons the radical wing determined the specifics of the Montagnard program. First, the failure of the Provisional Government and of Cavaignac's equally brief republican reign (July-December 1848) had discredited moderate republicanism and thus enhanced the standing of those on the left.[15] Second, the need to reach out to poor workers and peasants who suffered from the mid-century economic crisis helped to move the coalition's center of gravity toward the left. Finally, heavy government repression and the state's increasing disregard for basic liberties convinced those moderate republicans who decided to oppose Louis Napoleon of the need for tough countermeasures in order to preserve the republic. By 1850 these moderates had joined the democ-socs and acquiesced to their radical program.

This study focuses, then, on the embryonic mass political party whose members called themselves *démocrates-socialistes* or simply democ-socs. It analyzes the innovative ideology that Montagnard publicists fashioned out of unorthodox Christian beliefs and explores in depth the actual process by which this ideology was transmitted to humble Frenchmen in the rural provinces of the Center and South. This process of diffusion is placed in the context of the underlying socio-economic and cultural conditions that made certain rural dwellers receptive to the democ-socs' ideological appeal. The study's final section evaluates the extent to which these new political ideas took hold in rural communities, and it concludes with some suggestions about the ways in which the democratic-socialist politics of the Second Republic influenced the later development of both French republicanism and French socialism. During the Second Republic socialism was fused inextricably to the republican tradition. Future socialists would aim their criticism not so much at the republic per se as at its failure to live up to a social-republican ideal. The French Revolution gave birth to this republican ideal, but it was during the four years following 1848 that the French left defined the content of that ideal as socialism.

POPULIST RELIGION AND
LEFT-WING POLITICS
IN FRANCE, 1830-1852

CHAPTER I

THE ECONOMIC ROOTS
OF POLITICIZATION

The evolution of France's economy and social structure over the first half of the nineteenth century created an environment favorable to a broad political coalition of artisans and market-oriented peasants in 1848. By no means were economic circumstances directly responsible for the political allegiances of the Second Republic, but analysis of the period's economic conditions does help to explain the nature and meaning of mid-century democratic-socialist ideology. Moreover, a view of how the material conditions of peasants and artisans changed provides a sense of what made both groups receptive to the religious-based ideas of the republican left.

Beneath the seemingly placid surface of French farming, a number of important changes took place during the first half of the nineteenth century. Though French agriculture was neither more consolidated nor more mechanized in 1848 than it was in 1815, a quiet agricultural revolution produced a 50 percent growth in farm productivity during those years. As a result in large part of these advances in productivity, the number of peasant proprietors increased faster than did the size of the rural population, and the amount of peasant land grew at the expense of large-scale property owners. Increased output made it possible for peasants to remain on the land despite population growth, and they took advantage of improved grain yields to devote less land to growing their own food and more to cash crops. Thus, between 1815 and 1848 peasants increasingly shifted away from subsistence farming toward market involvement. By no means, however, did this commercialization of peasant farming make small cultivators prosperous, for with growing market involvement came both skyrocketing debt and growing vulnerability to economic fluctuations. Peasants went into debt to extend their holdings and to introduce new intensive methods of cultivation. Consequently, they perpetually owed money to land speculators, to insurers, and to the middlemen who marketed their products. Subsistence was not an issue in 1848; rather, by mid-century, peasant economic problems grew increasingly out of their commercial and financial difficulties. Thus, small cultivators, like their working-class compatriots, were open to an ideological appeal that promised a plausible means of severing their dependence upon those who possessed liquid capital. To this end, the democ-socs offered the peasantry an alternative society built on Christian moral values, unlimited credit, and democratized land ownership.

France's industrial situation resembled in many ways the agricultural one. During the first half of the nineteenth century the industrial sphere's façade of apparent stability hid major changes. Though this period registered few advances in technology, little growth in industrial concentration, and only a slight increase in the size of the labor force, industrial output expanded by 75 percent. This surprising development resulted almost entirely from the heightened exploitation of labor. Growing demand at home and intensifying competition caused by the extension of markets forced employers and master artisans to deepen the division of labor and resort to subcontracting in an effort to reduce costs of production. Such cost-cutting measures threatened artisans' skills and magnified alienation on the job. In some industries market expansion produced a situation in which commercial intermediaries known as merchant capitalists became the real employers of labor. It was they who assigned work, they who marketed finished products, and they who reaped the bulk of the profits. These merchant capitalists did not directly oversee production; they owed their economic position solely to the reserves of liquid capital that they possessed. As a result of these developments, master artisans who owned small workshops shared to an increasing degree the dependent status of wage laborers.

These threats to workers' skills and to the independence of master artisans made both groups receptive to a moral critique of capitalism that endeavored to bolster workers' dignity by fostering identification with a populist Jesus Christ. Skilled workers and master artisans refused to view labor as a commodity. And they ultimately turned to a democratic-socialist ideology that condemned the market system as immoral for its tendency to deny workers their individuality and to reduce their labor to just another salable good. As an alternative to wage labor, the democ-socs proposed to establish a system of producers' cooperatives, which would be founded with the aid of government credit and owned by groups of associated workers. In a process that might be labeled "collectivization from below" (see Chapter IV), cooperatist production would ultimately replace capitalist enterprise. This transformation, the democ-socs believed, would occur peacefully and result from the presumed ability of the cooperatives to outcompete their capitalist rivals. Ultimately, the exploitative system of wage labor would be replaced by a new economic edifice founded on the Christian tenets of fraternity and equality.

One of the salutary effects of recent work in French economic history is that we no longer measure French economic development by the traditional British yardstick. Maurice Lévy-Leboyer, T. J. Markovitch, J. Toutain[1] and others have shown that, despite inadequate coal reserves, slow mechanization in the textile industry, and lack of substantial industrial and agricultural concentration, the French economy grew considerably during the first half of the nineteenth century.[2] Though no "take-off" period can be pinpointed, both industrial and agricultural production advanced more than twice as rapidly as population between 1800 and 1850.[3] The important advances registered in commerce during the first half of the century testify to the growth in agriculture and industry. The tonnage of goods transported by road increased 34 percent between 1835 and 1851. Rail transport, just beginning in 1841, increased more than 1,000 percent by 1851. Personal travel advanced dramatically, as did postal communication.[4]

In the industrial sector, small artisan workshops made the overwhelming contribution to the steady growth in the output of French manufactured goods.* During the Second Empire artisans still made up more than three-quarters of the industrial work force, and the revenue from Artisan production was four times that of Industry.[5] In the agricultural sphere, the regions of central and southern France, where small farms predominated, displayed the most spectacular increases in yields.

Given the slow pace of mechanization and the lack of agricultural and industrial consolidation, how did the French economy manage to grow so rapidly? The primary source of agricultural growth during the first half of the nineteenth century was a dramatic increase in the productivity of the land. Cereal yields grew by 40 percent between 1815 and 1850,[6] and in some departments of central France grain yields doubled. Moreover, the joint effect of the vastly improved yields plus the creation of new arable land by drainage, conversion of pasture, and forest clearance resulted in a 70 percent growth in the amount of agricultural produce during the period.[7] This agricultural progress occurred before more than a tiny section of the railroad network was in place, before the introduction of harvesting machines, before the use of chemical fertilizers, before modern ploughs had replaced the old *araires*, and before the scythe had overtaken the sickle as the main harvesting tool. French cultivators produced a kind of quiet agricultural revolution by skillfully using the resources available to them: abundant labor and intensive cultivation of their small plots.

The fundamental cause of the marked increase in agricultural productivity was the introduction of mixed farming after 1830.[8] Stimulated by growing demand for agricultural products, especially in urban areas, and by the stepped-up efforts of agronomers, French cultivators began to plant such fodder crops as

---

*Throughout this chapter I have followed Markovitch in using "Industry" (capital "I") to refer to all enterprises that employ more than ten workers; "Artisanat" refers to all firms that employ fewer than ten and whose *patron* works alongside his hired labor in addition to directing the firm. Industry with a lowercase "i" refers to "Industry" and "Artisanat" combined—that is, to all production that does not belong to agriculture. T. J. Markovitch "Le Revenu industriel et artisanal sous la Monarchie de Juillet et le Second Empire," *Economies sociétés*, no. 4 (April 1967).

alfalfa, clover, and sainfoin on lands kept fallow under the traditional system of crop rotation. This substitution of planted meadows for fallow land both improved the prospects for successive crops by adding nitrogen to the soil and fed more livestock on a smaller space. Not only was the bigger and better livestock a benefit in itself, but the additional manure in turn enriched the soil. The improved soil produced better crops and better grazing, with the result that productivity spiraled upward. The introduction of mixed farming required little new capital investment and no new technology. It needed slightly more intensive labor, but the densely populated countryside was able to provide additional manpower without difficulty. Even the most modest peasants, therefore, could afford to switch to this new system of crop rotation during the two decades before 1850.[9] Perpetually short of capital but endowed with ample manpower, French cultivators turned to mixed farming as the way to bolster productivity.

The impressive decline of fallow lands during the first half of the nineteenth century testifies to the extent to which farmers applied new agricultural methods. Between 1815 and 1850, some 2 million hectares—nearly 30 percent—of fallow lands were eliminated. At the same time, planted meadows advanced by 1.5 million hectares, registering a 100 percent increase. During the decade 1815-1824, 35 percent of the land in the crop rotation system was left fallow. Two decades later the proportion of fallow had declined to 28 percent; by the 1850s it was down to 21 percent. Far from resisting innovation during the first part of the nineteenth century, French cultivators eliminated more hectares of fallow between 1815 and 1850 than they did in the second half of the century.[10]

Do the aggregate figures cited above mask substantial regional differences? Recent French *thèses* on the social and economic history of particular regions, as well as the Agricultural and Industrial Survey of 1848 and the observations of mid-nineteenth-century commentators, permit a more precise analysis of agricultural growth in selected provinces. Since this study is fundamentally an inquiry into the "republicanization" of France in the immediate wake of 1848, it will focus on those regions that voted republican from 1849 to 1851. Illustrations of agricultural developments, therefore, will be drawn for the most part from the departments of the Center and the South.

In these regions, and, as Ted Margadant demonstrates so convincingly, in the South in particular, the structure of the economy would facilitate political links between artisans and peasants.[11] Much of the industry of southern France was devoted to processing agricultural products. Thus any decline in demand for these goods affected both the peasants who grew the crops and the artisans who turned them into finished products. The situation was altogether different in the North. There economic crisis often triggered town/country antagonism, for the main agricultural crop was grain. After 1848 declining wheat prices harmed farmers and increased unemployment among agricultural laborers. But those reduced prices meant cheaper bread and thus benefited industrial workers, who enjoyed an increase in their purchasing power as a direct result of malaise on the farm. The mid-century crisis tended, therefore, to foster peasant-artisan solidarity in the South, whereas in the North it highlighted the conflicting interests of the agricultural and industrial sectors. For these and other reasons to be discussed below, the democ-socs were to find in the southern half of the country the more favorable terrain for their effort to build an alliance of peasants and artisans.

In the five departments of the Alpine region, agricultural output grew significantly between 1820 and 1851[12] owing primarily to the introduction of mixed farming. In the plains and foothills of the Drôme, for example, planted meadows covered 5,000 hectares in 1833 and over 32,000 twenty years later. Grain output grew by 50 percent between 1800 and 1850, and the new fodder crops spawned a fivefold advance in the number of horses, mules, and cattle. Wheat replaced rye in many Alpine regions, and the potato crop increased spectacularly.[13]

Both peasants and large landowners participated in this agricultural growth. In the flat regions of the Drôme and the Vaucluse, where agriculture showed the greatest progress, most communes comprised a handful of large owners (those who possessed more than thirty hectares) and a multitude of small proprietors (less than fifteen hectares). Domains larger than thirty hectares seldom represented more than 40 percent of any given commune in this region, and 75 percent of the plots were worked directly by their owner.[14] Middle-sized properties (fifteen to thirty hectares) were rare. Large proprietors introduced new agricultural techniques and then quickly communicated them to the local peasantry, many of whom worked part-time for the large owners of their communes.

The improved grain yields registered during this period enabled peasants to devote less of their land to cereals designed for their own consumption and thus permitted them to reserve more acreage for cash crops. Contemporary observers noted that it was small peasants, rather than large landowners, who specialized in such cash crops as wine, silk, and, to a lesser extent, madder.[15] The output of all three expanded rapidly during the first half of the century.[16] Wine was just beginning its take-off in the mid-1840s. Madder output in the Vaucluse soared from 2 million kilograms in 1800 to an average of 20-25 million between 1848 and 1852. In the Drôme the value of raw silk advanced from under 3 million francs in 1811 to 15 million in 1848. Virtually all of the Drôme's 361 communes produced some raw silk by 1851, and silkworm production expanded in the Isère and the Basses-Alpes as well.[17]

Accompanying this Alpine agricultural progress was an extensive subdivision of the land in which peasant property grew at the expense of large- and medium-sized domains. In the Isère, for example, large domains of fifty hectares or more* lost 15.3

---

* All those who have studied property distribution, including Vigier, Goujon, and Dupeux, agree that the classification of property as small, medium, and large depends on the region and the kinds of crops produced. In general, large domains begin at fifty hectares, medium at twenty; small or peasant property refers to domains of less than twenty hectares. In prosperous commercial farming districts, however, the bottom limit of large property is fifteen hectares; middle, five hectares. In an effort to develop a general model of property that allows for regional disparities, some historians have advanced a "social" definition of property. Large property in this model is defined as that which belonged to an important local notable who paid enough taxes to vote during the July Monarchy. Middle-sized property refers to domains cultivated by the owner, but large enough to require additional salaried labor. Small property is that

percent of their surface area between the date of the original cadastre (1820s and 1830s) and 1869. Medium-sized property (twenty to fifty hectares) declined by 18 percent, while small property (ten hectares or less) grew by some 23 percent.[18]

Not only did subdivision of Alpine land ensure peasants a share of the era's agricultural progress, but it also contributed to that development. Most often, it was the least productive of the large and middling domains that were split up for sale to land-hungry peasants. The highly productive large farms, for the most part, remained intact during this period.[19] The increasing cost of agricultural wage labor after 1830, the unpredictability of returns from sharecropping, the declining prices of most agricultural products, as well as the skyrocketing market price of arable land, were the primary economic factors that encouraged owners of relatively unproductive large domains to sell their land during the July Monarchy. Other factors included the attractions of city life and an unwillingness to commit time and energy to new agricultural techniques. Most often, these large owners sold their property to companies of land speculators who then made the terrain accessible to the peasantry by dividing the former domains into numerous small parcels and by allowing buyers to pay for their plots over a period of twenty to thirty years. The proud peasant owners of new lands immediately set out to turn previously uncultivated territory into productive farmland. By applying the new methods of mixed farming, they were able to improve vastly the output of lands cultivated by their former owners under the old system of crop rotation.[20]

The Agricultural and Industrial Survey of 1848 for the Aude signaled notable agricultural progress in that Mediterranean

---

which is sufficient to support a peasant family during a normal agricultural year. On small domains, the owner works his own land along with other family members, and no additional paid labor is engaged. Below small property is *propriété parcellaire*, or subeconomic property—that which cannot support an entire family. At least one family member must work elsewhere for wages or do piecework for others at home. See Pierre Levêque, "La Bourgogne, 1830-1851" (Doctorat d'Etat, University of Paris IV, 1977), vol. 6, pp. 91-92; Pierre Goujon, "Le Vignoble du Saône-et-Loire au XIXᵉ siècle (1815-1870)" (Doctorat du 3ᵉ Cycle, University of Lyon, 1968).

department. Mixed farming had been introduced in virtually every canton, and, as in the Alpine region, the subdivision of property contributed to agricultural improvement. The productivity of lands once neglected by large landowners improved significantly when, split into numerous small parcels, they passed into the hands of the peasantry.[21]

After 1815, mixed farming appeared in the Var, also a Mediterranean department, but here cultivators profited from improved per-hectare grain yields by vastly extending wine production.[22] At the beginning of the nineteenth century, Varois cultivators were already heavily involved in raising cash crops. The techniques of mixed farming simply allowed them to expand their market activity.

Two mid-nineteenth-century agronomers from the Nièvre, a department of central France, lauded the effects of the introduction of mixed farming in their region during the July Monarchy. J. B. Avril noted an average increase in Nivernais wheat yields from ten to fourteen hectoliters per hectare between 1840 and 1851.[23] O. Delafond argued that the Nièvre had witnessed "a veritable agricultural revolution between 1830 and 1848." Writing in 1849, Delafond summed up the causes of the Nièvre's agricultural fortunes: "Endowed with an excellent network of roads that facilitates the marketing of our products of the soil, and having created good natural meadows and extensive planted meadows, Nivernais agriculture has been able to abandon its old and ruinous system of three-field crop rotation. We have definitely entered the period of mixed farming."[24]

Recent findings by French economic historians confirm the mid-nineteenth-century views of Avril and Delafond.[25] According to Guy Thuillier's data, cereal yields improved so much in the Nièvre that by 1851 the department had registered a sizable grain surplus. This favorable food situation, combined with a rapidly growing Parisian demand for wine and the galloping subdivision of property—the number of *cotes foncières* taxed at less than ten francs increased 15 percent between 1835 and 1848—all stimulated a massive shift on the part of local cultivators into wine production.[26] Since vines benefit from intensive cultivation, the subdivision of property, which enabled (or forced) a peasant to devote all his energy to a tiny vineyard, led to markedly improved wine yields. During the four decades that followed the French Revolution, yields per hectare of wine increased by 54 percent. Export of wine from the Nièvre more than tripled between 1820 and 1840 as road and river transport improved significantly and as vineyard acreage grew by 21 percent.[27]

Further to the east, the two Burgundy departments of the Côte-d'Or and the Saône-et-Loire both demonstrated important agricultural progress during the July Monarchy. Fallow declined and wheat yields improved between 1830 and 1852 in all but one arrondissement of these two departments. At the same time, income from agricultural produce increased much faster than population, despite declining prices.[28] The wine-growing regions of eastern Burgundy resembled those of the Nièvre: small peasant property grew 10.6 percent between 1822 and 1846, and productivity was higher in the tiny vineyards than on the large domains.[29]

The agricultural growth that occurred in central and southern France produced two results that were to prove crucial for the politics of the Second Republic. First, agricultural progress brought increasing numbers of small peasants into the market either by providing a surplus of grain that they could sell or by allowing them to shift part of their land into cash crops. Second, it encouraged the subdivision of property both by enabling peasants to eke out a living on ever-smaller plots and by providing the capital and incentive to invest in new land. So long as they could make ends meet, either by working a small plot with the aid of their families or by supplementing the product of a sub-economic plot with family earnings from domestic industry or farm labor, peasants for the most part opted to remain in the countryside. The rural exodus did not begin in earnest until after 1850.[30] That agricultural output increased faster than population during the first half of the nineteenth century made it possible for the rural provinces to continue to support, however inadequately, their burgeoning numbers.[31] This inflated peasant population demanded and, as will be shown below, received more and more land, albeit in increasingly minute pieces. When plots became too small for grain production, even with the increased yields, peasants often shifted to cash crops like wine, as Thuillier discovered in his study of the Nièvre. A grain-producing peasant needed at least ten hectares of land to support his family in the middle of the nineteenth century, but he could make ends meet with only two to four hectares of vine.[32]

Clearly, the substantial agricultural growth of the first half of the nineteenth century did not occur in a vacuum. It was stimulated and sustained by a dramatic rise in demand for farm products. The combination of population increase, urban growth, and higher per capita consumption triggered a 26 percent rise in the demand for cereals, a 50 percent increase in the demand for meat, and a 25 percent rise in the demand for potatoes. Per capita consumption of wheat increased from 1.5 hectoliters per year in 1815 to more than 2.5 three decades later.[33] To a large extent, it was the French peasantry that met this increased demand by producing more and more for a market that extended beyond their respective localities. The political consequences of this new peasant commercial activity were profound. Between 1815 and 1848 large numbers of peasants were subjected more completely to the vicissitudes of the marketplace. At the same time, market production lifted them out of the mental and physical confines of their villages and put them into contact with other social groups. New contacts often introduced peasants to new political ideas, and under the relative liberty of the Second Republic these contacts helped them to translate grievances and aspirations into a nascent ideology.

A look at the mid-century commercial situation in central and southern France provides evidence of extensive peasant market involvement in these regions. The Rhône River, one of the main commercial arteries of pre-railroad France, had long facilitated peasant activity in extra-local markets. After 1815 new roads provided better access to the river, and peasants were encouraged to send more and more products to growing markets in Avignon, Lyon, and Marseille. Rhône commerce did not expand noticeably, however, until steamboats began to navigate the river in significant numbers during the July Monarchy.

Between 1835 and 1850, Rhône shippers increased the number of steamboats on the river from six to fifty-five.[34] Since the cantons that bordered on the Rhône were composed primarily of peasant property (less than fifteen hectares),[35] and since the number of peasant plots was growing rapidly during this period, small cultivators from the plains of the Alpine region almost certainly participated in the expanding market as much as large landowners. Despite obvious benefits, however, the peasants' increasing commercial activity was not without risk. The more they produced for the market, the more their fortunes depended on the commercial situation in places like Grenoble, Avignon, and Lyon and on national and international demand for silk, wine, olives, madder, and other cash crops negotiated in the urban centers. Unfortunately for the Alpine peasants, credit and capital remained in short supply, and the market was extremely unstable.[36] In the late 1840s a decline in the international demand for silk cloth set off a depression that extended downward from master silk weavers in Lyon to the peasants who raised silkworms in remote Alpine villages.

Already accustomed to producing for the market in 1800, the peasants of the Var expanded their commercial activity during the first half of the century. Cultivators raised olives for an international market in olive oil, and after 1820 they began to produce raw silk for French customers as tariff barriers and improvements in transport reoriented Varois commerce away from the Mediterranean region and toward the national market. Although wheat cultivation was still more important than wine production in 1815, grapes soon overtook grain as wine output increased fourfold between 1815 and 1848.[37] The improvement of roads and the growth of Marseille and Toulon, as well as better wheat yields, were responsible for the progress of the Varois wine industry.[38] Thus, in 1848, as in 1815, the Var's peasant cultivators were concerned mainly with the level of demand for their wine, olives, and silk, as well as that for such secondary products as flowers, fruits, and vegetables.[39] Varois trade brought a certain prosperity to the local peasantry, but, as the commercial crisis of 1848-1852 showed, heavy risks were involved as well. Any sharp decline in the demand for particular cash crops could leave small peasant producers in worse condition than the simple subsistence farmer.

The agricultural regions of eastern Burgundy registered increases in commercial activity similar to those of the Var. Between 1830 and 1852 the number of large Burgundy commercial houses taxed at more than Fr 200 increased by 30 percent.[40] During the same period, the number of large industrial enterprises (those taxed at more than Fr 200) in the region remained the same. Burgundy's commercial expansion, therefore, had little to do with large-scale enterprise. Commercial success, for the most part, resulted from the agricultural improvements mentioned above and from the vitality of artisan manufacture.[41] Both were stimulated by the growth of Lyon and the 1833 completion of the Canal de Bourgogne, which linked the Saône to the Seine and made the Paris market much more accessible to Maconnais vintners.[42]

Both the 1848 Agricultural and Industrial Survey and the Agricultural Survey of 1852 show that peasant involvement in commerce was not limited to selected localities, although it *was* concentrated in the Center and South. Using sampling techniques, Ted Margadant has demonstrated that 80 percent of the French cantons that responded to the 1848 survey exported agricultural products or craft goods to markets outside their own boundaries.[43] In the northern half of France these exports tended to consist of two commodities: textiles produced either by rural weavers or by factory workers, and wheat cultivated by large landowners or renters. By contrast, the cantons of southern France marketed such cash crops as wine, eau-de-vie, olives, and raw silk. Figures on property distribution show that in northern France, where most of those involved in agriculture were salaried workers as opposed to proprietors or renters, it was owners of domains larger than twenty hectares who marketed farm products. In southern France, on the other hand, where land was more evenly distributed, peasants were much more likely to work their own plots. Thus, exports from southern cantons came from small holders who owned under twenty hectares as well as from middling and large owners.[44]

The survey of 1848 portrayed the extent to which the agri-

cultural economy had evolved since the peasant rebellions of
1789. No longer did the size of the harvest serve as the measure
of agricultural success. More important after three decades of
rising yields were the level of demand and the selling prices of
agricultural produce. Significantly, the 1848 survey recorded no
complaints about food shortages. Although the severe mid-century economic crisis began with a serious grain shortage in 1846,
the situation had reversed itself by 1848 and quickly turned
into the sort of economic disaster characteristic of industrial
economies—a crisis of overproduction. What concerned a large
percentage of the French cantons surveyed in 1848 especially
those of the Center and South, was their inability to sell their
products.[45] Agricultural prices had plummeted, supply exceeded
demand, credit was lacking, and roads needed repairs to speed
the movement of goods. In canton after canton in southern and
central departments like the Hérault, the Aude, the Yonne, and
the Nièvre, local prosperity depended entirely on the short-
term commercial situation in agriculture.[46] When wine and other
farm products sold at a decent price, unemployment dropped
and local artisans and shopkeepers benefited from a healthy
demand for their products. Agriculture was the leading economic factor—that is, the prosperity of local manufacture depended upon the commercial success of farm products. Responding to the survey of 1848, the justice of the peace at Manosque
(Basses-Alpes) said: "Prosperity in agriculture depends on the
price of crops, that of silk and tanning depends on commerce,
and that of construction depends on good harvests and crop
sales." The justice of the peace at Servian (Hérault) agreed:
"When wine is selling at a good price, agricultural work is
abundant, and when landowners are prosperous, other industries do not suffer."[47]

The cash-crop-producing regions of central and southern France
could enjoy a certain prosperity when the commercial situation
was favorable. Because land was so extensively subdivided, a
large portion of the local population benefited from healthy
economic conditions. By the same token, however, a commercial
crisis like that of 1848 affected everyone in the locality. Small
cultivators and artisans suffered the most, and their plight be-

came particularly bleak in and around medium-sized market towns like Béziers (Hérault). Wholly dependent on wine distilling and the export of eau-de-vie, Béziers saw its relative prosperity turn into economic disaster when national and international demand for its spirits collapsed in 1848. Virtually no Béziers resident was spared. Agricultural laborers lost their jobs, and demand for artisan goods evaporated. Often in debt and operating on a small margin of profit, peasant proprietors suffered cruelly. Even those who owned or rented sizable domains enjoyed no immunity, for they were forced to sell at prices below their cost of production.[48]

The situation was altogether different in the grain-producing regions of northern France. Since people need bread even during economic depressions, the demand for grain did not decline as much as demand for such cash crops as wine and silk. Furthermore, low grain prices may have harmed the cultivators, but they bolstered the purchasing power of those workers who had to buy their food. Spending less on bread, miners and other laborers occasionally had money for other goods. Whereas in the South low agricultural prices depressed the entire local economy, in the North agricultural distress could mitigate industrial difficulties. In their responses to the survey of 1848, justices of the peace from northern cantons tended to complain about long-term trends in industry, such as increasing competition from foreign- and factory-made textiles, rather than about the short-term commercial situation in agriculture.[49]

In the South, therefore, the fortunes of agriculture and industry tended to fluctuate in unison, whereas in the North one tended to rise as the other fell. This fundamental North/South economic distinction was not without political consequences. In the North, political alliances of cultivators on the one hand and workers and artisans on the other were rare. In the South, the nature of the relationship between local agriculture and industry facilitated political links between peasants and workers.

We have seen how growth in agricultural output drew peasants away from subsistence farming and toward production for the market. At the same time, improvements in farm productivity encouraged both small peasant owners and landless agricultural laborers to purchase new land, even if such purchases meant increased indebtedness. Property ownership gave peasants a sense of independence, but that independence was often compromised by the debts they contracted in order to buy their new plots.

How can we be sure that peasant property ownership expanded during the decades prior to 1848? Statistics are, unfortunately, incomplete for the first half of the nineteenth century, but thanks to the painstaking labor of a nineteenth-century tax official, full information on changes in land distribution does exist for three departments of central and southern France: the Gers, Yonne, and the Isère.[50] This information shows that small peasant property increased at the expense of medium-sized and large domains. Between the time of the original cadastre (1820s and 1830s) and 1857, large property (greater than fifty hectares) in the Gers lost 10.6 percent of its *cotes foncières** and 11.4 percent of its surface area, while medium-sized property (twenty to fifty hectares) declined modestly. Small property (four to twenty hectares—columns 4 and 5 in table 1), on the other hand, added 5.2 percent to its number of *cotes* and 4.1 percent to its hectare area. Micro property (less than four hectares) grew the most with an increase of 26.8 percent in *cotes* and 22 percent in surface. In the Yonne, medium property lost more than large, while micro and small property gained accordingly. The evolution was similar in the Isère, except that property of between ten and twenty hectares declined significantly.

---

*One *cote foncière* represents the total amount of land one individual owns in a given commune. Thus, if all the land in commune X is shared by three owners, that commune has three *cotes foncières*. By the same token, a commune Y with a thousand different owners will have a thousand *cotes*. To say, for example, that large property in the Gers loses 10.6 percent of its *cotes foncières* means that the number of individual landed domains located within the boundaries of a single commune and encompassing more than fifty hectares has declined by this amount in the department as a whole. Clearly, when large property loses *cotes foncières*, the number of *cotes* in other property categories must grow. So if a *cote* of sixty ha. is divided into six equal pieces, and if each is sold to a different buyer, large property has lost one *cote foncière* and small property has gained six. The commune in which the sixty-hectare *cote* was located gains five *cotes foncières* in the process of subdivision, assuming none of the buyers already owns land in that commune.

TABLE 1 Percentage Change in the Number of *Cotes foncières* and in the Surface Area of Agricultural Holdings between the Original and the Revised Cadastres

Depart-ment	Date of Revised Cadastre	Micro Property 0-4 ha.		Small Property				Medium Property 20-50 ha.		Large Property 50+ ha.	
				4-10 ha.		10-20 ha.					
		C	S	C	S	C	S	C	S	C	S
Gers	1857	26.8%	22.0%	6.7%	6.0%	2.2%	2.2%	-2.8%	-3.6%	-10.6%	-11.4%
Yonne	1863	30.0	17.8	7.5	6.8	-2.5	-2.7	-11.0	-12.0	-5.6	-7.4
Isère	1869	51.1	38.3	7.1	5.3	-8.5	-9.0	-18.5	-17.9	-19.0	-15.3

KEY: C = *cotes*; S = surface.

In each of the three departments, a significant portion of the total taxable land was transformed from medium and large domains to micro and small property: 4.2 percent in the Gers, 4.5 percent in the Yonne, and 8.4 percent in the Isère. That the largest percentage increases consistently fall in the category of micro *cotes* (zero to four hectares) does not mean that the number of subeconomic farms grew at the same rate. Often, a new *cote foncière* of less than four hectares represented the purchase of land in one commune on the part of a peasant who already held terrain in a bordering commune. In other words, many of the *cotes* that appear subeconomic represent instead the new lands needed to make a formerly subeconomic plot viable.[51] Much of the rest of the increase in this first category signifies first land purchases by rural laborers who had put aside enough of their wages for a down payment on a coveted parcel.

Scattered evidence for other departments is consistent with the above figures. In the nine Côte-d'Or cantons for which complete data exist for the period 1822-1850, large property declined between 2.5 and 12.8 percent, while medium property lost between 23 and 36 percent of its terrain. The neighboring Burgundy department of the Saône-et-Loire showed a similar movement away from large- and medium-sized property. In six fully documented cantons large domains lost between 2.5 and 43.4 percent of their surface area, while medium property declined between 15 and 35.9 percent (see table 2).[52]

The Limousin, a backward region dominated by small landowners, showed the same kind of property division that occurred in the Alps: small property grew by chipping away at large domains.[53] Property subdivision took place most rapidly in the Limousin during the July Monarchy and the Second Republic, and here property was more evenly distributed than in most other regions of the country.

In the Var, the number of small peasant property owners increased dramatically between 1815 and 1848. Census returns for the period show a sharp decline of landless laborers without any significant rural exodus. Clearly, the only way that such a development could occur would be for landless laborers to acquire property. Indeed, changes in the classification system of

TABLE 2   Decline of Large and Medium Property in Burgundy, 1822-1850

Department and Canton	Large Property		Medium Property	
	% Decline by 1850	Size Range (ha.)	% Decline by 1850	Size Range (ha.)
Côte-d'Or				
Auxonne	−2.7	50+	−34.4	30-50
Beaune Nord	−2.5	50+	−26.2	a
Châtillon-sur-Seine	−4.4	80+	−36.1	50-80
Dijon-Est	−10.2	50+	b	b
Précy-sous-Thil	−12.8	50+	b	b
Saint-Jean de Losne	−7.4	50+	−27.5	30-50
Saint-Seine-l'Abbaye	−6.6	80+	−23.2	50-90
Saulieu	−3.5	90+	−24.4	50-90
Seurre	−2.5	50+	−39.4	a
Saône-et-Loire				
Beaurepaire	−2.5	50+	−14.9	a
Chapelle de Guinchay	−43.4	50+	−35.9	a
Coude	−12.5	50+	b	b
St.-Gengoux-le-Royal	−14.4	50+	−20.3	a
St.-Germain-du-Bois	−12.9	50+	b	b
St.-Martin-en-Bresse	−9.5	50+	b	b

a Less than 50 ha., but more than Fr 1,000 in taxable revenue.
b No data.

the Var census reflect the growth in the number of peasant smallholders registered during this period. The classification scheme of the ancien régime divided the agricultural population into a hierarchy of *propriétaires* (well-off farmers), *ménagers* (peasant property owners), and *travailleurs* (landless agricultural workers). By 1849 the bottom category had been split into two parts—*cultivateurs* and *journaliers*—to account for the new status of those day laborers who had bought land. *Cultivateurs* referred to those who both owned some land and hired out their labor, and this formed by far the larger of the two new categories. The term *journalier* represented the small number of agricultural laborers who remained landless.

As former wage workers acquired land, they devoted less of their time to paid labor. As a result, the Var suffered a shortage of agricultural hands, which in turn engendered a dramatic increase in agricultural wages. But the wage hike did nothing to check the Var's labor drain. On the contrary, farm workers took advantage of their higher incomes to buy land.[54] Thus, during the first half of the nineteenth century the old distinction between the rural proletariat and the relatively well-off *ménagers* tended to disappear as rural laborers bought land.

Although cadastral information shows clearly that small property advanced at the expense of medium and large holdings during the first half of the nineteenth century, can we be certain that *peasants*, and not members of higher social classes, bought these new *cotes* of less than ten hectares? Paradoxically enough, the soaring cost of arable land during the July Monarchy indicates that it was indeed peasants who purchased many of the new *cotes*. Since land prices increased on the average from 500 francs to 1,275 francs per hectare between 1830 and 1846,[55] agricultural property became a sound investment only for those who intended to work it themselves. The low rate of return and high initial outlay made land purchase unwise as a long-term bourgeois investment.[56] Land buying could be profitable for middle-class capital only in certain choice wine-growing regions or as a speculative venture whose immediate goal was to resell the terrain in small pieces to land-hungry peasants. Indeed, it made good economic sense for bourgeois and ex-noble proprietors to *sell* their land. It fetched them a high price at a time when increasing costs of rural labor and declining prices of agricultural products provided ample incentive to unload all but the most productive farmland.[57] For the peasant, on the other hand, land was not a mere capital investment. Land meant social status, the possibility of economic independence, an improved standard of living for his family, and a more secure future for his children.

The agricultural growth of the second quarter of the nineteenth century encouraged peasants to pay the high prices demanded for land during this period. Improved yields and stronger consumer demand as well as the expectation of continued progress all reinforced the peasants' traditional desire to expand their holdings.[58] Propertyless agricultural laborers showed the same land hunger, and the increased wages that resulted from agricultural improvement enabled many of them to acquire new plots of land, most often in tiny parcels of less than five hectares.[59]

By no means, however, did either peasants' production for an extra-local market or their modest increases in property ownership contribute much to improving their lot. Market involvement subjected peasants to the hazards of commercial fluctuations, and property purchases often deepened their burden of debt. Yet if the peasants' material situation did not markedly improve, their social condition had begun to change. Involvement in an extra-local market liberated them from old constraints at the same time that it imposed new limits. The commercially oriented peasant was freed from the Malthusian scissors that had plagued his ancestors. But, released from the social and cultural isolation of his rural world, he found himself subjected more completely to the laws of supply and demand. Property ownership gave him more mastery over his work, while the market assumed mastery over the fruit of that work.

The agricultural laborer, newly turned proprietor of a subeconomic plot, was not necessarily subject to the laws of supply and demand. But the debts he contracted in order to acquire his parcel reduced his social isolation and forced him to confront hitherto unknown pressures. Beyond the farmer who employed him, he now had to face a new array of social superiors—moneylenders, notaries, justices of the peace—all with different demands. Indebtedness undercut the advantages of the laborer's newly obtained land and potentially increased his sense of social inferiority.

Rural indebtedness was not, of course, limited to agricultural laborers. Virtually every major study of rural France in the first half of the nineteenth century cites peasant indebtedness as a fundamental blight on the rural landscape.[60] Rural indebtedness was not merely the result of the exploitation of poor country folk by crafty urban usurers. Rather, it formed part of an evolving rural dialectic in which economic progress both stimulated peasants' liberty and deepened their dependence. The capital that peasants borrowed during the period of constitutional monarchy often enhanced their wealth, and, by providing property, gave them control over their own labor. At the same time, however, the need to borrow made them increasingly dependent on those who could advance credits. The excess demand for capital and France's primitive banking system—a system that did not, for the most part, extend into rural France—put the moneylender in a particularly strong position. If a peasant wanted to buy land or make improvements, he had to accept the creditors' terms. Most charged high to usurious interest rates—15 percent and more for short-term loans at a time when 10 percent was considered usurious. The peasant's traditional land hunger plus the improved agricultural prospects motivated him to accept the lender's terms. In addition to the burden of the debt, the sums owed to various creditors made peasants that much more vulnerable to the capriciousness of the market. When crop sales and prices were high, the peasant could handle his notes; when sales and prices plummeted, as they did after 1847, the peasant often was unable to repay his loans. Operating on a narrow profit margin even in the best of years, the small cultivator had no cash reserves to draw on during periods of decline.[61] Throughout the July Monarchy, then, peasants extended their landholdings and day laborers acquired their plots. But peasants who produced commercial crops confronted both the uncertainties of the market and the demands of capital, while the worker-proprietor, whose crops were primarily for home consumption, had somehow to pay his debts.

The small winegrower faced a particularly tenuous situation. Not only did he owe money to creditors and operate in an extensive and vulnerable market, but he also depended on wholesalers to sell his products. Most small wine producers could not, for example, afford to hold back part of their harvest in an effort to take advantage of price increases later in the season. Debt and necessary family expenses forced them to sell their whole stock to wealthy intermediaries just after the harvest. Moreover, most peasants had neither the expertise nor the financial means to market their own wine.[62] In the Maconnais and the Beaujolais, as in most regions, there were no cooperative entrepôts that would have permitted small growers to pool their resources for the stocking and sale of wine. Only those with substantial private capital could meet the high cost of marketing Burgundy wines in the distant urban centers that demanded them.[63] As skilled cultivators who put extensive effort and expertise into their labor, the small winegrowers confronted a particularly frustrating contradiction. On the one hand, they managed independently the complex task of wine production; on the other hand, like all small businessmen, they had no ability to determine the value of that product.

What, then, is the political significance of these developments in French agriculture? As has been shown, the substantial progress of French agriculture during the first half of the nineteenth century stemmed not from land consolidation or enclosure. It resulted simply from the widespread introduction of new methods of cultivation and from a shift into cash crops. In addition to expanding the French food supply, agricultural progress provoked an increase in the amount of peasant property and facilitated the extension of market relations into the French provinces. But as a consequence, peasants sank deeper into the quicksand of indebtedness, and they faced the uncertainty of volatile swings in supply and demand. The penetration of commercial capitalism into the countryside did not compromise the future of the mass of French peasants, as some historians have argued.[64] Capitalism engulfed the peasants and, for better and worse, subjected them to its laws.

The peasants' confrontation with a conquering market helped make them receptive to Montagnard ideology. Involvement in the market facilitated exposure to the carriers of these new ideas while it created new grievances and stirred up aspirations for change. During this period peasants tended to express these aspirations in the form of religious ritual. And the democ-socs, republican apostles of populist religion, were to build electoral support in the rural regions of central and southern France by transforming the peasants' pragmatic religiosity into a rudimentary commitment to socialist democracy. Nineteenth-century rural communities sought to harnesss spiritual power for the effort to solve worldly difficulties, and the democ-socs argued that the democratic and social republic was the only form of government that could do just that.

In many ways, the progress of French industry over the first half of the nineteenth century resembled that of French agriculture. Industrial output expanded significantly without either major consolidation of enterprise or mechanization of production. In 1850 French industry was only slightly more concentrated than it had been in 1800. Moreover, it continued to specialize in the same consumer-oriented products in 1850 as it had a half-century earlier. The 75 percent growth in industrial output registered during this period was the result of intensified exploitation of labor and the subjection of independent artisans to the commercial power of merchant middlemen.

Although we lack precise statistics on the size of French firms in the middle of the last century, available data suggest strongly that the vast majority of the nation's enterprises were still very small (fewer than five workers). According to the census of 1851,[65] three-quarters of French workers belonged to small industry and commerce—construction, clothing, food, transportation, printing, luxury goods—and within this sector "masters" narrowly outnumbered workers. This means that the hypothetical average French atelier employed just one worker in addition to the master artisan. Even in what the 1851 census terms large industry—mining, textiles, metallurgy—the ratio of masters to male workers is as high as one to five. When female workers are included, the ratio becomes one to ten, hardly indicating a preponderance of huge factories.

These figures must be considered suggestive rather than definitive. The 1851 census fails to make clear what is meant by "master," and, more seriously, it erroneously bases the distinction between large and small industry on the kind of goods produced rather than on the size of the firms in question.[66] To achieve a sharper picture of the relationship between the two sectors of French industry, data from the surveys and census of the 1860s must be used. Statistics gathered for the Industrial Survey of 1860-1865, plus the professional census of 1866, permit a determination of the average number of workers per firm in Industry and Artisanat, as well as an indication of the relative size of the two sectors (see table 3). Assuming that the number of bosses is roughly equal to the number of firms, the figures indicate that 95 percent of French enterprises employed fewer than ten workers. In other words, the Artisanat represented 95 percent of all industrial concerns in the early 1860s. In the Artisanat sector there was about one worker for every boss, while in industry the ratio of workers to bosses was about fourteen to one. Since the *artisans-patrons* were effectively part of the labor force, the figures show that 72 percent of the overall industrial work force belonged to the Artisanat during the Second Empire.

These figures undoubtedly overestimate the number of workers employed in large industry. In the textile sector, for example, tens of thousands of rural outworkers were reported as employees of large firms when in fact they toiled individually.[67] And although Markovitch counts firms that employed between ten and twenty workers as part of large industry, these were in reality small enterprises and belong in the category Artisanat. Correcting for this overestimation of large industry, it appears that some 95 percent of all industrial firms and about 80 percent of the labor force belonged to the artisan sector. As late as the

TABLE 3   Working Population, 1860-1865

Type of Industry	Bosses	Workers	Number of Workers per Boss
Industry (more than 10 workers)	80,000	1,150,000	14.5
Artisanat (fewer than 10 workers)	1,420,000	1,600,000	1.1
Total	1,500,000	2,750,000	1.8

SOURCE: T. J. Markovitch, "Le Revenu industriel et artisanal sous la Monarchie de Juillet et le Second Empire," *Economies et sociétés*, no. 4 (April 1967), 85-87.

mid-1860s, then, French industry had shown little movement toward consolidation.

Perhaps the basic reason for the predominance of small-scale artisan manufacture in mid-nineteenth-century France was the existence of a large reservoir of skilled labor.[68] Having grown steadily throughout the eighteenth century and increasing some 30 percent between 1800 and 1850, the French populace provided the principal resource of the nation's industry. The importance of this labor force was heightened by France's relative deficiency in coal and iron ore, as well as by its inadequate network of road and water transport. Britain early on developed a mechanized factory system, in large part because manpower was short and high internal and external demand encouraged increased production. Possessing a completely different set of resources, France had no good reason to imitate the British model. Understandably, entrepreneurs based their enterprises on the economic trumps they possessed: labor and craftsmanship. Thus it was the production of finely crafted finished products for which high levels of skill and intensive labor were required—fine silk, wool, and printed cottons, leather goods, and tableware—and the cultivation of agricultural cash crops that fueled French economic development in the nineteenth century. Wisely playing from strength, French manufacturers conceded inferiority to British basic industry and set out to capture international markets in finished goods. The profits from these consumer goods were then rechanneled "upstream," where they helped to finance French basic industry—mechanized spinning and ironworks. In a sense, French industry developed backward, since it was the secondary enterprises that supported the primary ones.[69]

Between 1810 and 1840, consumer-oriented manufacture accounted for 75 percent of the value of France's total industrial output (not including construction). By 1880, after four decades of steady industrial growth, consumer goods still constituted 70 percent of the nation's manufactured products.[70] Thus, even in the second half of the nineteenth century consumer industries continued to fuel economic expansion.

Not only had French industry failed to consolidate, but as

most French economic historians now agree, mechanization played only a minor role in the French economy between 1815 and 1850.[71] Despite the paucity of steam-powered machines, however, French industrial output grew an average of 2.5 percent per year during this period.[72] The industries that did use new technology do not account for the bulk of this growth, since nonmechanized artisan manufacture grew at least as fast as large-scale enterprise. During the decade 1835-1844 artisan production represented 70 percent of the total revenue from French industrial output; thirty years later the artisan share had risen to 77 percent.[73]

How did industry manage to expand its production by 75 percent between 1815 and 1848, when its structure seemed to change so little?[74] Though mechanization and industrial consolidation languished, important structural change did nonetheless take place. Increasing competition among manufacturers and the subordination of manufacture to commerce forced a "rationalization" of artisan production. As improved transportation connected artisan-producers with an extra-local market, they were subjected to intensified competition from firms outside their localities. At the same time, artisans who once marketed their own goods now found it necessary to sell them to middlemen who had the capital and expertise to operate in the growing markets. Thus, profiting from their positions of strength, the merchants who increasingly controlled both access to the market and availability of credit were able to force down wholesale prices during the second quarter of the nineteenth century.[75]

As wholesale prices dropped, master artisans and other employers had no choice but to cut unit costs of production. They accomplished this task by lowering wages, by resorting to subcontracting, and by intensifying division of labor.[76] This heightened exploitation of the country's skilled work force permitted industrial output to increase significantly in the absence of new technology and alterations in the small-scale form of production. As a result of these developments, artisans were "proletarianized"—that is, subjected to a stepped-up work process that reduced the importance of their skills—without losing their status as small-scale skilled producers.[77] Masters and workers alike saw their incomes decline,[78] and both chafed under the reign of a more efficient division of labor. Indeed, small bosses and their workers often found their interests converging in the mid-nineteenth century. Proud of their expertise and dedicated to their trades, these artisans did not take lightly the degradation of their work.

Beginning in the 1840s, artisans sought to challenge the growing power of merchant capitalists by advocating the establishment of producers' cooperatives. Each cooperative would be jointly owned by all those associated with it. Because most French firms were small and employed uncomplicated technology, it seemed conceivable that a group of associated workers could raise the capital necessary to own and operate their businesses. In many ways, the producers' cooperative was as much a "moral" solution to workers' problems as an economic one. By abolishing wage labor, cooperation promised to realize "equality" and "fraternity," the two primary goals that workers in the 1840s increasingly viewed as religious imperatives. Yet although cooperation offered a solution to the immorality of wage labor, it left open the question of how to eliminate the competition that mercilessly forced down wholesale prices.

Growing competition threatened the livelihoods of France's independent town and rural artisans at least as much as it affected the well-being of those employed in the nation's small ateliers. Craftsmen working alone obviously could not reduce costs through division of labor. They could maintain their incomes in the face of falling wholesale prices only by working more intensively, longer hours, or both. Of course, when demand declined, it was senseless to try to make up for falling prices by working more; the market simply was not there.

The Parisian tailoring industry provides a perfect example of a trade forced to undergo structural change as a result of commercial developments that took place during the July Monarchy. The rise of ready-made clothing and the proliferation of outwork put severe pressure on the tailor's workshop after 1830.[79] In order to compete with the lower-priced ready-made ware, work processes within the tailoring trade had to be altered radically.

Rather than making a whole article of clothing, the tailor now performed a series of repetitive tasks. The ready-made clothing industry, itself composed of small workshops and *faconniers* working at home, did not threaten the existence of the tailor's small atelier; it simply reduced the status—and often the income—of the tailors by forcing a rationalization of their work. As Christopher Johnson has shown, many of the tailors' strikes of the 1840s were directed not so much against masters as against the entrepreneurs of the ready-made clothing industry.[80]

A number of other trades in Paris and the provinces underwent the same kind of structural change. By 1850 a finely honed division of labor was no less common in the small atelier than in the large *fabrique*. Moreover, in large cities like Paris the division of labor existed not only within a single atelier but also among a group of ateliers, each specializing in one aspect of a craft. By mid-century the knife makers of Thiers and Paris had nineteen different specialities, while Parisian leather dressers (*corroyeurs*) adopted twenty-six different tasks. Toolmakers (*taillandiers*) took on twenty specialities; fine jewelry craftsmen, twenty-three, and makers of artificial jewelry, twenty-two.[81] Since the skilled artisans of Paris and other French cities could produce better-crafted goods than the large-scale *fabriques*, the introduction of a more rigorous division of labor often sufficed to maintain their competitive advantage over domestic and foreign mechanized rivals.[82] The price they paid to keep this advantage, however, was very high. Work became more and more routine, and real wages spiraled downward.

The market pressures that altered the *structure* of such trades as tailoring and knife making simply lowered the incomes or sped up the work of skilled craftsmen in other fields. The silk workers of Lyon, whose industry consisted mainly of small ateliers of one to five workers, suffered not so much from the degradation of skills as from the commercial omnipotence of merchant capitalists. The latter furnished all the raw silk, ordered work to be done, provided credits, set prices, and determined standards of quality.[83] Unable to market his own wares, the master silk weaver, often the owner of several looms and director of a small atelier, was at the mercy of a powerful group of Lyon merchants. The masters' strenuous efforts to prevent merchants from lowering wholesale prices during the July Monarchy were to no avail. Journeymen silk weavers, who suffered indirectly from the wholesalers' control over the market, identified with their bosses and supported their efforts to limit the merchants' prerogatives.[84]

The situation was similar in the prosperous wool industry of Bédarieux in the Hérault. A small-scale version of Lyon, the Bédarieux wool industry consisted of a multitude of small artisan workshops that turned out wool cloth for an extensive market dominated by merchant capitalists. The literate Bédarieux weavers took pride in their work and sought upward mobility for their children. They regarded the merchants' pressure to lower prices and speed up the tempo of their work as immoral.[85]

It was not just within the traditional artisan crafts that commercial middlemen exercised growing power. In the lumber industry of central France, for example, the competition from peasants who worked part-time as loggers and the declining demand for French timber enabled Parisian lumber merchants both to reduce the incomes of loggers and to quicken the pace of their work.[86] During the July Monarchy the annual period of unemployment increased year by year, and when loggers did work, they labored longer hours for reduced pay.[87]

Although the amount and tempo of the work changed, the structure of the logging industry, which was not unlike that of the Lyon silk weaver's atelier, remained the same. Small teams composed of a master lumberman (*compagnon de rivière*) and five journeymen (*flotteurs*) continued to build log trains upstream and guide them down to Paris. The *compagnon de rivière*, the logging equivalent of a master artisan, exercised complete command over the work process and had full authority to hire and fire the journeymen, whose wages he paid. At the same time, however, he was at the mercy of the Parisian merchants who controlled the lumber market. Like the Lyon merchant capitalists, the lumber wholesalers had the power to fix the master's pay and to decide how often he worked. The *compa-*

gnons de rivière, like so many other master artisans, suffered a frustrating disparity between independence on the job and subservience in the marketplace. Journeymen *flotteurs*, who lived in the same neighborhoods as their masters and shared the latter's culture and values, blamed the Paris merchants and not their bosses for their growing economic distress. After 1848, masters and *flotteurs* banded together to protect their livelihoods and to defend the democratic and social republic.[88]

Outside the relatively weak textile, metallurgical, and coal industries, the mid-century captains of French enterprise tended to be merchants who possessed capital rather than entrepreneurs who built factories. These merchants had absolutely no interest in consolidating production or in taking direct charge of manufacture itself. They benefited from the intense competition that reigned among the multitude of small producers and from the highly seasonal demand for handcrafted goods. During periods of peak demand, merchants pressed the ateliers into full production; when demand slackened, they simply stopped buying from them. In this way they could maximize sales without having to worry about fixed costs during the off-season. Master artisans, on the other hand, had to maintain their shops, equipment, and often their employees the year round. Worse, competition and the inventory that merchants could stockpile kept down wholesale prices even during the periods of intense demand. Gone were the days when the *chef d'atelier* could benefit from the high prices of the peak season to recoup the losses he incurred the rest of the year.[89] Throughout the country, this tightening commercial situation reduced master artisans almost to the level of their workers by making them all the employees of merchant entrepeneurs.

Although the subservience of the Artisanat as a whole—masters and workers—to a commercial bourgeoisie was a nationwide phenomenon in the mid-nineteenth century, scholars have only recently realized its importance. Older historians, locked into a twentieth-century model of labor conflict that necessarily opposed workers and bosses, were at a loss to explain the frequent cooperation of these two groups during the Second Republic. Ignorant of the structure of artisan industry in which the real employer was the merchant capitalist, historians like Guillaume and Vidalenc could do no better than cite "paternalism" or the "corporatist heritage" as reasons for the master-worker alliance they observed after 1848.[90]

The justices of the peace who responded to the Survey of 1848 had a more precise understanding of the situation. "In our workshops, the boss is nothing more than a kind of head worker," reported the judge from the canton of Villenauxe in the Aude. A boss, the judge added, was hardly more secure than his workers. He depended on commercial middlemen for work orders, credits, and raw materials.[91] "Often," wrote the judge at Béziers, "the boss has no other advantage over his workers than the self-satisfaction of directing the work."[92] Typically a property owner who paid taxes, the *chef d'atelier* endeavored to manage his business efficiently, and he could only be frustrated by the distinction between his leadership position in the productive sphere and his subservience in the realm of commerce.

Justices and workers alike complained about the excess competition in most trades. In a twenty-eight-page manuscript attached to the survey response from Auxerre (Yonne), a master typesetter named Rousseau summed up his grievance:

> The small bosses who employ five or six workers hardly differ at all from their employees. The bosses' only advantage is the ability to work *for themselves*. This is only a slight benefit, since competition is so stiff that each boss is forced to undersell the other. In doing so, he must either lay off workers or make them labor at an inhuman pace. If the workers complain, the boss can only respond that he, too, is working just as hard, and that they have no choice but to work this way since the market price is so low. If the worker asked, "Why do you ["tu" used] work at such a price?" the boss could only respond: "If I didn't do it, my neighbor would. Then I would be forced to close my workshop and starve to death."[93]

Rousseau was a vocal member of the démocrate-socialiste movement and a champion of workers' causes; thus he cannot justly be accused of special pleading on behalf of the *patronat*. Rousseau's position resembled that of the master silk weavers of Lyon. Director of a tiny workshop, he was more a chief worker than a small entrepreneur.[94]

In many ways, then, skilled workers all over the country and large numbers of peasants in central and southern France faced a similar predicament. In the atelier, pressure from commercial entrepreneurs routinized artisans' labor and kept wages low; in the countryside, market expansion stimulated indebtedness and accentuated economic vulnerability. Both artisans and peasants were relatively independent at work but subservient in the marketplace. The démocrates-socialistes understood the common predicament of these skilled workers and peasants, and they fashioned an ideology that resonated with the moralistic and pragmatic religiosity of these classes. During the July Monarchy the left-wing opposition to Louis Philippe developed a critique of laissez-faire liberalism based on precepts of Catholic morality. This opposition argued that ordinary Frenchmen lived in misery because the French economy was built on an immoral ethic of unbridled competition, egoism, and human exploitation. The left maintained that the economy should rest instead on the Catholic principles of fraternity and cooperation. The establishment of republican institutions in February 1848 enabled the democ-socs to conceive of a means of realizing in the material world the progressive promises they believed were embedded in the Christianity of the Gospels. In so doing, they transformed a moralistic Christian critique of French society into a project for socialist democracy. Deeply religious, the democ-socs considered themselves the apostles of a new kind of republic—a democratic and social republic grounded in the universal truths of Catholic morality. After 1848, this sacralized republic would appeal to peasants and artisans who suffered the rigors of a market economy in crisis.

CHAPTER II

POLITICAL OPPOSITION AND POPULIST RELIGION DURING THE JULY MONARCHY

Although intellectual historians and students of Romanticism documented long ago the resurgence of Christian language and moral concepts among certain intellectuals after the Revolution of 1830, the July Monarchy as a whole is not particularly well-known as an era of religious restoration. Louis Philippe's France is more commonly seen as a period of industrial development, bourgeois enrichment, and liberal ascendancy. Leading Orleanist political figures, such as Odilon Barrot and Adolphe Thiers, as well as the king himself, were steeped in Enlightenment culture and had little interest in religion and theology. Their intellectual passions centered on the scientific study of history, an endeavor that in their view traced the evolutionary process by which the middle classes overcame religious superstition and achieved political power for themselves. The Orleanist regime believed that the Catholic clergy, much of which had remained Legitimist, should be removed from positions of power and influence and relegated to the task of keeping the people in line.[1]

While the conservative government of the *Juste Milieu* kept alive the secular teaching of the Enlightenment and Revolution, its left-wing political opposition—both bourgeois and working class—increasingly turned toward Catholicism for the intellectual tools with which to criticize the regime. It was not just a small circle of Romantics who returned to Christian precepts. Rather, a heterogeneous array of republican and socialist intellectuals, Romantic artists and writers, working-class leaders, and miscellaneous reformers all adopted a vocabulary and overall frame of reference remarkable for their Christian content.

Influenced by the bourgeois leaders to whom they looked for

guidance, ordinary urban workers also demonstrated a renewed religiosity during the July Monarchy. Skilled craftsmen were attracted to a sort of populist Christianity that sought to dignify their humble condition through an identification with Jesus Christ. Jesus, workers were told, was a simple artisan, just like themselves. Like Louis Blanc and Etienne Cabet, many urban workers came to believe that "true Christianity"—as opposed to the corrupted beliefs of the Church hierarchy—provided the moral basis for an alternative to laissez-faire capitalism, for an economic system based on human equality and fraternal cooperation. The workers thus viewed Christianity not so much as a set of abstract beliefs but as the ideological basis of a program of reforms to be realized in the material world. For the worker of the 1840s, the promise of Christianity—equality, brotherhood, sharing, an end to exploitation—became the goals of political and social change.

Parallel with these urban developments, popular religious expression in the countryside reached new levels of intensity. The decline of Church influence after the Revolution did not lead peasants to abandon religious practice and devotion; rather, they simply turned to an unorthodox mixture of pagan and Christian forms. Thus, by the beginning of the July Monarchy, saint worship reached an intensity unknown since the Middle Ages, religious processions occurred more frequently and more fervently than in the recent past, and villagers participated in an increasing number of religious festivals.[2] These forms of popular religion expressed a longing for practical and earthly solutions to everyday concerns, and they embodied the populist and incipiently democratic belief that rights over religious ritual and meaning belonged to the people as a community and not to the priest. When villagers did turn to their priest, it was not for his intellectual and spiritual gifts but for his supposed magical powers to perform practical services.[3] Beginning in the mid-1820s, Church leaders, determined to subdue this popular religiosity and reassert their authority, acted to undo the effects of the Revolution. In many regions of rural France, these attempts to counter popular practices considered pagan and superstitious produced alienation from a priesthood increasingly unwilling to depart from doctrinal purity to satisfy peasant demands.

Thus, during the July Monarchy bourgeois intellectuals, working-class leaders, skilled craftsmen, and ordinary peasants all experienced a renewed Christian religious fervor. For intellectuals and workers, this religiosity promised the ideal of moral community as an ideological alternative to laissez-faire liberalism; for the peasantry, it expressed the desire to harness sacred power for material ends, and it asserted the right of the community to control religious practice. After 1848 this widespread religiosity would provide a common language with which intellectuals, workers, and peasants—groups separated by vast cultural differences—could communicate with each other. And in the aftermath of the June Days it would facilitate a political alliance based on a common desire to realize fundamental Christian promises.

In reacting against the austere materialism and individualism of the Enlightenment and Revolution, the Romantic movement of the early nineteenth century sought to reintroduce into public discourse such traditional moral imperatives as community solidarity and human brotherhood. In so doing, Romantics taught their followers a sense of pity for the weak and disinherited.[4] Lacking any new moral language or set of philosophical conceptions, the Romantics drew heavily on Catholic precepts. George Sand, for example, asked Sainte-Beuve in 1835 to help her find a "religious and social truth one and the same."[5]

Virtually all the prominent thinkers of the republican, socialist, and working-class movements of the July Monarchy echoed the religious sentiments of the leading Romantic writers of the period. Unlike the revolutionaries of 1789-1793, the opponents of Louis Philippe did not confront a government organically tied to the Catholic Church. On the contrary, the rulers of the July Monarchy were outspoken Voltairians who believed, with Thiers, that religion should be reserved for the uninstructed masses. Since the regime had marked its distance from Catholicism and the Church, the opposition could embrace the Catholic religion without appearing to support those in power.

At the same time, republicans and socialists separated themselves from the established Church by coloring their religiosity with intense shades of anticlericalism.

It was Henri de Saint-Simon who formulated the ideas that underlay the religiosity of the July Monarchy's oppositionist intellectuals. He argued for a "new Christianity" in which "morality would form the basis of a real religious doctrine, and dogma and ritual would serve primarily to reinforce that morality in the spirit of all Christians."[6] Following Saint-Simon's lead, intellectuals who considered themselves republicans, democrats, socialists, communists, or some combination of the four labels set out to rejuvenate Christianity by resurrecting an original doctrine that they believed had been perverted by the established Church.[7]

Pierre Leroux, Saint-Simon's disciple who turned to Romanticism in the 1830s, argued in his influential *Encyclopédie nouvelle* that the origins of organized Christianity were profoundly democratic. According to Leroux, Christian doctrine was originally formulated in a democratically elected *concile*, a sort of revolutionary convention in which popularly elected bishops turned proposed texts into Christian law by majority vote:

> The bishops were the elected representatives of the Christian people. And when three hundred and eighteen bishops and priests, drawn from all the provinces of the Empire, gathered in Nicaea they formed a veritable *convention*. The role of this *convention* was none other than to represent a victorious Christianity and to make its laws.[8]

Here Leroux takes a position on religion precisely opposite to that of his revolutionary forebears. Whereas the men of '89 to '93 argued that Catholicism and revolution were incompatible, Leroux sought to identify Christianity with the revolutionary tradition. He used a revolutionary yardstick to legitimize primitive Christianity. Thus, Leroux justified Christian belief not because it represented divine gospel but because it emerged from the same kinds of institutions that created the democratic republic: "the last real councils of humanity [i.e., councils of bishops] dedicated themselves to the future—as did the *Con-*

vention [of 1793] in decreeing simultaneously the rights of society and the rights of man."[9] Moreover, just as the established Church threatened the Revolution, so it also menaced true Christianity. As the democratic *concile* gave way to papal rule, the vital spirit of Christianity, first subordinated to the interests of ecclesiastical power, was finally all but snuffed out by the modern clergy.[10]

The Christian message of Fourierist leader Victor Considérant, though similar to that of Leroux, was much less anticlerical. Believing he could convince the clergy to support his quest for a "regenerated Christianity," Considérant argued that Fourier's teaching was "quite simply the realization of Christianity in society" and that phalansterians were none other than "the Christians of the nineteenth century."[11] In 1843 he proclaimed:

> We call on all priests and Christians to unify your efforts with ours for the task of preparing the Kingdom of God on earth. . . . Seek, declared Christ, seek first and above all the Kingdom of God and His justice, and as a reward for your faithful service all worldly goods will be yours. It is in the spirit of this divine formula that we, representatives of social science, endeavor to forge our union with you.[12]

Just as there was no necessary opposition between Christianity and the Revolution for Leroux, so was there no contradiction between religion and science for the Fourierists. Indeed, Considérant believed that the role of "social science" was to realize the fraternal promise of Christianity, to establish the Heavenly City on earth. For *La Démocratie pacifique*, Christianity's fraternal promise was the abolition of wage labor: "The work of Christ is not yet complete, for the wage system [*salariat*], the latest remnant of antique slavery, is still alive. . . . Work is still a painful burden which exhausts the worker, since each man is not paid according to his work, as the justice of the heavenly city would require."[13]

As chief of the most important working-class movement of the 1840s, Etienne Cabet preached a Catholic message more fervent even than that of the bourgeois utopians. The Icarian leader proclaimed that communism was simply Christianity in practice. In his view, the teachings of Jesus and the message of communism both emphasized, above all else, human fraternity and the essential equality of all men. The special role of communism, according to Cabet, was to realize in the material world Christianity's promise of equality. Cabet went so far as to declare in *Le Vrai Christianisme* that "if all the *philosophes* who believed in the need for community arose from their graves to form a governing assembly, they would choose Jesus Christ as their president."[14] Cabet's chief lieutenant, a traveling salesman named Chameroy, claimed that profound Christian belief had led him inexorably to communism. Icarians referred to Chameroy as Cabet's Saint Paul, and his Christian faith typified that of other movement activists. Speaking to a group of workers, one of Chameroy's colleagues affirmed that "communism is nothing but Christianity reformed to its primitive purity— one cannot really be a Christian without being a communist."[15]

Cabet was not the only early communist leader who considered Jesus Christ the founder of his movement. Alphonse Laponneraye, destined to become a leading democratic-socialist journalist during the Second Republic, embraced communism in the early 1840s. In the introduction to his collected works of Robespierre, whom he considered a communist, Laponneraye described Jesus, Rousseau, and Robespierre as "three names which exist in an inseparable unity and which are logically related to each other, like three terms of the same theorem."[16]

Even communists who placed themselves to the left of Cabet echoed his Christian sentiment. In 1846 the short-lived ultra-communist paper *La Fraternité* proclaimed that "since God had created all men equal [their struggle for] social equality and fraternity was simply God's will."[17] This effort to justify communist doctrine on the basis of Christian teaching was widespread enough in 1843 to move a dumbfounded Friedrich Engels to comment at length on the phenomenon:

> It is absolutely remarkable that, at a time when English socialists in general are opposed to Christianity and are forced to put up with all the religious prejudices of a gen-

uinely Christian population, the French communists, belonging to a nation well-known for its unbelief, are themselves Christians. One of their favorite maxims is
"Christianity equals communism," and with the help of
the Bible they seek to demonstrate the truth of this maxim
by the fact that the first Christians had to live under a
system of community ownership.[18]

Engels's only error was to underestimate the religiosity of the
French workers, a subject that will be treated below.

The thinker best known for espousing Christian socialism
during this period was Philippe Buchez. An atheist in his early
years, Buchez founded the Carbonari movement that flourished
underground in France during the 1820s. He discovered the
Gospels while still a leader of the Carbonari movement, and in
1825 he came under the influence of Saint-Simon's *Nouveau
Christianisme*. In arguing for the contemporary relevance of
the Gospel's morality, Saint-Simon's work helped move the ex-
atheist toward a commitment to Christian moral values. Buchez
was appalled, however, by the religious cultism and sexual lib-
ertinism of Saint-Simon's heir, Enfantin, and in 1829 he broke
with the movement. Buchez then decided to develop his own
brand of socialism—a doctrine, like those of the era's other
socialist theorists, that was to be firmly grounded in Catholic
morality.[19]

Buchez regretted that the teachers of his youth had never
introduced him to Christianity's moral truths, and in 1832 he
proclaimed that it was these verities that made him a Catholic:
"I discovered that the moral code which presided over modern
society, the moral code which I had obeyed for so long without
ever knowing that it had a name, was the moral code established
by Jesus Christ."[20] Since, for Buchez, the essence of that morality was equality, any social system based on inequality was
necessarily immoral. It was for moral reasons, therefore, that
Buchez sought to reform French society. Like the other socialists
of his time, he aimed to realize in practice the promise of Christian doctrine:

As long as material inequality exists among men, the only sentiment which can provide the proper basis for social morality, as for individual morality, is the desire to wipe out that inequality. . . . The Christian era will not have reached its culmination until it realizes the equality that the earliest Christians proclaimed as the keystone of their dogma.[21]

Buchez believed that this inequality could be remedied by mobilizing credits from the state and other lending institutions for the establishment of producers' cooperatives. Not only would these cooperatives "free workers from the servitude that capitalists have imposed on them," but they would turn Christian moral principles into political reality: "One can hardly imagine how Christian morality could ever become a political reality if we could not establish something like producers' cooperatives in our society."[22]

Buchez's most important contribution to the politics of the 1840s was his sponsorship of the workers' newspaper, *L'Atelier*, founded in 1840. Edited by the woodcarver A. Corbon, *L'Atelier* combined Buchez's social Christian message with moderate republican political views and a certain working-class consciousness. *L'Atelier* subscribed to the view that a sharp antagonism existed between workers and owners of capital, and it championed the idea of producers' cooperatives as the means of freeing workers from their dependence on capitalists.[23] Although *L'Atelier* demanded the extension of suffrage during the years prior to 1848, its basic message was moral rather than political. Following Buchez, *L'Atelier* urged the working class to draw on the moral values of early Christianity—that is, on the original teachings of Christ, before his message was perverted by the established Church. The fundamental principle of this original Christianity, according to *L'Atelier*, was fraternity. This sacred notion of a brotherly bond uniting all men was never put into practice, argued Corbon, because the Catholic Church violated its very premises by establishing hierarchic authority and allying itself with temporal power.[24] Christian fraternity thus remained purely spiritual and theoretical. The role of revolution in the nineteenth century, announced *L'Atelier*, would be to apply the principle of fraternity to the material world: "The coming revolution must proclaim loud and clear that it is Christian." Political gradualists, the editors of *L'Atelier* believed that this revolution would be the result not of violent upheaval but rather of a vast associationist movement based on producers' cooperatives, the symbol of Christianity's principle of fraternity.[25]

Despite its pro-Catholic position, there was little in *L'Atelier*'s message to comfort Church authorities. Corbon and his colleagues contradicted fundamental tenets of Catholic teaching by arguing that salvation could be attained in the here and now. Moreover, the Church would play a role in assuring earthly salvation only if it cooperated with the associationist revolution: "The priest will be summoned to make a formal decision concerning whether to serve the revolutionary process or to oppose it. If he opposes it, he will be considered a heretic and prosecuted as such."[26] In a neat reversal of roles, *L'Atelier* proclaimed that it, and not the Church, would decide who was a heretic. Like Saint-Simon, Corbon and his colleagues defined heresy as the failure to strive for the moral and physical improvement of the working class.[27]

The democratic movement of the 1840s, led by lawyers and journalists affiliated with the left-most parliamentarians of the July Monarchy, has commonly been considered heir to the secular spirit of Jacobinism. Yet, despite the movement's neo-Jacobin reputation and outward disdain for the various socialist sects of the era, it nonetheless was smitten by religious impulses similar to those of the socialist theorists analyzed above. *Le Dictionnaire politique encyclopédique du langage et de la science politique* (1842), bible of this democratic movement,[28] defined democracy as an eclectic mixture of Catholicism and Protestantism. From the former, democracy took the idea that personal inclination cannot take precedence over the authority of the law; from the latter, it borrowed the notion that no universal laws exist separate from or above the collection of individual interests and rights. Democracy would conciliate "the particular and the universal, the individual and society, through an organization of power where everyone will have a place."[29] For the authors of *Le Dictionnaire politique*, the true Christians of the nineteenth century were none other than "confesseurs de la doctrine démocratique." Like *L'Atelier*, *Le Dictionnaire* defined association as "la religion des révolutions futures" and referred to the society that would emerge from an associationist revolution as the "promised land." Democracy was simply the earthly realization of the unfulfilled Christian promise of equality: "Christianity is the religious dogma of equality, democracy is the political expression of that dogma. And Association is the practical means by which it can be realized."[30]

The religious fervor of Louis Blanc—notwithstanding his reputation as a Jacobin socialist[31]—was no less apparent. Writing in *La Revue du progès*, Blanc argued that eighteenth-century Voltairianism was no longer appropriate for the progressive forces of his own era. The left needed an injection of religious sentiment to combat the haughtiness and egocentrism of the July Monarchy:

> To carry on with Voltaire's tradition in today's world would be dangerous and infantile. Each era has its own task. The task of our own epoch is to breathe life back into religious sentiment, to combat the insolence of skepticism and to turn idle banter into serious discourse. . . . It is, therefore, in the name of religious sentiment, and in order to assure its triumph, that we denounce the iniquities and the ceremonial farces which serve to discredit religious sentiment by cloaking themselves in its garb.[32]

The bourgeoisie legitimized it rule, Blanc maintained, by presuming to represent the Christian values to which all Frenchmen subscribed. Blanc hoped to undermine a legitimacy he considered false by arguing that leftists alone respected the spirit of Christianity. France's governing Voltairians violated Christ's teaching by opposing the struggle for liberty, equality, and fraternity—the revolutionary trinity—which the radicals believed to be embedded in the Gospels themselves. If the democrats could prove an exclusive right to true Christian credentials, Blanc believed, they would be able to assume the religious authority that the government had unjustly usurped. In proposing an alternative standard of Christian belief, Blanc could claim in effect that democrats were more Christian than their conservative opponents. At the same time, he demonstrated the extent of his own religious commitment and anticipated one of the major propaganda themes of the démocrates-socialistes. Was he also responding to an emerging popular religiosity that took seriously the Christian promise of equality and brotherhood?

Blanc himself certainly believed that the Parisian working class possessed strong religious sentiments. In his view, the violent anticlericalism and anti-Christian hostility expressed during and after the revolution of July came not from Parisian workers but from the Orleanist bourgeoisie. The socialist writer asserted that it was "members of the bourgeoisie dressed in black suits and yellow gloves," and not Parisian workers—as has often been supposed—who sacked the Saint-Germain Auxerrois Church on 14 February 1831, the anniversary of the duke of Berry's death.[33] According to Blanc's account of this event, the workers stayed out of the fray when angry Orleanists ransacked the Church to punish the clergy for allowing a commemorative mass to turn into a Legitimist demonstration. Moreover, workers abandoned a republican demonstration the following day when it left the Palais Royal to parade in front of the archbishop's residence. The workers had no desire to attack the Church, wrote Blanc: "Their sole cry was 'Give me work and give me bread!' "[34]

Blanc's attempt to absolve the Parisian workers of violent anticlericalism is not implausible. Since the Church was not inextricably tied to governmental power in 1831, as it was in 1789, it seemed less responsible for the plight of the popular classes. Moreover, urban laborers sought tangible benefits from their participation in the July revolution, and when these were not forthcoming, they rightly blamed the government and not the clergy. Yet, suggestive as it is, Blanc's account is not disinterested enough to provide a fully credible or complete picture of the religious attitudes of French workers during the July Monarchy. Evidence of working-class religiosity must be gleaned from other sources: bourgeois thinkers known to have influenced the working class; nonpolemical accounts of working-class behavior; workers' memoirs; popular literature; and songs written and sung by members of the laboring class.

Georges Duveau has pointed out that the mentality of workers in the 1830s and 1840s cannot be dissociated from that of the liberal and republican bourgeoisie. Thirsting for education during this period, artisans looked to sympathetic members of the middle class for enlightenment. Far from resenting bourgeois republicans, workers respected their knowledge and, more often than not, they were glad to follow bourgeois leadership.[35] Joseph Benoît, a communist militant in the 1840s who later joined the international and the Paris Commune, wrote that "the workers of that epoch [1836] . . . were driven by an insatiable thirst for knowledge and for instruction in political and social science. . . . And it is for that reason that they spread the ideas formulated by Louis Blanc, Pierre Leroux, and others."[36]

In his *Mémoires de Léonard*, Martin Nadaud, the mason turned Representative of the People in 1848 and senator under the Third Republic, demonstrates the extent to which he felt the influence of republican and socialist leaders during the July Monarchy. Nadaud explains, for example, that upon seeing Louis Philippe for the first time his initial reaction was to find the citizen-king sympathetic. His spontaneous emotion vanished, however, as he remembered what Raspail and Cabet had said in their newspapers: not only had the king humiliated France over the Prichard affair with the British, but he had sabotaged the Glorious Revolution of 1830 by installing the reign of the moneyed bourgeoisie.[37] Throughout his memoirs Nadaud emphasizes the respect and admiration he felt for all those who were sympathetic to his fellow workers. Despite his communist affiliation in the 1840s, Nadaud considered anyone who defended the people both a political ally and an intellectual mentor.[38]

During the July Monarchy workers in general had more confidence in bourgeois theorists and political leaders than in their fellows. Whereas newspapers edited entirely by workers, such as *L'Atelier* and *La Fraternité*, attracted an almost exclusively middle-class readership, workers tended to read Cabet's *Le Populaire*.[39] Indeed, Cabet had become so popular among Lyonnais workers in the mid-1840s that they soundly rejected a challenge to his leadership organized by a group of their peers.[40] During the years prior to 1848 popular legend had it that if Pierre Leroux, Proudhon, Cabet, Considérant, Cantegrel, and others were closeted together in a single room, they would ultimately come up with a formula designed to guarantee human happiness.[41] More than revealing a penchant for wishful thinking, this legend shows the extent to which workers exalted intellectual schemes and looked up to bourgeois social theorists.

Given the religious orientation of the socialist and republican personalities to whom activist workers looked for political and intellectual guidance, it seems safe to assume that the religious precepts so important to political discourse in the 1840s, at the very least, did not offend politically conscious French workers. Indeed, there is substantial evidence that workers shared their bourgeois mentors' religiosity—albeit tinged with anticlericalism. Moreover, it is highly likely that precisely these shared religious beliefs and common religious vocabulary allowed bourgeois intellectuals and publicists to communicate with and command the respect of an urban working class so culturally different from the left-wing elite. In many ways, Christian language and belief served as a cultural intermediary that linked middle- and working-class activists.[42]

That Etienne Cabet, the socialist who equated Christianity and communism, enjoyed the largest and most exclusively working-class following of any 1840s political leader testifies to the religiosity of politicized workers.[43] Le Populaire, whose thirty-five hundred subscribers (it had, of course, many more readers) were largely skilled urban craftsmen, trumpeted appeals to Christian purity and continually advertised its belief in communist-Christian identity. Jesus was the first communist, according to the Icarian paper, and the goal of the communist movement, was simply to fulfill the eighteen-century-old Christian promise of human equality and fraternity. Rank-and-file Lyonnais Icarians registered agreement with Le Populaire when they declared that communism was the "veritable Christianity as applied to the relations of life."[44]

Although the other socialist sects had no sizable working-class following, their ideas nonetheless did filter down to urban workers. Writers like Eugène Sue popularized Fourierist and Saint-Simonian concepts—religious and otherwise—in their novels, and much of this literature was serialized in mass-circulation newspapers and published in cheap editions.[45] Literate workers had access to these publications in the reading rooms (*cabinets de lecture*) established in Paris and major provincial cities between 1820 and 1845. In addition to novels and newspapers, the reading rooms stocked the writings of Cabet, Louis Blanc, Pierre Leroux, and other authors to whom literate workers looked for guidance.[46]

Illiteracy did not prevent workers from being exposed to this political-religious material. Literate artisans read aloud to illiterate comrades gathered in habitual cafés and meeting places. And in quiet workshops, like those of the tailors, workers were read to while they cut and sewed.[47] Charles Remusat, a government minister during the 1840s, reported that the literature read by workers to each other during this period was "ultrademocratic," by which he meant the writings of Blanc, Cabet, Leroux, Considérant, and the like.[48]

Next to Cabet, the middle-class theorist most popular among the "lower orders" was probably Felicité de Lamennais, the abbé turned propagandist of a populist Christianity conceived as the moral basis to a future democratic society. Lamennais's *Paroles d'un croyant* (1834) was one of the most influential writings of the early nineteenth century, and his *Livre du peuple* (1837), published in several cheap editions, reached both peasants and workers through colportage and the cabinets de lecture. So popular was the *Livre du peuple* that it sold more than ten thousand copies during its first few days on the market.[49]

It is not difficult to see why Lamennais's books appealed to economically squeezed workers who sought to bolster their declining status or why readers were attracted to the abbé's religious views. Lamennais proclaimed—his books read like sermons—that God created all men equal but that princes had made them unequal. Democracy was the only political system consistent with Christian teaching because it guaranteed the human equality that Jesus promised. "God did not create you to be a

simple herd driven by a few powerful men," Lamennais exhorted. "He created you to live freely in a society of brothers."
"The rulers," he continued, "will tell you that the arbitrary
domination of a few and the slavery of everyone else represents
God's established order. . . . Let them know that their god is
in fact Satan . . . and that your God is destined to defeat theirs."[50]
In identifying God with the people and placing Him on the side
of the unprivileged, Lamennais anticipated Louis Blanc's struggle to wrest the mantle of religious legitimacy away from the
ruling elite and bestow it on the democratic movement. He
sought to deny conservatives the moral authority they enjoyed
as a result of what he considered an unholy association with
Catholicism.

Lamennais did not limit his critique to the political structures
of the July Monarchy. He attacked the essence of the capitalist
economy itself as anti-Christian and contrary to God's will.[51]
Modern labor conditions were worse than those of slavery, for
the vast majority was forced to toil for the benefit of a dominant
but idle elite who felt no obligation even to guarantee the subsistence of their employees. Setting the tone for a generation
of social theorists, Lamennais argued that the road to reform
lay in achieving the Christian promise, "in constructing the
City of God [by] realizing progressively . . . His work in humanity."[52]

It is highly likely, then, that French workers were receptive
to and influenced by the religious ideas of the July Monarchy's
republican and socialist leaders. But what made them open to
these ideas, and how did they manifest their own religious
commitment? The workers' profound respect for bourgeois theorists has already been noted, but there is perhaps a more basic
reason for workers' deep religious feelings. Outside the largest
cities, religious tales and other Christian writings composed a
major part of the reading matter accessible to the popular classes.
Thus, the books with which workers learned to read were mostly
religious. Proudhon, for example, taught himself to read the
Bible, and so did many other self-educated workers. One Jean
Dessoliaire, a tailor, taught his daughter to read using Lamennais's *Paroles d'un croyant*, and the father of worker-poet Fré-

déric Mistral read and re-read just three books during his life-time: the New Testament, *L'Imitation de Jésus-Christ*, and *Don Quixote*. Furthermore, as printing innovations slashed publication costs during the July Monarchy, more and more workers began to read the cheap editions of the Gospels and the lives of the saints that flooded both urban and rural France after 1830.[53] And just as workers' more formal education often rested on religious material, so the informal religious teaching they received from their parents sometimes resonated with overtones of populist morality. Joseph Benoît credited his mother with enriching his life with religious meaning:

A Christian mother developed in me all the best sentiments, as much through her words as through examples of her charity. This is how my mother helped to complete my education. Every day my heart was filled with the love of my fellows, and especially of the poor, whom I had learned to consider as brothers deprived of God's treasures.[54]

Growing class consciousness contributed as well to workers' receptivity to the July Monarchy's resurgent religiosity. Politically aware workers increasingly sought to dissociate themselves morally and ideologically from a commercial bourgeoisie that, like the Philippist political leaders, remained overtly Voltairian.[55] Far from being a dangerous class in many ways indistinguishable from common criminals,[56] skilled French workers often exhibited an almost severe moral rectitude and abhorred the lax morals and frivolous behavior of their social betters.[57] Encouraged by the populist Catholic literature of the 1830s and 1840s, many workers began to equate moral laxity with an insensitivity to suffering and exploitation. It was only a short logical step to the belief that both resulted from a lack of Catholic faith on the part of the wealthy classes. The clergy itself was not unsympathetic to such a view during the 1840s, and churchmen often held the bourgeoisie responsible for working-class anticlericalism.[58] The religious question, then, was fast becoming one of the principal issues through which workers expressed their growing apprehension of class antagonism.

Beyond the books and newspapers they chose and the leaders they followed, how did French workers demonstrate their religious commitment during the 1840s? The celebrations and solemn observances in which they took part often had substantial religious content. For example, the 1845 funeral of an Icarian tailor who died in prison followed Catholic ritual to the letter, as did the commemorative ceremony at his graveside a year later. Typographical workers, holding a banquet to celebrate their successful negotiation of a *tarif*, referred to the fete as a "Sainte Communion."[59]

One of the best direct records of working-class mentality is the collection of songs written and sung by workers during the July Monarchy. Gathering in working-class singing societies like La Lice chansonnière or simply meeting clandestinely in basement *goguettes*, such songsters as Jules Vinçard, Louis Festeau, Pierre Dupont, Gustave Léroy, Charles Gille, Eugène Pottier, and others less well-known sang to Parisian workers and their bohemian consorts. Many of their songs were printed on single sheets of low-grade paper and sold on street corners for a few centimes apiece. The works of these songwriters seem to have been well-known among the Parisian working class, and they helped to inject a certain political and social content into the all-too-brief hours of leisure passed in neighborhood cafés.[60]

Like most worker-intellectuals of this period, songwriters felt the influence of the July Monarchy's various socialist currents. Vinçard, the son of a modest artisan, apprenticed as a carpenter and joined the Saint-Simonian movement in 1831. Festeau's skill as a jewelry maker enabled him to graduate into the commercial middle class, and he took Fourier and Considérant as his political mentors. Gustave Léroy, a brush maker, was a moderate socialist close to Ledru-Rollin and *La Réforme*. Charles Gille, illegitimate son of a corset maker, entered his mother's profession and joined Marc Caussidière's Babouvist-oriented secret society in the mid-1830s. Gille hawked copies of his own songs for twenty centimes apiece, and he quickly became one of the most popular working-class singers. Eugène Pottier, canonized by twentieth-century socialists as author of the "Internationale," was a Fourierist affiliated with *L'Atelier* in the 1840s.[61]

Perhaps the most famous songster-poet of mid-century was Pierre Dupont, friend of Baudelaire and intimate of the republican elite. During the Second Republic, Dupont's "Chant des ouvriers," "Chant des paysans," and "Chant du vote" nearly equalled the "Marseillaise" in popularity. Virtually without exception, the songs of these prominent working-class poets, as well as the verses aired in France's more obscure goguettes, expressed Christian sentiments similar to those of the socialist and republican leaders of the 1840s: Christian morality would undermine the corrupt system of capitalist exploitation and form the basis of a new regime of cooperation and harmony.[62] Socialism represented the fulfillment of the original Christian promise of equality and fraternity. Thus, the verse of Reims cobbler Jean-Louis Gonzalle blamed the workers' plight on the faithlessness of modern capitalism:

Carthage was faithless, England is the same,
For they embody, harsh and extreme, the spirit of business.
Such a spirit respects no other gods, no other laws
Than love of the stark and horrible "every man for himself."
. . . .
Do not extoll our industrial expansion!
Far from improving the material conditions
Of the working people, it exploits and decimates,
It creates beneath them a horrifying abyss.[*63]

A new Christian faith could, however, turn the new industry to the workers' benefit: "De la vapeur subissons la puissance, / Mais l'avenir n'est qu'à Dieu [Today, we must endure the power of steam, / But the future, the future is in the hands of God]!"[64] Jules Vinçard viewed his songs as an appeal for "the fraternal

---

* Carthage était sans foi, l'Angleterre est de même,
C'est l'esprit de négoce, alors qu'il est extrême,
De n'avoir d'autres dieux, de n'avoir d'autre loi
Que des amours de brute et affreux *tout pour soi.*
. . . .
Qu'on ne me vante pas l'essor industriel!
Loin d'ameliorer le sort materiel
Du peuple travailleur, il exploite et décime,
Il creuse sous ses pas un effroyable abîme.

union of all men, of all families and of all nations—an effort
to translate into acts the thoughts of Jesus."[65] In "Alerte" (1836)
Vinçard proclaimed that God would unite "all the world's workers . . . in a new faith," a faith that ultimately would abolish
"aggressors" and "oppressors."[66] Similarly, in "Le Salaire"
Charles Gille urged his fellow workers: "Rally to the cause of
order; I mean the order of God, an order which is none other
than Fraternity."[67] Unlike most worker-poets of the 1840s, Pierre
Dupont directed his message to peasants as well as artisans. In
"Le Noël des paysans" ("The Peasants' Christmas") he paid
homage to the egalitarian message of Jesus Christ:

> My poor friends. It was Jesus
> Who illuminated our dark night with the
> Brilliant light of clarity.
> Let us drink to his sainthood
> For with Him was born equality.**[68]

The analysis of religiosity during the July Monarchy has, to
this point, been limited to middle- and lower-class intellectuals
and urban artisans. What about the rest of the population, the
vast majority of Frenchmen who lived in the countryside and
in small villages? How did the religious sentiments of peasants
compare with those of their urban compatriots during the first
half of the nineteenth century? The religious history of rural
France, like all aspects of nineteenth-century provincial life, is
mired in the complexity of the nation's vast regional differences.
Nonetheless, a number of generalizations can be suggested concerning both popular religious expression and the Catholic
Church's role in rural communities between 1800 and 1850.

Historians have tended to believe that the Enlightenment
inaugurated a process of "dechristianization," a process that,
heightened by the Revolution of 1789, continued unabáted until
our own day. Recent studies, however, reveal a more complex

** Jésus fait dans notre nuit noire
  Pauvre gens! Luire une clarté:
  A sa sainté nous devons boire,
  Avec lui naît l'égalité.

series of events in which the religious commitment of the different levels of society must be distinguished.[69] According to this new historiography of religion, the period from the sixteenth to the late eighteenth century was an era of intensive *Christianization* in the French countryside. Only marginally Christian at the beginning of the sixteenth century, the peasantry became the object of a Counter-Reformation-inspired campaign to stamp out what the Church considered "paganism" and "superstition." Although this campaign failed to suppress the old peasant religion completely, it succeeded admirably in suffusing that religion with the rituals, symbols, and beliefs of Catholicism. Thus the agricultural rites and popular festivals of peasant tradition were assimilated into Christian culture without entirely losing their pagan flavor.[70]

The Church's mission to Christianize the peasantry continued well into the second half of the eighteenth century, the period during which the middle and upper ranks of society began to detach themselves from the tutelage of the Catholic clergy. The Revolution erupted, therefore, at a moment when Catholic orthodoxy was receding in the urban centers but gaining considerable ground in the provinces, though peasants often demonstrated a remarkable ability to dilute Counter-Reformation orthodoxy with their own customs and beliefs.[71] Among elites and urban dwellers, then, the events of 1789 simply heightened a dechristianization already underway; among the peasants, the Revolution abruptly halted a still incomplete process of Christianization.

The decade of Revolution disrupted the operation of the Catholic Church to the point where it could not fill clerical vacancies for want of ordained priests and could not hold mass or catechism classes for lack of funds to rebuild destroyed or damaged churches. Between 1800 and 1825 the number of French priests declined steadily, as did the number of usable churches.[72] Thus, by the beginning of the July Monarchy, the population of such provinces as the Paris Basin, the Orléanais, Berry, and the Limousin had only marginal contact with the Church.[73] Yet the evaporation of Church presence in the countryside between 1800 and 1830 did not dispel popular religious fervor. On the contrary, this vacuum of clerical power encouraged the resurgence of a popular religiosity that reflected the fundamental insecurity and uncertainty of rural life in the early nineteenth century. In essence, this peasant piety exhibited a belief in the practical utility of sacred and supernatural forces and found expression in saint worship and quasi-Christian magical ritual.[74]

For a number of intersecting reasons, popular religiosity reached its nineteenth-century peak at the beginning of the July Monarchy. By 1830 the postrevolutionary generation, largely ignorant of Catholic doctrine, had reached adulthood and now set the tone for their communities' religious expression.[75] Moreover, most of the priests trained before the Revolution were now dead, and the Church had not produced enough young curés to fill their places. Finally, the severe cholera epidemic of 1832 traumatized rural France and fanned popular devotion to the cults of healing saints.[76] Desperate for protection from the deadly epidemic, peasants began to shift their interest from worship of Church-sanctioned saints to such newly resurrected popular idols as Saint Roch, believed to have cured plague victims in the fourteenth century.[77]

Alarmed by a phenomenon they considered pagan, Church leaders endeavored to restore more orthodox religious belief in the countryside. In the mid-1820s the Church began to recruit new curés from the ranks of the peasantry, and it established missions to rechristianize the population. The diocese of Blois, for example, had no bishop until 1826, and many of its parishes lacked priests. But beginning in 1826 the newly appointed bishop moved to restore Church power, and he opened a large seminary at the end of the decade. The nation as a whole followed the Blois example, and by the 1840s the Church exhibited renewed strength.[78] Ordinations rose steadily during the 1830s and continued to grow until 1868, when they reached their all-time peak.[79] As a result, attendance at Sunday and Easter mass increased dramatically in parishes all over the country.[80]

By no means did this "Catholic restoration" take place evenly throughout the country, nor did the renewed strength of the Church have the same consequences nationwide. Clergymen imposed their leadership most successfully in regions such as the North where an influential and devout rural elite reinforced the Church's power. By contrast, in such provinces as the Limousin and Provence, where support from local *notables* was either lacking or waning, the Church found it more difficult to restore its authority. Moreover, traditions of clericalism or anticlericalism inherited from the revolutionary period conditioned local responses to the Catholic restoration, as did the Gallican or ultramontane affiliation of the parish clergy.[81]

Between 1820 and 1848 priests' attempts to impose doctrinal purity gave rise to severe conflict between peasants and their *curés*. These conflicts often resulted in a popular anticlericalism that did much to detach the rural population from the Church in the years prior to 1848. Seldom, however, did this anticlericalism engender atheism.[82] The peasantry simply turned away from the Church and looked elsewhere for an outlet for its religious sensibilities. After 1848 democ-soc politicians were to provide that outlet.

During the first half of the nineteenth century priests continually complained of their parishioners' disrespect for official religious belief and ritual, and they ruefully admitted that the villagers practiced a religion fashioned after their daily needs. In 1850 the curé of Selle-en-Hermais in the diocese of Orléans summed up the religious behavior of his flock:

> They [the village population] practice certain customs that have something to do with religion. They recite the formula of prayers, but they don't pray; they attend mass, but they hear nothing; *they believe in a God which they fashion for themselves*; they fervently pray to God when they are sick, when they believe themselves bewitched, when their animals are sick; they constantly ask God for temporal goods, but never for spiritual ones.[83]

Priests from the diocese of Digne (Basses-Alpes) similarly lamented the unorthodox and populist religious impulses of their parishioners. In the 1841 Spiritual Survey the curé of Blégiers reported: "When I consider the spirit of this region, I still see some religious faith. There is, at least, a certain *exterior* of religion . . . [but] the people love to meddle in all that concerns the Holy Ministry; and they want to manage [conduire] and dominate the priest according to their own ideas."[84] Responding to the same survey, the curé of Bayasse à Fours wrote that "the [people's] religious spirit is somewhat bizarre, for it conforms to their own whims. They want their own kind of religion [réligion à sa mode]. . . . But despite this, there still are, generally speaking, religious sentiments."[85]

The curés do not accuse their parishioners of abandoning religion; rather, they lament the villagers' stubborn efforts to determine what religion means and how it is to be practiced. The spiritual surveys reveal the populist and incipiently democratic character of mid-nineteenth-century rural piety. Ordinary people exercised a kind of popular sovereignty with respect to religion: they, and not the priest, decided which beliefs and rituals were important.

For rural dwellers in the first half of the nineteenth century religious practice was often inseparable from elaborate processions to honor patron saints and joyous dancing to celebrate religious holidays, baptisms, weddings, and funerals.[86] Rural churchmen found these popular rituals profoundly disturbing, for they revealed the peasants' refusal to embrace the clergy's separation of sacred and profane. Curés believed religious rituals should be devoted exclusively to solemn and pious observance. Perhaps even more important, rituals should be orderly and dignified—that is, under firm priestly control. Peasants saw things differently. They made no distinction between sacred and profane and viewed religious ceremonies as both solemn and joyous, spiritual and earthly. Sunday was not just a day of worship—though mass remained important to perhaps the majority of peasants in the first half of the last century—it was also a day of relaxation and amusement. To the horror of many rural clergymen, festive dancing regularly followed morning mass, and the religious observance of Catholic holidays often ended with dancing, feasts, and flirtatious encounters. On a more practical level, religious events often provided the occasion for discussing agricultural problems.

Churchmen complained not that profane celebration competed with pious observance but that peasants insisted on linking the two. In 1838 the curé of Ahny (Côte-d'Or) declared that, although most of his parishioners attend Sunday mass, "dances begin right after vespers and often continue well into the night."[87] Three years later a priest from Châteauneuf Miravail (Basses-Alpes) wrote: "On Ascension Day there is a huge gathering, not because this multitude is attracted by a sentiment of devotion—which might seem on the surface to be the case—but rather to give itself up to all sorts of disorders [e.g., dancing]. For many years this day has tormented the priests of Châteauneuf."[88] Châteauneuf's curé and many of his colleagues filled their spiritual survey with a long litany of religious holidays that regularly turned into profane celebrations complete with dancing and heavy drinking. "On the day after Pentecost," wrote the curé of Peypin (Basses-Alpes), "virtually all the people form a long procession called the tour of the countryside. Most people come not to sing praise to the Lord, but to discuss their crops."[89]

Priests worried most about the religious celebrations devoted to their parishes' patron saints. These fetes almost always began with a solemn religious observance and then degenerated into dancing, flirtation, feasting, and general merrymaking. The curé of Mison deplored how, during a procession to honor the patron saint, the young men of the village, "accompanied by a few musicians, place themselves among the girls who traditionally march in front of the married women. What is more, the difficulty and length of the procession's path occasions considerable dissipation."[90] Another Basses-Alpes curé asked his bishop to outlaw one lengthy procession in his locality: "We must forbid this procession of Gaubert, given the long distance from the church to the chapel of Cousson [the procession's destination] . . . and the dissipation that results from the chapel's remoteness [from the church]."[91] That this procession took its participants beyond his supervision profoundly disturbed the curé of Gaubert. So forcefully, however, did rural dwellers act to maintain sovereignty over their spiritual lives that curés hesitated to voice disapproval in public. When clergymen did attempt to assert Church orthodoxy over popular practice, severe conflict often resulted.

Not only did peasants consider religion a means of festive self-expression, but they also believed it possessed the magical power to improve their everyday lives. Priests constantly complained during the first half of the nineteenth century that peasants looked to them not for spiritual guidance but for practical services. As the curé of Villambalin (diocese of Orléans) observed: "people who ordinarily never set foot inside the church will come to have a gospel said in the hope of curing a sickness. . . . Some of them would go to mass if we didn't preach to them, if we never spoke of Hell or of confession. . . . People don't like a curé who preaches."[92]

Believing the curé capable of invoking divine intervention on their behalf, peasants asked him to bless virtually everything connected with their everyday lives. The priests of Autun (Saône-et-Loire) were expected to bless sick animals, new houses and barns, wells, ovens, vines, trees, and gardens.[93] In Autun and elsewhere priests routinely blessed fields before each harvest and performed various rituals designed to ward off storms, floods, and insects. Each Easter Monday throughout the first half of the century a priest from Nevers led a procession whose purpose was to bless the Loire River in order to prevent floods. And in the Basses-Alpes priests sometimes led, sometimes followed anxiously, processions undertaken to "conserve the fruits of the earth."[94] Throughout eastern Burgundy peasants marched in religious processions to ensure successful harvests, prevent droughts, end bad weather, and strengthen livestock.[95] Priests in Languedoc offered prayers against hail and storms, and peasants throughout southern France believed their curés possessed the power to ward off forest fires and violent storms.[96] Peasants also turned to religion for solutions to personal problems. They asked the curé to bless a son's shirt to bring him good luck on the eve of the conscription lottery; they took communion before a long trip; and young women had the curé pray for them to find a suitable fiancé. In addition, priests were expected to bless the clothes of a newborn baby and to cure sick family members.[97] Père Tiennon, peasant hero of Emile Guillaumin's *Vie* d'un simple, typifies much of France's peasantry in the mid-nineteenth century: "Though Tiennon was far from being an obedient disciple of the Church, he hardly ever missed ceremonies in which the success of crops was at stake."[98]

Occasionally peasant demands for practical priestly services could prove uncomfortable and even hazardous for rural men of the cloth. During times of drought villagers from several parishes of the Nièvre undertook processions to the Fountain of Notre Dame de Fauboulain to ask for rain. After the customary prayers, each pilgrim removed one of his shoes, filled it with fountain water, and then proceeded to douse the good curé. Uncomfortable as this might have been, priests fared even worse during periods of unseasonably cold weather. The ritual designed to ward off the cold required curés to bless a huge bonfire, and on at least one occasion a priest narrowly missed being roasted alive when his clerical robes caught fire.[99]

Not all rituals and prayers were addressed to God. Peasants in most regions paid homage to various saints as a means of preventing natural calamities, curing disease, and procuring certain services. Frédéric Mistral told of a Provençal ritual in which villagers plunged a bust of Saint Anthime three times in the local river in the hope of ending a dry spell.[100] Similarly, in 1850 peasants of the Poitiers region placed small packets of oats on the tomb of Saint Rodegonde in order to obtain a good harvest.[101] In the southeast villagers paid homage to Saint Brigitte "in order to preserve themselves from the disasters of the wind." On the Sunday closest to Saint Eloi's Day rural processions sought protection for their domestic animals, and on or near Saint Michel's Day peasant processions appealed for protection from the plague.[102]

Terrified by the recurrent cholera epidemics of the July Monarchy, villagers showed particular fervor for Saint Roch and other healing saints. For example, in the early 1830s the Basses-Alpes commune of Peyruis replaced its fête patronale with a day of homage to Saint Roch. "The new Saint Roch Day draws a large gathering of people," noted the local curé, but "less for its religious significance than as a day of dissipation . . . abuses [of Church orthodoxy] are everywhere."[103] Priests unwittingly encouraged such saint worship—and often provoked anticlericalism as well—by blaming the people themselves for the epidemic. When the archbishop of Sens (Yonne) and the curé of Béziers (Hérault) insisted that the epidemic represented God's punishment for popular atheism and immorality, their respective parishioners turned to fervent saint worship.[104] With medicine powerless to stop the epidemic and organized religion unwilling to intervene, the task of combatting cholera devolved to the healing saints.

In many rural regions peasants sought saintly cures from self-appointed healers, most of whom were elderly women. Acting as intermediaries between the sick and the supernatural, these healers performed rituals designed to obtain from certain saints both the diagnosis and the cure for a number of ailments. The curé of Broin-sur-Seurre (Côte-d'Or) reported that a woman in his parish "claims the ability to cure certain illnesses . . . called saints' diseases [maux des saints]." Parishioners "come from all over to consult her" for the diagnosis and treatment of the diseases of Saint Louis, Saint Phillibert, and Saint Marion.[105] Her technique was to soak three ivy leaves, each representing one of the saints, in holy water for forty-eight hours, accompanied by prayers that the curé found "mysterious and unrecognizable." If at the end of the forty-eight hours one of the leaves showed a mark, the patient had the disease of the saint that the leaf represented. If all three were marked, he was plagued with all three maladies. The healer's cure began with a mass and featured a nine-day fast during which the patient's diet was limited to a tasteless waffle that had to be eaten before dawn. It ended with a pilgrimage to the place where locals honored the saint who both carried and cured the given ailment. Clearly exasperated by his parishioners' faith in this healer, Broin's curé wrote that "the fast is observed with an exactitude that the Church never sees for its own fasts." Even worse, his flock often disputed the rules he made, but seldom did they challenge hers. What is striking about the healer of Broin-sur-Seurre and others like her is that they did not feel estranged from the Catholic religion. The priest reported that the "saints' disease lady" came to mass every Easter and made a point of speaking to him. Perhaps she considered herself an adjunct member of the clergy, for her relationship to her patients resembled the priest's to his congregation. She said mass, recited special prayers, prescribed fasts, led processions, and continually exhorted her suppliants "to have faith."[106]

Although many of the religious practices discussed above, such as blessing fields, crops, new houses, and barns, accorded with Church orthodoxy, many did not. And it was the peasants' rejection of the Church's effort to distinguish the orthodox from the superstitious that proved problematic for France's rural clergymen. Bishops undoubtedly had their reasons for ruling that blessing crops before the harvest conformed to orthodoxy while performing rituals to prevent storms did not. But peasants could not comprehend such subtleties. If a priest could guarantee a good harvest, he could prevent rain. Since peasants above all sought practical services from their religious observance, and since priests willingly provided those the Church considered orthodox, a curé who refused to perform practical rituals that were popular but unorthodox risked provoking the wrath of his peasant parishioners.

Many curés understood the danger of conforming to Church doctrine and accepted, albeit reluctantly, the people's sovereignty with respect to religion. As the curé of Quinson (Basses-Alpes) put it: "The people cling superstitiously to their own practices, and they would rebel against the priest who would want to suppress them one iota. Long experience has proved this to me. A religion that is serious and holy does not enter easily into the people's spirit."[107] A priest from Digne held a similar view: "The people must be treated very carefully. . . . They are likely to attack the priest who . . . shows himself a rigid observer of diocesan regulations."[108] Despite their recognition of the risks involved in enforcing Church orthodoxy, many of the clergymen ordained during the 1830s and 1840s tended more and more to oppose the people's unorthodox religious expressions. These new priests had felt the influence of Enlightenment rationalism, and they sought to disprove the liberals' charge that the Church encouraged superstition. Thus, clerical opposition to popular forms of piety mounted during the second quarter of the last century, and this opposition often provoked violent conflict between priests and parishioners.[109]

In 1840 the curé of Brignoles (Var) found himself the object of a riotous *charivari* after he refused to respect what he considered the pagan tradition of blessing local livestock during the festival of Saint Eloi. The Brignoles peasants grew so enraged over the curé's rejection of a rite they considered fundamental that they physically attacked both the police chief and the subprefect who were called in to placate the crowd.[110] A similar conflict occurred in 1840 during a religious procession in the Basses-Alpes village of Bras-d'Asse when a group of peasants violated an 1836 diocesan ban on a popular ritual in which village youths carried a statue of the Virgin while dancing. The Church considered it bad enough that these youths claimed the Virgin for themselves, but to dance with her constituted pure blasphemy. When the Bras-d'Asse curé attempted to prevent this ritualistic embrace of the Virgin, a tense confrontation ensued. In a subsequent statement to his bishop, the priest wrote that his parishioners regarded their violations of Church orthodoxy as legitimate efforts *"to reconquer their supposed rights."*[111] Rural Frenchmen thus viewed the ability to shape their own religious expression as a sacred right and felt justified in defying the curé when he acted to deprive them of their religious sovereignty. These villagers clearly considered themselves, and not the curé, the arbiters of proper religious practice. The curé's role was simply to preside over the customary religious rituals in which the villagers fervently believed. The peasants of Brignoles and Bras-d'Asse, like those of many other French regions, were by no means resolutely anticlerical; they desired the curé's acceptance of their ritual and attacked him only when he refused.

In southeastern France conflict arose frequently over a "superstition," as the curé of Mirbeau (Basses-Alpes) described it, "that priests have the power to attract or to dissipate storms."[112] Another Basses-Alpes curé reported the same superstition in his parish, and he added that villagers "attribute to evil forces phenomena that have natural causes."[113] Even in this relatively remote Alpine department priests in the 1840s attacked peasant beliefs from the perspective of scientific rationalism. Not only did this popular belief violate the curé's understanding of nature, but it threatened to undermine clerical authority. As the curé of Rougon put it: "The priest runs the risk of being paralyzed because storms occur often in this region, and I have heard a large number of gross ignoramuses claim to have seen the priest up in the sky moving the clouds."[114] In September 1848 conflict over a priest's refusal to exorcise hailstorms became so severe in Les Mées (Basses-Alpes) that Digne's police chief told the prefect there would be serious disorder in the village if the curé were not fired before the next storm. Les Mées's peasants believed that "as a result of his presence in their church . . . the anger of the heavens would come down on them."[115]

One of the popular rituals that provoked the most conflict during the 1830s and 1840s was the annual procession to commemorate Corpus Christi.[116] Considered by the peasants the most important procession of the year,[117] Corpus Christi joined the Catholic celebration of the Eucharist with a pre-Christian agricultural rite designed to guarantee a rich harvest. The occasion enabled the people to reiterate their identification with Jesus Christ and at the same time ask God for an abundant crop. The clergy did not approve of the unorthodox content that the peasants had injected into the celebration, and Church attempts to stamp out these non-Christian elements triggered numerous conflicts between villagers and their curés.

Trouble arose in the commune of Breux (Meuse) in 1825 when a new curé attempted to assert Catholic orthodoxy and clerical prerogative over town custom with respect to Corpus Christi. According to local tradition, the honor of carrying the dais during the procession, an event in which the entire village participated, went to four members of the municipal council chosen by the mayor. The curé, however, believed that this honor should be bestowed on the village's most devout Catholics. Told that the town councilors in question had not observed Easter that year, the curé decided to give the dais honor to four townsmen known for their regular church attendance. When the councilors declined to relinquish the dais, the curé angrily canceled the procession and stalked back into the chapel. Profoundly disappointed, the villagers broke into a noisy demonstration against the priest that became so raucous that local judicial officials contemplated calling in troops.[118]

Conflicts between peasants and their curés were by no means limited to the problem of "pagan" ritual or to the confusion of religion and magic. Priests' attempts to forbid Sunday work gave rise to vociferous protest from Midi peasants, many of whom labored for others during the week and reserved Sunday for their own plots. In addition, villagers and priests constantly fought over the cost and circumstances of burial. Peasants resented the fees charged by curés for presiding over funerals, and in many regions they believed that the right to perform funerals belonged to them and not the priest. In the Eure department, where confraternities of charity (confréries de charité) experienced a resurgence in the aftermath of the Great Revolution, confraternity members had become accustomed to presiding over all burials.[119] When a villager died, these lay members of the community donned ecclesiastical robes and performed the Church's traditional service for the dead. But as the Church replenished itself in the 1830s and 1840s, newly ordained priests endeavored to restore clerical control over funerals.

The situation came to a head in 1842, when the bishop of the Eure ruled that lay people had no right to wear clerical garb or to lead funeral services. These prerogatives belonged exclusively to ordained ministers of the Church. The confraternities disagreed and their members resented that the clergy "wants to snatch away from the people its religion, its devotion."[120] So strong was peasant belief in their confraternities that many preferred burial by excommunicated charité members to interment by ordained priests. These rural people had not become irreligious, for the charités imitated traditional priestly functions and recited standard Catholic prayers; rather, they believed religion belonged to them and profoundly distrusted the attempts of a clerical oligarchy to dilute their authority over religious observance. As one charité spokesman put it: "The voice of the peasant is every bit as powerful for God as that of a Bishop with his mitered head."[121] One could hardly ask for a clearer statement of the peasantry's populist and incipiently democratic conception of religion.

In regions where curés retained the ability to preside over funerals, peasants increasingly challenged their right to decide who merited Christian burial. Whereas curés reserved Church-sanctioned funerals for those who had been good Catholics, the people sought Catholic burials for all those who had been decent human beings. In a typical incident from 1829, the peasants of Le Luc (Var) demanded a proper Catholic burial for one Louis Charles, a wealthy liberal landowner who, true to his lifelong Voltairianism, refused last rites. Magnanimous and paternalistic, Charles had endeared himself to the townsmen, who expected him to be buried with honor—that is, by the Church. The curé had other ideas. He ordered Charles interred, without ceremony, in the corner of the cemetery reserved for sinners. Furious over the curé's decision, the population of Le Luc turned out to march behind Charles's casket in boisterous defiance of their priest.[122]

In most such incidents of this period the crowd did not extend its defiance of the curé to a rejection of religion itself. On the contrary, villagers often took religious law into their own hands and provided their own Christian burial for a deceased friend rejected by the Church. In 1847 a crowd of two hundred people in the Var town of Barjols forced its way into the town's locked church and conducted an ad hoc funeral service, complete with traditional prayers and holy water.[123] Similarly, in 1834 the mayor of Gaillefontaine (near Rouen) led a sizable crowd into the village church and performed the mass for the dead over the coffin of a deceased friend denied a Catholic burial by the curé.[124] These striking events demonstrate how anticlericalism developed out of conflicts within the community of believers over the meaning and uses of religion. Anticlericalism was not, therefore, associated with irreligion during the July Monarchy, and peasants could free themselves from clerical tutelage without denying their Christian or crypto-Christian faith.

Beyond these accounts of outward manifestations of piety and of conflicts between priests and parishioners, there are other

sources that provide information about peasants' religious beliefs during the first half of the nineteenth century. A number
of recent studies have argued that an analysis of the literature
to which villagers were exposed can provide additional insight
into popular mentality.[125] In the view of Geneviève Bollème
and others, the pamphlets, songs, almanacs, and brochures of
the *Bibliothèque bleue* both depicted and helped to shape the
culture of the rural masses in the eighteenth and early nineteenth centuries. Whether popular literature reflected popular
culture remains in dispute, however. Robert Darnton has argued
that this literature, written by anonymous urban authors, represented not popular culture but the popularization of elite culture.[126] Nevertheless, analysis of the religious publications of
the *Bibliothèque bleue* casts doubt on the notion that this material depicted the religious views of the eighteenth-century
French elite. The popular religious literature of the late eighteenth and early nineteenth centuries is filled with striking parallels to the provincial piety discussed above.

The religious songs, brochures, and popular books of 1750-
1848 show a preoccupation with saints and a practical view of
religion consistent with the peasants' outward piety. They exude
a joyous spirit that mirrors the festive way in which peasant
communities celebrated Catholic holidays. And, just as French
peasants everywhere feted Corpus Christi more exuberantly and
elaborately than any other holiday, the popular literature of the
time extolled with special fervor the image of a popular Jesus
Christ, humble man of the people.[127]

The literature of the *Bibliothèque bleue* may have mirrored
certain aspects of rural piety, but did it influence popular religious mentality? Did it in fact reach a rural audience during
the period 1750-1848? Scattered evidence indicates that it did.
Divided into a large number of small chapters and written to
resemble the rural folk tales traditionally transmitted by mem-
ory, the literature of the *Bibliothèque bleue* was designed to be
read aloud.[128] By 1750 most villages had at least one literate
resident, and a tradition of public storytelling provided a ready-
made forum in which the books of the *Bibliothèque bleue* could

be exposed to illiterate villagers who could not afford to buy them from the *colporteur*.[129]

By the beginning of the nineteenth century popular literature had come within the financial reach of well-to-do peasants and prosperous rural artisans. Both Jean-Pierre Gilland and Agricol Perdiguier, sons of peasants, wrote in their memoirs of buying literature from colporteurs early in the century.[130] But it was not until after 1830 that popular books found their way to the peasantry in significant numbers.[131] During the July Monarchy the number of books sold through colportage reached an all-time high as technical improvements in printing and paper making drastically reduced the prices of the colporteur's literature and the primary education law (1833) gave an unprecedented boost to literacy. Whereas 45 percent of the young men examined for military recruitment could read in 1829, the proportion able to read skyrocketed to 63 percent by 1848.[132] In the late 1830s and 1840s an army of some thirty-five hundred colporteurs sold more than nine million volumes per year in provincial France.[133]

In addition to peddling printed literature, colporteurs responded to the widespread rural saint worship of the July Monarchy by selling massive quantities of lithographed images of the various saints. By 1842 the Epinal firm of J.-C. Pellerin alone turned out nearly a million images a year, and approximately three-quarters of them were religious—mostly saints, but including portraits of Jesus Christ and the Virgin Mary as well. Lithographs of saints enjoyed such a high demand that all the images sold in the provinces during this period, even those that had nothing to do with religion, were called saints.[134]

It is unfortunately impossible to determine precisely who bought the popular literature and imagery sold annually in the provinces in the 1840s. But humble peasants and artisans likely formed the bulk of the colporteurs' clientele. The rural middle class just was not large enough to account for more than a fraction of the ten million items sold annually. Moreover, departmental archives abound with accounts of colporteurs arrested for selling literature to the peasantry. For example, in 1833 the justice of the peace from Saint-Florentin (Yonne) complained about "colporteurs who frequent local markets where they peddle to crude and ignorant peasants [a literature] that is blasphemous and obscene."[135]

Though it is difficult as well to determine which kinds of popular literature these rural dwellers preferred, available evidence indicates that primarily religious literature appealed to peasant buyers in the 1840s. Reine Garde, a simple seamstress and budding Provençal poet, told Lamartine in 1847 that, apart from *Robinson Crusoe*, the only books written for and of interest to the common people were the religious works of the *Bibliothèque bleue*: "With the exception of the Evangelists and of the one who wrote the *Imitation of Christ*, authors of our era did not think of us when they wrote their books. . . . Every author thinks of those like himself. . . . With the exception of *Robinson Crusoe* and *The Lives of the Saints*, what has been written for people like us?"[136]

Reine Garde was not alone among working-class writers in considering religious books appropriate for popular readers. A. Corbon, worker-editor of *L'Atelier*, published a popular edition of the Gospels in 1837, and Agricol Perdiguier urged his fellow *compagnons* to read it. Perhaps the best indication of lower-class attachment to religious literature during this period appears in the memoirs of one Poujet, son of a humble peasant. Poujet depicted the *veillées* of the 1840s in which his father lovingly read from a pocket-sized Bible: "We loved the Bible. It contained extraordinary stories which we enjoyed enormously. The stories were about ordinary people [Le peuple en était là]."[137] This statement does much to explain why religious literature appealed to peasants in the 1840s: they believed that the Bible and the popular religious writing diffused by colporteurs during the July Monarchy depicted their lives—"Le peuple en était là." Perhaps the nonreligious literature of the *Bibliothèque bleue* did represent a popularization of elite culture, but the religious books did not. Indeed, analysis of the basic religious texts of the *Bibliothèque bleue* indicates that ordinary villagers had good reasons to consider this literature relevant to their lives. These works advanced a sort of populist Catholic message that proclaimed the worth and dignity of common men.

The religious collection of the *Bibliothèque bleue* featured the *Bible des Noëls*, which recounted with vivid imagination the birth of Christ, and the various *Vies des Saints*, which celebrated the glory of saintly existence.[138] Often set to the music of traditional drinking and love songs, the *Noëls* were sung by colporteurs as they trudged from village to village hawking their literature. Rural dwellers easily associated the familiar melodies with the new words, and thus the *Noëls* could pass quickly into the villagers' repertoire of songs for the veillée and their local fetes.[139]

The *Bible des Noëls*, by far the most widely circulated religious book of the period, emphasized over and over the notion that Jesus Christ was a humble son of the people. Presented as a very human infant born into suffering and near misery, the Jesus of the *Noëls* became an object not simply of religious reverence but of personal identification as well. The poor families of rural France saw themselves in the Holy Family of the *Noëls*, and this literature suggested that Jesus belonged to them. The *Bible des Noëls* proclaimed, for example, that when Jesus was born, only the rural dwellers showed devotion for the holy child: "The bourgeois did not comfort him, and neither the well-to-do farmers nor the merchants visited him." The *Noëls* also stressed that Jesus had lived "to break the chains that bind us." On the whole, Catholicism appeared as the poor people's religion, as a faith based on the suffering and good works of a man very much like themselves.[140] Writing in 1884, socialist leader Benoît Malon beautifully captured this popular identification with Jesus in describing his own thoughts as an eight-year-old boy. Sitting in a church shortly after the Revolution of 1848, the young Malon envisioned Jesus as a living human being and imagined that he personified the suffering of the boy's rural existence:

> From where I sat . . . I saw . . . a cadaverous Christ portrayed with heartbreaking realism. His white chest was pitifully emaciated, and huge red spots marked his hands and feet. His huge dying eyes pierced all the way to the bottom of my soul. . . . The great Christ appeared more

and more pale and more and more pathetic in his agony.
. . . He became for me the personification of the suffering
of those threatened by the "great sorrow" and the "horrible
massacres" that the curé predicted for the future.[141]

Interestingly enough, confirmation of the popular identification with Jesus Christ came from the Catholic clergy as well.
The events of 1789 had convinced the hierarchy of the need to
restore obedience and respect for established authority. And to
undo the new and potentially subversive symbolic content of
the Jesus image, religious leaders sought to restore a distant
and authoritarian God to the center of Christian attention by
preaching a *Christianisme de la peur*. Neglecting Jesus Christ,
churchmen in the early nineteenth century instead raised the
specter of a terrible and vengeful God intent on punishing sin
and disobedience with the eternal agony of Hell, an agony they
lavishly evoked for the benefit of their parishioners.[142] In ban-
ishing Jesus from its discourse, the clergy implicitly acknowledged that Jesus had become the symbol of a nascent egalitar-
ianism. At a time when festive and magical populist religion
was on the upswing, this Christianisme de la peur no doubt
contributed to alienating the peasants from the brand of Catholicism that their curés represented.

Just as the *Bible des Noëls* fostered popular identification with
Jesus, so the *Vies des Saints* brought Catholicism closer to the
people by stressing the religion's practical uses. By the mid-
eighteenth century the *Vies des Saints* had introduced the idea
that one need not simply wait passively for death and disaster
to strike: religion could be used to struggle against death, disease, and natural catastrophe. Thus, these tales of saintly virtue
featured various prayers and semimagical recipes for protection
against storms, the plague, and other maladies. In offering such
practical remedies, the *Vies des Saints* suggested that it was
religion that gave common people a certain earthly power. More
than a mere means to salvation in an afterlife, religious faith
promised the possibility of personal betterment in the here-and-
now. Thus, the popular literature of the late eighteenth century,
like the popular religious expression of the early nineteenth

century, presented Christianity not as a set of obscure and distant doctrines but as a practical and communitarian antidote to personal misfortune.[143]

The *Noëls* and the *Vies des Saints* dignified the common people by identifying them with Jesus Christ and helped to free their spirits from the drudgery of everyday life. Associated with the melodies of drinking and love songs or presented as colorful and exciting narratives, both the *Noëls* and the *Vies* turned traditional religious tales into a forum for group participation and exuberant individual expression. One eighteenth-century collection of religious songs, for example, advertised its purpose as to "banish profane songs and to raise the soul up to God by filling it with the Holy Spirit."[144] Such an invitation to joyousness accorded well with the festive way in which rural people celebrated religious occasions, and it encouraged villagers in their growing struggle to retain their own rituals.

On the eve of 1848, therefore, both peasants and urban workers represented a reservoir of religiosity that could be tapped for political purposes. During the Second Republic the *démocrate-socialiste* left would prove capable of harnessing the fervor of these anticlerical believers. By claiming to be the true representatives of Christ and offering the earthly realization of Christianity's promise of equality and an end to exploitation, the Montagnards would succeed in channeling this sentiment into a rudimentary, but nonetheless genuine, left-wing *prise de conscience*. Peasants and workers already believed in a populist Jesus; the Montagnards would simply suffuse that belief with republican imagery. The people believed religion had practical utility in the here-and-now; the democ-socs would argue that the Red Republic, through the introduction of democratic institutions, could realize on earth many of Christianity's promises. Not only would religious language and symbols serve as a means by which peasants, workers, and members of the middle class could communicate with each other. But through an ideology grounded in the tenets of early Catholicism democ-soc propagandists would transform the economic malaise and populist religiosity of peasants and artisans into a commitment to democratic socialism.

CHAPTER III

THE MONTAGNARD PARTY:
AN INNOVATIVE FAILURE

In September 1848 the left wing of the republican movement, under the leadership of Ledru-Rollin, set out to construct a coalition with socialists of all degrees, from Louis Blanc to Etienne Cabet. The social basis of the Paris union was to be a nationwide alliance of skilled workers, peasants, and modest middle-class democrats. Determined not to repeat the failures of the Provisional Government, these republicans endeavored to build a coalition that would unite the whole of the French left and address the needs of humble workers and peasants. As the coalition took shape in the fall and winter of 1848-1849, it developed a strategy designed to establish contact with a politically unschooled rural population and to disseminate an ideology grounded in the moral principles of early Christianity and endowed with an explicit program of radical reforms. In addition, the new political union set out to establish a disciplined and hierarchic national party, an organization that anticipated the mass parties of the twentieth century.

This left-wing coalition did not emerge painlessly. Blanquists, radical republicans, and utopian socialists harbored strong suspicion and even antagonism toward one another. Often, personality clashes and opposing political strategies divided the various branches of the French left more than significant doctrinal differences. But their conflicts proved important enough to prevent them from uniting behind a single candidate for the presidential election of fall 1848.

It was the landslide victory of Louis Napoleon that provided the sense of imminent danger needed to complete the fusion of the left. A shared fear of the new prince-president, combined with the persistent efforts of those dedicated to unity, succeeded in creating a united French left in time for the crucial electoral campaign of spring 1849. Members of the new coalition, in keeping with their dual political origins and with the kind of socialist ideology they developed, called themselves démocrates-socialistes, or simply democ-socs.[1]

Fearing a premature assault on the young republic, most radical and socialist leaders opposed the workers' rebellion of June 1848, despite their deep sympathy for the workers' plight. La Réforme's editorial of 23 June 1848 portrays the agony of the radical republicans' decision to oppose the uprising:

> We are writing these lines with our hearts torn apart by a bitter distress, and our agony is cruel. On the side of the people, there are terrible grievances of suffering and despair; there are accumulated grudges which are for the most part legitimate. On the side of the republic there is our enlisted principle, the great principle of the republic, and whatever the faults of the individuals might be, there has been no violation by the government of sovereign rights.*[2]

Even so prominent a working-class leader as Martin Nadaud could not support his comrades' assault against the young republic: "I was [at that time] an ardent revolutionary. But for me to have joined the [June] combat, someone would have had to show me what obstacle there was to overcome. Since both the republic and universal suffrage were accomplished facts, I believed my main responsibility was to consolidate these two important conquests."[3]

Although the left dissociated itself from the uprising, it nonetheless suffered heavily from the workers' defeat. The failure of the radicals and socialists to support the rebellion isolated them from much of the Parisian working class, but their stance did not prevent conservatives from blaming them for the uprising. As a result, radicals and socialists lost what remained of the power that the February revolution had brought them. The

---

* La Réforme, founded in 1843, became the house organ of radical republicanism during the July Monarchy. Interested mainly in political and institutional reforms before 1848, it devoted considerable attention to the social question after the February revolution.

republican left never enjoyed the confidence of the provinces, and now their working-class support had evaporated as well.[4]

Bleak as their situation was at the end of the summer of 1848, the left's leaders resolved not to give up. Recognizing the need for a united opposition in the face of conservative reaction, Ledru-Rollin and his followers initiated a fall banquet campaign designed to ally reform-minded republicans with those who called themselves socialists. Ledru-Rollin chose the fifty-sixth anniversary of the First Republic, 22 September 1848, to launch the effort to unite the former left wing of the Provisional Government with the socialist leaders who opposed it during the hectic spring of 1848. Addressing a banquet crowd that included 150 left-oriented deputies from the Constituent Assembly, Ledru-Rollin sought to rally democrats and socialists around a definition of the Republic on which they all could agree. He argued that it was impossible to be a republican without desiring social reforms, that there could be no "real republic" without the *droit au travail*—a guaranteed job for everyone—and without institutions of credit designed to aid the modest worker. Unless the Republic was "consolidated by social institutions," declared Ledru-Rollin, "it would exist only in name, not in fact." The founder of the journal *La Réforme* hoped to convince his audience that, since the only true republic was necessarily democratic and above all social, leftists need not advocate socialism. The word "socialism" aroused fear and played into the hands of the right. What France needed was an "applied republic," the only regime that could "bring about for each person a proper equilibrium of dignity and well-being." To apply the true principles of the republic, Ledru concluded, the left required nothing more than unity.[5] Although Ledru-Rollin had made clear his support for the droit au travail, a fundamental worker's demand derived from Fourierism,[6] his speech did little to conciliate the socialists.

Ledru was perhaps more interested in drawing socialists into his own camp than in creating a genuine republican socialist coalition. Cabet, on the other hand, downplayed distinctions between republicans, democrats, and socialists in his appeal for unity at the same banquet:

I drink to the union of all democrats, even though I mean the union of all socialists, because there are no real democrats who are not socialists and there are no real socialists who are not democrats and republicans . . . the words "republican," "democrat," and "socialist" are therefore inseparable: republic, democracy, socialism are essentially the same thing.[7]

Despite Cabet's communist label, his position was not incompatible with Ledru's. The latter argued that all those who believed in democracy and who advocated social reforms were "real republicans," whereas Cabet deemed all republicans who desired social reforms to be in reality socialists. "To improve the lot of the people," declared the Icarian apostle, "that is socialism." Although Ledru-Rollin clung to the distinction between socialism and "applied republicanism," both he and Cabet agreed that the goal of republican politics was social amelioration.

This first banquet failed to produce a political alliance, but the speeches revealed a common ground on which republicans associated with *La Réforme* and so-called utopians like Cabet could build a coalition. Both groups called themselves republicans, both believed in democracy, both saw social reforms as the object of the republic, and, most important, both ultimately fashioned a commitment to democratic socialism out of the ideals of early Christianity.

While Ledru-Rollin continued to set himself apart from the socialists, other reform-minded republicans decided to assume the socialist label. By calling themselves socialists, these left-wing republicans sought the right to define the term their way. In so doing, they hoped to unite all social reformers around a new understanding of socialism. Speaking to two thousand guests at the second major banquet of the fall 1848 season, veteran republican lawyer d'Alton Shée declared his allegiance to socialism. He argued that all those who opposed social inequality and who sympathized with the plight of the poor had to consider themselves socialists. In his view, reformers who sought "to create a large and powerful democracy to regenerate the old world" were socialists, "regardless of whether they called themselves republicans, democrats, or revolutionaries."[8] D'Alton Shée distinguished "formal" democrats like Cavaignac from real democrats, and he maintained that "socialism is applied democracy . . . it is the construction of social equality." He told the assembled guests that republicanism and socialism were two inseparable parts of the society they all hoped to create: "The Republic is the form; socialism, the essence." Later in the evening the socialist philosopher Pierre Leroux appeared to accept d'Alton Shée's overture toward republican-socialist unity. Before the cheering crowd, Leroux drank to "the union of all democrats, without exclusion and without exception, provided that they profess the following truth: 'The Republic is not only democratic, but social in its essence.' "[9]

Following d'Alton Shée's lead, the left-wing Paris daily *La République* announced, in what would become the characteristic religious discourse of the democ-soc coalition, that "socialism is the only road to salvation." The paper then went on to plead for "a *fraternal* union between *les républicains-démocrates* and *les républicains-socialistes*." Echoing Cabet, *La République* argued that no real distinction existed between the two groups: "If one is a true republican, he is therefore a democrat. And if he is a democrat, he must be a socialist."[10]

Ledru-Rollin failed to convince the entire left to support his candidacy for president of the Republic.* But the fall 1848 banquet and press campaigns for republican unity spawned two Paris-based organizations—La Propagande démocratique et sociale européenne and La Solidarité républicaine—that joined republican reformers and socialists under the banner of democratic socialism. La Propagande démocratique et sociale led an innovative campaign to blanket the provinces with left-wing propaganda, and La Solidarité républicaine represented the first French effort to establish a centralized national political party.

---

* The French left, for the most part, opposed the institution of the presidency, and thus it participated only halfheartedly in the fall 1848 presidential campaign. Left republicans and socialists feared that the establishment of a strong executive power would revive France's monarchical traditions and compromise popular sovereignty.

These two groups helped to revive the republican movement by initiating a new appeal to rural voters, and they contributed to the relative success of a unified left in the legislative elections of 1849. Although there is no direct evidence of ties between the two associations, both were established in early November 1848; both included among their officers Agricol Perdiguier, the *compagnon* turned Representative of the People; and both modeled their organizational framework on that of the national administration.[11] Each established a central committee in Paris and sought to open branches in every department capital and subbranches in every arrondissement and canton in the country. The goal of both organizations was to unite republicans and to bring the rural population into the republican orbit by exposing it to democratic-socialist propaganda.[12] Whether or not the two groups actually worked together, there was a division of labor between them: La Propagande concentrated on propaganda distribution, La Solidarité on political organizing. The former constituted itself as a business enterprise and was able to escape political repression. The latter, openly a political organization, succumbed early to Louis Napoleon's assault against his republican opposition.

La Propagande démocratique et sociale européenne was first conceived in October 1848 by Gabriel Mortillet, a former leader of the Club de la Révolution, one of the most prominent clubs of spring 1848. Mortillet sought to centralize the dissemination of left-wing propaganda and to encourage its diffusion in the countryside. To this end, he wrote to all Paris democratic and socialist newspapers and organizations to solicit their participation in his new organization. Appalled by "the political ignorance of the proletariat and the lower-middle class," he considered it "urgent and indispensable to instruct all laborers." For Mortillet, "propaganda was the key to revolution":

> In order that our propaganda produce a powerful action, it must spread throughout the entire country. Democratic and social publications must be distributed in all our cities and all our towns. It must penetrate into the smallest vil-

lages, and if possible into each house. [With a nationwide organization], we can in a short period of time inundate France with literature, enlighten the laboring population, and assure the triumph of the democratic and social republic.[13]

Mortillet may have been overly optimistic about how long it would take to enlighten the people, but he did realize clearly that their education would require hard political labor. Neither the Provisional Government nor the Parisian clubs of spring 1848 had paid more than lip service to the need to propagate republican ideology in the provinces.[14] But Mortillet understood that good organization and a serious nationwide propaganda effort were needed to convert the people to republican politics.

Jules Ballard, veteran of numerous small business ventures, became chief administrator of Mortillet's propaganda outfit, and the two men put together an editorial committee evenly divided between republicans who labeled themselves democrats and republicans who called themselves socialists. Included were three deputies (Perdiguier, Beaune, and Pierre Leroux), one former club president, and four newspaper editors.[15] Their job was to decide which writings would be disseminated by the organization and to divide this literature into two categories. The first embraced theoretical pieces on political, social, and economic issues by recognized socialist authors. La Propagande intended these works to stimulate discussion and controversy and "took no responsibility for the doctrines developed in these writings."[16] The second category included "socialist writings which proposed solutions to pressing political problems."[17] La Propagande gave top priority to the second group and assumed responsibility for the contents of its literature. In addition to these two kinds of writings, La Propagande distributed songs, engravings, drawings, and caricatures "that could serve the democratic and social cause"; portraits, busts, statuettes, medals, and medallions that reproduced the features of socialists and Montagnard representatives";[18] and low-priced lithographs, often with political messages conveyed through religious imagery. A characteristic lithograph disseminated by La Propagande bore the caption "Le Jugement de Dieu" and portrayed Louis Napoleon and other European rulers fleeing in fright from the angels of death.[19] The organization also sold subscriptions for newspapers whose political line was acceptable.

Publishing nothing itself, La Propagande acted as a commercial intermediary between writers and publishers on the one hand and readers on the other. Mortillet and his associates simply sought to facilitate the spread of democratic-socialist propaganda into the provinces by centralizing sales. A provincial political leader or local bookstore owner would no longer have to buy literature from dozens of different publishers, for the whole range of democ-soc writings would be available through La Propagande's catalogue.[20] Given the transportation problems that still existed in the mid-nineteenth century, the ability to buy from a central depot was a great advantage. Being innovative propagandists, Mortillet and Ballard based their socialist enterprise on the principles of their era's commercial capitalism. Just as commercial middlemen marketed the products of France's master artisans, so the directors of La Propagande sought to take over the sales operations of the multitude of small left-wing publishers. Instead of marketing their own works, the latter would produce exclusively for Mortillet and Ballard.

Though La Propagande displayed no interest in making a profit, it nevertheless became a solid commercial venture. It lasted from November 1848 to the coup d'état—a long time for a démocrate-socialiste organization—and was considered a business success by the police officials who surveyed it. La Propagande kept afloat financially by selling large quantities of low-priced materials. It sold more than a million copies of Felix Pyat's "Toast aux paysans," nearly forty thousand of Proudhon's "Les Malthusiens" as well as "a considerable number" of the "Evangile socialiste," a text illustrating the democ-socs' belief that the Gospels provided the basis of modern socialist politics (see Chapter IV).[21]

Typically, La Propagande would buy *petits livres* from a publisher for five centimes apiece and then sell them for six centimes each to peddlers and other provincial contacts, who would in turn hawk the literature for eight to ten centimes. La Propagande thus covered its own expenses and provided a small income for the provincial correspondents. Another common practice of the organization was to buy up huge quantities of overstocked writings at exceptionally low prices. It then found provincial buyers through its network of engagé sales representatives. In so doing, La Propagande marketed socialist material that other publishers could not move, and it contributed to the diffusion of new political ideas into the countryside.[22] The sale of political literature in the provinces was not without precedent. But whereas the liberal propaganda peddled earlier in the century cost rural buyers fifty centimes to five francs apiece, La Propagande's merchandise sold for as little as two francs per hundred copies.[23] Technical innovations in printing, improved transportation, and reduced postal charges permitted this price decline and thus enabled Mortillet's literature to reach a peasant and working-class audience.[24]

In the spring of 1849 Louis Napoleon's police considered La Propagande démocratique et sociale européenne the most dangerous oppositionist organ in the country, "a real force within the state."[25] The government, however, was virtually powerless to act against it. The repressive legislation instituted after the June Days restricted the operations of private organizations that met regularly for political purposes, and it effectively outlawed many other political groupings through a catchall clause against "secret societies."[26] But the new laws could not touch an organization like La Propagande whose statutes and operations were purely commercial. As a business devoted to selling literature, La Propagande enjoyed immunity from the law against political societies, and as an aboveboard enterprise fully in accord with business law, it could not suffer prosecution as a secret society. Thus, the commercial nature of La Propagande frustrated police efforts to repress it and contributed largely to the organization's political success. The police report on La Propagande's administrator, Ballard, lamented that "the courts would find [in Ballard's correspondence] nothing more than a list of the names of the main provincial buyers—mostly bookstore owners and local democrats." In an imaginary conversation, the police summed up Ballard's enviable position:

I [Ballard] can publish that which seems useful to the party and destined for success. I will have correspondents in the provinces in each department. . . . [As a result] we will develop a real network of propaganda that has all the advantages of a *political organization* without any of the problems. I will have in my hands the names of all the men of action and initiative in each of the eighty-six departments, but I will correspond with them in a purely commercial manner. . . .[27]

Mortillet confirmed the police view of his organization. "The central office is concerned with nothing other than propaganda in the form of printed literature and drawings" he explained. Local branches could take on other "democratic activities," but the Paris headquarters would stay out of direct political involvement. All of La Propagande's activity was conducted aboveboard, and the enterprise scrupulously stayed within the law. Ballard carried on his work, as the police put it, "apart from all conspiracies and apart from all secret societies. . . . The petits livres are his barricades, and these aren't the least dangerous barricades we face."[28]

La Propagande intended to use professional colporteurs to sell its literature in the provinces, but new restrictions on freedom of the press passed in July 1849 made colportage of political materials too risky. The main links in provincial propaganda distribution thus became small-town bookstore owners, other shopkeepers, café proprietors, and members of the liberal professions. La Propagande mailed shipments of literature to democsoc bookstore owners, who then took charge of local sales. Other materials were sent directly to small-town Montagnard leaders who had occasion, in the course of their work as doctors, lawyers, veterinarians, notaries, or merchants, to sell or give the literature to peasant clients (see table 4 and Chapters V and VI). The police considered liberal professionals "the most dangerous of all propagandists, because they escape all repression and all surveillance."[29]

La Propagande survived the intensified repression that followed the abortive republican uprising of 13 June 1849 in Paris,

TABLE 4   Individuals Known to Have Been Local Correspondents for La Propagande démocratique et sociale européenne

Name	City	Department	Profession (politics)
Anstell, Ignace	Selestat	Bas-Rhin	
Ballay	Lyon	Rhône	Book dealer
Choffel	Toulon	Var	Metal worker (Proudhonian)
Collée, Abraham	Brignoles	Var	House painter (Icarian)
Dark, Marie-Rose	Poligny	Jura	Concièrge
Dubois, S.-B.	Saint-Die	Vosges	
Dubosc, Pierre	Marseille	Bouches-du-Rhône	Journalist
L'Allemand, Joseph	Provins	Seine-et-Marne	Café proprietor (socialist)
Olivier, Germain	Arles	Bouches-du-Rhône	Pharmacist
Ortlieb, Zenon	Saint-Marie-aux-Mines	Haute-Rhin	Pharmacist (Fourierist)
Pierre J.	Ste.-Menehould	Marne	Wine seller
Prodier	Clermont-Ferrand	Puy-de-Dôme	Seller of novelties
Roberge, Eugène	Belleville	Seine	Book dealer
Salomin	Strasbourg	Bas-Rhin	Bookstore owner
Silberling	Strasbourg	Bas-Rhin	Former solicitor

SOURCES: Dictionnaire biographique du mouvement ouvrier français; APP AA 432.

and in late 1850 the organization began to expand operations. Its first move was to sell shares of stock in an effort to gather the funds necessary to broaden its activity. Mortillet hoped to raise twenty-five thousand francs by offering one thousand shares at twenty-five francs apiece. La Propagande's directors sought to democratize ownership of the enterprise by dividing each of four hundred of those shares into twenty-five coupons worth one franc apiece, a price that laborers could afford. By mid-1851 Mortillet's enterprise had attracted only sixty investors at twenty-five francs, but its increased activity had enabled the organization to enlarge its sales dramatically. Monthly receipts rose from nearly nil in January 1851 to twelve hundred francs the following July, a sum that more than covered La Propagande's expenses.[30] La Propagande's experiment in democratic financing—tried as well by a number of republican newspapers (see Chapter VI)—worried the government. Not only did the new funds enable republicans to continue their work, but organizations like La Propagande could circumvent the legal restrictions on political conclaves by convening shareholders' meetings.[31] In the face of heavy political repression, these democ-socs demonstrated remarkable resourcefulness. They had become masters at using free enterprise to foster socialist politics.

In early November 1848 three of Ledru-Rollin's political allies, Charles Delescluze, Agricol Perdiguier, and Martin-Bernard, announced the formation of La Solidarité républicaine. Martin-Bernard, a typesetter turned lawyer, was a veteran of conspiratorial politics who helped Blanqui and Barbès to found La Société des familles and La Société des saisons in the late 1830s. His participation in Blanqui's uprising of May 1839 cost him a long stint in a Mont-Saint-Michel jail cell, but in 1848 he won a seat in the Constituent Assembly. Perdiguier, chronicler of France's *compagnonnages*, was a moderate republican of peasant stock also elected to the Assembly in 1848. Delescluze, a journalist, was a close associate of Ledru-Rollin.[32]

Bankrolled in part by Ledru-Rollin, La Solidarité represented the first French attempt to establish an organized national political party.[33] Unlike the republicans of spring 1848, the democsocs understood that universal suffrage could not be expected to produce automatically a left-wing majority within the French electorate. La Solidarité républicaine was the first political group during the Second Republic to set as its explicit goal the systematic exploitation of the political potential of the rural masses, who still constituted two-thirds of France's population. Neither the provincial *notables* in April 1848 nor Louis Napoleon in the presidential election the following fall had needed to campaign for rural support. Their personal reputations had sufficed to win a population unfamiliar with electoral contests. As the directors of La Solidarité realized, however, the results of these elections implied no fixed political affiliation, and a campaign of political education could attract the rural populace to the republican cause. Hence, "the purpose of La Solidarité . . . lies in the active effort to propagate socialist doctrines. It has a special responsibility to spread this propaganda wherever knowledge is the most limited and the people are the least enlightened."[34] In founding La Solidarité, Martin-Bernard and his colleagues demonstrated that they grasped the significance of France's abrupt change from restricted to universal suffrage. Whereas the Provisional Government had alienated urban workers and neglected the rural masses, La Solidarité determined to earn the support of both groups. It was the only political group that created an organization appropriate to the new mass politics of 1848.

Martin-Bernard, Perdiguier, and Delescluze became, respectively, president, vice-president, and general secretary of the organization. They named a seventy-member General Council to oversee the operations of a smaller Central Committee based in Paris. Composed mainly of middle-class professionals, the General Council included thirty-five parliamentary deputies, six doctors, four journalists, six men of letters, six businessmen, seven other professionals (engineers, veterinarians, and the like), and six workers. The three founding officers, as well as the members of the Central Committee and the General Council, were drawn from all the main republican and socialist currents of the July Monarchy—"radicals" of La Réforme, utopian socialists, Icarian communists, and veterans of Blanqui's secret societies. Among the General Council members whose pre-1848 political affiliations can be identified, thirteen had been radical republicans, nine veterans of July Monarchy secret societies, five communists, seven assorted socialists, and the rest ex-compagnons or members of workers' associations.[35]

The original circular sent to prospective members of La Solidarité républicaine succinctly summed up the founders' goals: "The Solidarité républicaine has been created for the purpose of uniting under a single umbrella all the scattered elements of democratic opinion, to give them a coherent leadership and to constitute on a solid and durable foundation the great party of the democratic and social republic."[36] La Solidarité's correspondence stressed two central themes: the need to unite all republicans who desired social reforms, and the importance of creating a centralized, nationwide political organization. The purpose of this centralized organization was to "create or support democratic newspapers, enlighten the voters, assure the legality of electoral contests, spread all writings capable of instructing and moralizing the population of the cities and the countryside, aid workers' associations, create defense councils for all members of La Solidarité républicaine, come to the aid of members stricken by unemployment or sickness . . . and finally to do everything possible to ensure that the republican dogma will be embraced and applied."[37]

The party statutes established a hierarchic organizational structure in which the Paris Central Committee presided over a national network of branches in each department, arrondissement, and canton. La Solidarité's founders believed such a structure would endow the French left with "the power of centralization from which springs the force of our *Patrie* and the glory of our great Revolution."[38] Once all committed republicans had achieved unity and forged a centralized organization, explained President Martin-Bernard, the party could then prepare "for the day when the nation . . . would be obliged to embrace real democracy."[39] In the event of another 24 February, republicans would not again be taken by surprise. "We will have a political personnel already created," Martin-Bernard told the leader of Lyon's Solidarité républicaine. One of the organization's primary goals, therefore, was to train committed republicans for future roles in postrevolutionary government and administration. From the failure of the Provisional Government democsocs like Martin-Bernard had learned the importance of being ready to exercise power. For Charles Delescluze, La Solidarité républicaine was a "revolutionary government" waiting in the wings for circumstance to catapult it into national office.[40]

La Solidarité's founders established what may well be France's first political party. Before 1848 France had known only parliamentary alliances, political tendencies such as legitimism or republicanism, underground conspiratorial organizations like the Carbonari and Blanqui's Société des saisons, and semiclandes-

LIBERTÉ, ÉGALITÉ, FRATERNITÉ.

LA

SOLIDARITÉ RÉPUBLICAINE

ASSOCIATION

POUR LE DÉVELOPPEMENT DES DROITS ET DES INTÉRÊTS DE LA DÉMOCRATIE.

L'UNION FAIT LA FORCE.

EXTRAIT DES STATUTS.

ARTICLE PREMIER. — « Une Association est formée entre les républicains des départements et des possessions françaises d'outre-mer, sous le titre de : la *Solidarité Républicaine*, pour » assurer, par tous les moyens légaux, le maintien de gouvernement républicain et le développement pacifique et régulier des réformes sociales qui doivent être le but et la conséquence » des institutions démocratiques.

ARTICLE 12. — « Sont nommés Membres du Conseil général les citoyens dont les noms suivent :

ANTOINE (Xavier), propriétaire.
AUBERT-ROCHE, ancien commissaire-général de la Marne, de la Haute-Marne, des Ardennes et de l'Aube.
BAC (Théodore), représentant du peuple.
BARENNE (Lucay), rédacteur en chef de la République.
BAUDIN, docteur-médecin.
BEAUNE, représentant du peuple.
BENOIST.   Id.
BÉRARD (Puiseux), tailleur à Clichy.
BERNARD, homme de lettres.
BOUQUET (J.-B., ancien adjoint du 12e arrondissement.
BRAYARD Toussaint), représentant du peuple.
BRIVES.   Id.
BRUTINEL-VIDAL, professeur de mathématiques.
BRUYS, représentant du peuple.
BUTTURA (Antoine).   Id.
CASTENET, ouvrier tailleur.

COMMISSAIRE, ancien commissaire du Jura.
CORNIER (Bienvenu), adjoint.
CRÉVAT (V.), ancien commissaire de l'Aube.
DAJEAN, avocat.
DELAILLE (Camille), rédacteur de lettre.
DELESCLUZE (Ch.), anc. commissaire-général du Nord et du Pas-de-Calais.
DEMOUTRY (Aimé), représentant du peuple.
DETOURS.   Id.
DEVILLE.   Id.
DUPUY.   Id.
DUBOS (Gouvray), docteur-médecin.
FOSSEVEUX, anc. médecin aux armées de la république.
GAMBON, représentant du peuple.
GOSSET, libraire.
GOUHAIN-CORNILLE, homme de lettres.
GREPPO, représentant du peuple.

FARGIN-FAYOLLE, représentant du peuple.
HÉROUARD, ancien commissaire de l'Orne.
RIGONNET, ingénieur civil.
BOUIS, docteur-médecin.
HUZET, ouvrier mécanicien.
JONCHARDET, représentant du peuple.
JOLY NEAU.   Id.
LAGARDE, rédacteur de la Réforme.
LAMBERT (Louis), homme de lettres.
LAMENNAIS, représentant du peuple.
LEBON (Napoléon), ingénieur.
LEBROUSSET, représentant du peuple.
LEFRANC (Pierre), représentant du peuple.
LEMAITRE aîné, homme de lettres.
MARTIN-BERNARD, représentant du peuple.
MATHÉ (Félix).   Id.
MATHIEU (de la Drôme).   Id.

MEYNARD, représentant du peuple.
MIE (Auguste).   Id.
NADAUD, ouvrier maçon.
OLIVIER (Démocrate), représentant du peuple.
PÉCOT-OGIER.   Id.
PERDIGUIER (Agricol).   Id.
PILETTE, ancien commissaire du Nord.
PYAT (Félix), représentant du peuple.
RIBEYROLLES (Carnot), rédacteur en chef de la Réforme.
SIGAULT (Gustave), représentant du peuple.
SCHOELCHER.   Id.
SERVIENT, ancien gouverneur du Louvre.
SIGNARD, docteur-médecin.
THOMASSIN, docteur-médecin.
TREMPLIER (Léon), ingénieur-métallurgiste.
VIGNERTE, représentant du peuple.

ARTICLE 19. — Les moyens d'action que pourra employer le Conseil général consisteront à créer ou soutenir des journaux démocratiques, à éclairer les électeurs, à assurer la pureté des élections, à répandre tous les écrits propres à instruire, en la moralisant, la population des villes et des campagnes, à faciliter les associations de travailleurs, à créer des conseils de défense pour tous les Membres de la *Solidarité républicaine*, à venir en aide à ses Associés nécessiteux en cas de chômage ou de maladie, à chercher les moyens de leur procurer du travail ; enfin, à ne rien négliger pour faire aimer et pratiquer le dogme républicain.

Le Président, le citoyen MARTIN-BERNARD.
Le Vice-Président, le citoyen Agricol PERDIGUIER.
Le Secrétaire-Général, le citoyen Ch. DELESCLUZE.

On reçoit les adhésions au Local provisoire de l'Association, 10, *boulevard Montmartre*, à PARIS.

Typographie et lithographie FÉLIX MALTESTE et Cie, rue des Deux-Portes-St-Sauveur, 22

1. Poster Announcing La Solidarité républicaine

tine republican pressure groups such as the July Monarchy's société des droits de l'homme et du citoyen. Never had any tendency or organization attempted to create a political apparatus ready to replace the old officeholders in the event of a revolution or other political crisis. La Solidarité républicaine, inspired by the centralist ideology of the Jacobins and by the organizational techniques of La Société des droits de l'homme,[41] became the first political society to endeavor consciously to prepare a future governmental debut. To direct this preparation, Martin-Bernard and his colleagues established in Paris a kind of shadow cabinet whose "ministries" would be responsible for developing administrative expertise and for monitoring government activity. In an early January 1849 meeting the members of the organization's Central Committee established a list of commissions that paralleled the government ministries, including Interior, Police, War, Foreign Affairs, Maritime Affairs, Finance, Justice, Religious Affairs, and Public Education. Demonstrating their socialist orientation, the Central Committee members added a new ministry to the traditional roster—that of Workers' and Farmers' Associations.[42]

Not content merely to keep track of the government in Paris, the Central Committee required the organization's provincial branches to provide it with detailed monthly reports on the political situation in their localities. Like the prefects and the procureurs généraux in the established government, representatives of the local Solidarité républicaine committees were to "send to the central committee a report containing precise information on the needs and attitudes of the population, the behavior of local government functionaries, the maneuvers of political groups, and on anything that could facilitate the activity of the central committee and be of interest to the democratic and social cause."[43] Martin-Bernard and his associates believed in hierarchic organization, and the statutes of their society stipulated that the Paris "General Council will direct the activity of the departmental, arrondissement, and cantonal committees." All local officers were appointed by the Paris General Council for the first year; subsequently, the branch officers would be elected by their own members, subject to approval by the Paris governing board. The General Council reserved the right to delegate to the main departmental committees the power to nominate and approve local officers. Individuals' annual dues of four francs were divided evenly between the members' department committees and the Paris main office.[44]

La Solidarité established its local branches in one of two ways: by sending representatives from Paris to set them up, or by relying on provincial leaders to do the honors. According to the Paris police, the central organization employed ten "traveling propagandists" whose job was to help organize local branches. Imitating the methods of inspectors for insurance companies, La Solidarité's emissaries financed their voyages by counting on each newly formed local branch to contribute to their travel expenses.[45] In major provincial cities the editor or publisher of the local left-wing newspaper often established his town's branch of La Solidarité républicaine, as did Albert Laponneraye, the influential editor of Marseille's *La Voix du peuple*. The managers and editors of the republican newspapers of Lyon, Montpellier, and Poitiers performed a similar service in their respective home towns.[46]

Two examples, from the Hérault and from the Loir-et-Cher, can provide insights into the ways in which La Solidarité's regional committees were founded. In the Hérault a local leader took it upon himself to establish a Solidarité républicaine branch. After reading Solidarité's statutes in *La Fraternité*, Carcassonne's republican paper, Louis Viot wrote the Paris office. He wanted to open a branch of the organization in his native Saint-Pons in order to bring the democ-soc gospel to the backward population of his region, and he hoped that the Paris headquarters could provide him information on the incumbent deputies from the Hérault.[47] Viot clearly took seriously La Solidarité's pretension of being a nationwide political party.

Shortly after Viot received the go-ahead from Paris to form a Solidarité républicaine committee in Saint-Pons, the Paris police raided and then shut down the national headquarters. Undaunted, Viot decided to organize a local branch anyway. He claimed his committee was a literary society and held meetings at a local café. When the police raided the locale, they found

Viot speaking in favor of progressive taxation to the assembled Solidarité membership. On the table in front of the orator lay three issues of Proudhon's paper *Le Peuple*, the statutes of the literary society, a proposal for the establishment of progressive taxation, and a petition to the National Assembly to restore the *milliard des émigrés.** While police hesitated over whether to indict Viot, he turned his committee into an electoral organization and prepared for the legislative elections of May 1849.[48]

In the Loir-et-Cher it was a representative of the Paris Central Committee, a journalist named Jean Benoît, who organized the departmental Solidarité républicaine committee.[49] Benoît began his effort by making contact with local sympathizers in Blois. Once he grasped the local political situation, he organized a meeting of the city's leading left-wing republicans and socialists. This group included a doctor, a high school teacher, a tanner, a merchant, and a house painter, who together formed the nucleus of Blois's Solidarité républicaine. Benoît then moved on to Saint Aignon, in the southern part of the department, where he organized a second committee. Like the main branch in Blois, the Saint Aignon group consisted of artisans, shopkeepers, and members of the liberal professions.[50]

Having established the two principal Solidarité républicaine committees of the Loir-et-Cher, Benoît then allowed the local members to complete the organization in their department. Their first step was to form a study group called the Cercle littéraire de la solidarité, which quickly became a kind of political club for Blois's left-wing artisans. Seeking to reach the rural population, Solidarité member Laforie founded a monthly newspaper called *La Solidarité démocratique du Loir-et-Cher*. To facilitate department-wide circulation of the new paper, Laforie set up editorial committees in each of the three arrondissement capitals of the Loir-et-Cher. These committees in turn organized a network of rural correspondents charged with selling subscriptions to peasants and sympathetic café proprietors (at 1 franc, 20 centimes a year, even some peasants could afford to

---

* The *milliard des émigrés* was a socialist proposal to "restore" to the nation's poor a billion francs in tax money paid during the Restoration to nobles whose lands had been expropriated after 1789.

subscribe).[51] Thus, by March 1849 the new democratic-socialist coalition of the Loir-et-Cher had established the organizational infrastructure that would enable the department's democ-socs to wage a well-fought electoral campaign in the spring of 1849. Only in major regional capitals like Marseille and Dijon did widely known republican leaders direct Solidarité républicaine committees. In provincial towns the organization's governing boards closely resembled those of the Loir-et-Cher. That is, they were cross-class local alliances of bourgeois professionals and *fonctionnaires*, shopkeepers and skilled artisans. Whereas a committee of republican notables directed La Solidarité at Dijon, the capital of Burgundy,[52] in the nearby cantonal seat of Châtillon (Côte-d'Or) the committee was more modest and more representative of the local Solidarité movement: a lawyer too poor to vote during the July Monarchy served as president, a locksmith assumed the vice-presidency, and a doctor, pharmacist, café proprietor, and coppersmith rounded out the governing board.[53]

In Chalon, headquarters of La Solidarité républicaine in the Saône-et-Loire, the directors included an ex-leader of Dijon's Société des droits de l'homme, a wealthy landowner, a liquor dealer, a solicitor, two café proprietors, a baker, and a fisherman. The governing council in Louhans, an arrondissement capital in the Saône-et-Loire, consisted of a lawyer (president), an insurance agent, and the son of a notary.[54] La Solidarité républicaine of Tours, like that of Blois, was organized by Jean Benoît. Its officers included two architects, a doctor, a carpenter, a well-off peasant, and a bank teller. The two Solidarité officers in Château-Renault (Indre-et-Loire) were a locksmith and a house painter.[55] In Metz the Solidarité president was an architect; in Sens (Yonne) a doctor presided. The large left-wing community of Niort (Deux-Sèvres) displayed its egalitarian credentials by naming one Joseph Maichain, a peasant and assistant mayor, president of the republican society.[56]

Châtillon in the Côte d'Or is the only town for which precise information on the rank and file of La Solidarité exists. The local society's sixty affiliates included thirty-eight artisans, eleven small merchants and shopkeepers, and eleven low-ranking fonctionnaires and members of the liberal professions.[57] The list of those arrested in a police raid on Solidarité's headquarters provides the only clue to the social composition of the Parisian rank and file. Apart from one national officer, Louis Tremplier, vice-treasurer and metallurgist by profession, none of the others netted in the raid held leadership posts. The police booked twelve office employees of La Solidarité républicaine, six artisans, two doctors, one traveling salesman, and one city hall employee.[58]

Solidarité's records show that by the end of January 1849 the organization had established itself in sixty-two of France's eighty-six departments, with a total of 353 branches.[59] The police claimed knowledge of some 300 of these committees and estimated national membership at over thirty thousand.[60] It is likely that some of the local groups affiliated with La Solidarité républicaine existed prior to the parent association's founding. Nonetheless, Martin-Bernard and his colleagues demonstrated impressive organizational skills in putting together a network of 350 branches in less than three months.

It was precisely this nationwide network of Solidarité républicaine committees that so frightened the police of Louis Napoleon. Never had a French government faced an opposition that had organized so successfully in the provinces. Expressing the government's fears, the procureur général of Aix wrote:

> Right in the heart of the State, an organization rivaling that of the State has extended its tentacles throughout the entire surface of France. With its committees at the department, arrondissement, and cantonal levels, it stands in opposition to the legitimate authorities of our departments, arrondissements, and cantons. It is a private society in the midst of the society at large. This rival organization is the ultra-democratic party. It is a formation which is disciplined and endowed with a network of communication that links members from one end of the country to the other. This faithful membership is capable of planning unified actions and of responding in unison to a single directive.[61]

For Minister of the Interior Léon Faucher, La Solidarité républicaine was "a state within the State," and the Paris prefect of police termed Solidarité an attempt to "create a secret government within the midst of the legitimate one."[62] In portraying Solidarité as a rival government, Faucher and his colleagues revealed just how seriously they took its challenge. They viewed the republican organization as a nascent political party that could conceivably use France's new democratic institutions to destroy their hegemony.

Formidable as the young organization was, the national administration undoubtedly exaggerated the threat it posed. Official perceptions cannot be taken as a wholly accurate measure of Solidarité's power. Rather these alarms indicate the extent to which conservatives feared the democratic path to revolutionary change. Indeed, the government's fear of democracy seemed to equal the left's faith in the democratic promise.

When Faucher closed down La Solidarité's national headquarters on 29 January 1849, the organization had already accomplished some of its primary goals. It had set the stage for a well-fought electoral campaign in the spring of 1849 and had helped create a broad democratic-socialist alliance. Two weeks after La Solidarité républicaine was officially outlawed, a group of former members of the General Council met quietly in Paris to plan electoral strategy for the spring. Discussion focused on how to use for electoral purposes the ties between provincial and Parisian republicans that La Solidarité had established.[63] In both the Saône-et-Loire and the Loir-et-Cher members of dissolved Solidarité républicaine committees met discreetly to continue their efforts to spread propaganda and prepare the elections. In some cases the outlawed Solidarité républicaine simply reconstituted itself as the local electoral committee, the only overtly political organization still immune from government harassment in early 1849.[64]

Although many local branches of the aborted party remained virtually intact during the electoral contest of May 1849, the government's decision to outlaw La Solidarité seriously damaged the démocrate-socialiste cause. Faucher's action decapitated the nascent political formation and deprived the opposition of effective national leadership for the duration of the Second Republic. Without a central Solidarité républicaine committee in

Paris to direct and coordinate the provincial affiliates, the démocrates-socialistes could no longer contend realistically for governmental power. Moreover, when tens of thousands of rural Frenchmen rose up in December 1851 against Louis Napoleon's coup d'état, the lack of a nationwide, Paris-led organization was sorely felt. Without a centralized infrastructure, the opposition could not capitalize on this massive rebellion.[65]

Yet the government's repressive measures by no means dissolved the movement's accomplishments or eliminated its influence (see Chapters V-VII). La Solidarité had firmly rooted its organization in such departments as the Côte-d'Or, the Hérault, and the Loir-et-Cher.[66] And, together with La Propagande démocratique et sociale européenne, it had helped to create a democratic-socialist movement that, as will be suggested below, succeeded in attracting rural support by disseminating an ideology that articulated the economic and spiritual needs of humble Frenchmen. In breaking down personal and doctrinal barriers on the left, the two organizations enabled French democrats and socialists to work together to forge widespread popular allegiance to the democratic and social republic.

The first anniversary celebration of the February revolution put the final touches on the left's new democratic-socialist alliance. Although the government had deprived this coalition of its organizational structure, the democ-socs had endowed themselves, as will be shown in Chapter IV, with the rudiments of a unifying ideology. All major leftist factions were represented at this commemorative banquet, held appropriately in the Salle de la Fraternité on 25 February 1849. Old enemies like Delescluze and Proudhon, having dueled the previous fall, now showed outward signs of accord.[67] Proudhon praised Ledru-Rollin, and former Blanquist conspirators embraced republican deputies. When Ledru-Rollin proclaimed himself a socialist before the banquet crowd of three-thousand, he made the gesture that enabled him to assume the leadership of a united democratic-socialist movement.[68] Thus, by late February 1849 the once disparate factions of the French left, now allied as démocrates-socialistes, had created a political force that was prepared to meet the challenge set out by Félix Pyat's "Toast aux paysans." Published immediately after the banquet and then distributed profusely by La Propagande démocratique et sociale européene, the pamphlet urged democ-socs to devote themselves to making the peasantry republican.[69] The first anniversary celebration of the February revolution launched a nationwide electoral campaign whose success no one would have predicted in the somber aftermath of the June Days.

CHAPTER IV

THE IDEOLOGY OF THE DEMOC-SOCS

Despite the intense repression that followed the June Days, France's republican movement came back to life in the fall of 1848. In conjunction with efforts to build a nationwide organization, left republican leaders forged an innovative and highly coherent democratic-socialist ideology. This new doctrine dissipated the verbal fog of the revolution's early months and endeavored to explain mid-century economic and social conditions. It contained, moreover, plans for a reformed society founded on Christian morality and egalitarian politics.

The ideology developed in the démocrate-socialiste press and disseminated by Montagnard spokesmen and organizations after September 1848 differed in a number of important ways from the tangled doctrine that spilled forth from the revolutionary clubs of springtime 1848.[1] During the reign of the Provisional Government, "pure republicans," "democratic republicans," and "socialists" were all at odds with one another. But by the beginning of 1849, when the pure republicans had either joined the reaction or resigned themselves to political impotence, the rest of the republican left agreed to a common political strategy and rallied to an eclectic socialist ideology. Democrats overcame their distaste for socialism and embraced the social question, while socialists affirmed their commitment to democratic procedures and institutions. Moreover, the left's preoccupation with urban problems in spring 1848 was replaced by the Montagnards' focus on the rural provinces.

In articulating their ideology, the démocrates-socialistes transformed the Christian-moral critique of French society developed during the July Monarchy into a project for socialist democracy. The political conjuncture of February 1848 enabled the republican left—united after June—to conceive of a means by which to realize in the material world the progressive promises they believed to be embedded in the Gospels. The democsocs held that universal suffrage, the cornerstone of the new republic, would permit the ascension of a government committed to instituting a set of practical measures that would transform Christian moral ideals of justice, equality, and fraternity into tangible reality. The promise of equality would find worldly expression in participatory democracy, free and universal education, and state-guaranteed economic opportunity. Fraternity would be realized by replacing competitive and hierarchic capitalist enterprise with a system of cooperative production.

Historians, for the most part, have viewed the 48ers' religiosity simply as proof of their political naiveté and backward-looking romanticism.[2] Analysis of the actual ideas of the democsocs shows, however, that religion did not represent for them a retreat from contemporary reality. Rather, religious concepts provided the intellectual tools with which they fashioned a penetrating economic and political critique, a comprehensive alternative vision, and a concrete program for the realization of that vision. Just as peasant and worker religiosity was by no means incompatible with anticlericalism and a receptivity to new political ideas, so middle-class republicans saw no contradiction between Christian moralism and a forward-looking project for economic and social change. For the democ-socs, the dynamic fusion of early Christian spirituality and republican institutional reality would produce—without violent trauma—a socialist society dedicated to economic growth, personal liberty, and individual well-being.

Beginning in early 1849, the democ-socs set out to transmit their ideology to millions of newly enfranchised Frenchmen.*

---

* I identify as spokesmen of the démocrate-socialiste left all those who meet the following conditions: they directed or contributed regularly to major Second Republic newspapers, almanacs, and other periodicals that declared allegiance to the démocrate-socialiste ideology; they supported the left-most candidates in the elections of the period 1849-1851; and they endorsed the electoral platform of the Montagnard representatives to the National Assembly. Others taken as democ-soc ideologues are those who presided over the major organizations affiliated with this extreme left group, such as La Propagande démocratique et

In an ambitious campaign of propaganda, they promised peasants an alternative society built on Christian moral values and democratized land ownership. And they offered workers emancipation from wage labor through the establishment of producers' cooperatives founded on government credits and sentiments of Christian fraternity. Unlike the left of February-June 1848, which abandoned the peasantry in an unsuccessful attempt to win the workers, the democ-socs of 1849 were able to gain widespread allegiance among both groups. The key to the Montagnards' success was their ability to articulate the populist and communitarian spirituality of peasants and workers in the form of a program of material improvement.

In an essay entitled "Bases de la politique" (1849), Gabriel Mortillet, founder of La Propagande démocratique et sociale européenne, argued that the original Christian message of the Gospels contained the entire moral code on which to build a democratic-socialist society. Nineteenth-century socialists had only to rediscover the pure teaching of early Christianity, a teaching that had been distorted by the Catholic Church, and apply it to the modern world.[3] In Mortillet's view, "The whole of morality was contained in the concept of fraternity . . . the admirable principle that was elaborated on every page of the Gospels."[4] Since socialism was a system based on cooperation, and since fraternity was the principle that taught cooperation, the Gospels' fraternal message provided the moral foundation that the democratic-socialist republic required.

Albert Laponneraye, editor-in-chief of the most important democ-soc newspaper outside Paris, shared Mortillet's belief in the fundamental importance of Christian fraternity. Writing in *La Voix du peuple*, Laponneraye proclaimed that Jesus Christ was "the first to preach fraternity and love, *the two bases of democracy*. Jesus Christ was not, therefore, merely the redeemer of humanity from the divine point of view, He was the emancipator of humanity in the here-and-now."[5] Similarly, one

---

sociale européenne. Although the démocrates-socialistes used interchangeably the labels "democ-soc," "Montagnard" ("Mountain" in English), or simply "socialist" to describe themselves, I shall use only "democ-soc" and "Montagnard" in this chapter.

of the toasts delivered before a Montagnard banquet on Christmas Eve 1848 commemorated "the birth of Christ, that divine regenerator of society whose democratic and socialist message is still so poorly understood."[6] For Saint-Simonian songwriter Jules Vinçard, Jesus Christ was "a man of supreme genius . . . [who] introduced to the world the fundamental principles of socialism."[7] Journalist Louis Langomazino called Jesus "a poor worker . . . who founded a religion full of love and charity and who regenerated the world."[8]

So revolutionary was the moral doctrine of the Gospels, according to the democ-socs, that Jesus' Christian teaching sufficed as the basis for socialism in the nineteenth century. M. Legenvue, director of La Ligue sociale, a propaganda organization dedicated to "La République démocratique et sociale," declared that "for us Christianity . . . is at once the foundation and the keystone of the new social edifice that must henceforth shelter the world."[9] For the editors of La République, "socialism was simply . . . the introduction into the political realm of the immortal principles of the Gospels."[10] Thus, all those who believed in the Gospels—as opposed to the Church's corrupted teaching—possessed the moral qualities required by the democratic and social republic: "Our reverence for Christianity . . . is equaled only by our disdain and fear of Catholicism—that self-serving and degrading plague of our society. . . . The principles of Christianity that you put forward—love one another, do unto others that which you would have them do unto you—are the fundamental laws of the democratic and social republic."[11]

As the above statements make clear, the democ-socs viewed Christian precepts both as a body of moral principles designed to guide human conduct and as a set of laws—much like a bill of rights—that should be put into practice and be guaranteed by the institutions of a modern republic. In declaring that socialism was "the Gospels in action," Louis Blanc summed up this practical and operational view of religion.[12] The benefits of Christianity, in the Montagnards' view, would no longer be limited to the spiritual realm; divine power and inspiration could be harnessed to improve the material life of human beings. According to La République:

God is no longer separated from humanity, [for] . . . the action of God is revealed through the constant improvement of the moral, intellectual, and material condition of all the underprivileged and especially of the workers who live under constant exploitation by capital. God reigns just as much over the earth as he does in heaven. . . . For the action of God is revealed as well through the liberation of all peoples, by universal association, by the application of the divine principle of fraternity proclaimed by Jesus. . . . It [the action of God] is revealed through the abolition of all monopolistic privileges, and through the destruction of all obstacles which stand in opposition to the regime of liberty, equality, and human fraternity that we so ardently desire.[13]

If socialism harnessed divine power and represented the Gospels in action, it also performed services similar to those of the saints who were so central to populist religiosity. According to Montagnard journalist A. Roubaud: "Socialism is an angel that has descended to earth from the heavens in order to relieve and to heal the ills and sufferings of humanity. . . . [With socialism] the whole society . . . would become invulnerable to the torments which have gripped it since the beginning of time, and with socialism we would have the veritable reign of democracy, that is, of God."[14] By presenting socialism as the realization of divine and supernatural power, Montagnards expressed ideas that were highly compatible with the utilitarian and incipiently democratic religiosity analyzed in Chapter II. It is significant that both La République's ode to a utilitarian and humanitarian God and Roubaud's plea for a saintly socialism appeared on the eve of the legislative election of 13 May 1849, the first national electoral contest in which republicans actively sought peasant votes.

The démocrates-socialistes identified so strongly with Jesus Christ that virtually every political banquet they held during the Second Republic opened with a toast to Jesus Christ, the first republican, or to Jesus Christ, the founder of socialism.

Their newspapers and campaign literature overflowed with reverent homage to a Jesus portrayed as father of their movement. A short-lived socialist newspaper was even entitled *Le Christ républicain*, and songs with such titles as "Jésus républicain" and "Le Christ socialiste" became commonplace.[15] Louis Blanc deemed Jesus Christ "the sublime master of all socialists," and Pierre Leroux argued that all socialist republicans were "veritable disciples of Jesus."[16] Democ-socs liked to imagine that if Jesus returned to earth, he would be on their side:

> If Christ came down to earth . . . [the conservatives] would call Him a utopian, an anarchist, a revolutionary [all names the right called the Montagnards]. They would charge Him with vagrancy and place Him in chains . . . Christ would not be with the Honnêtes Modérés [i.e., the Party of Order]. He would be with the poor and the oppressed. . . . He would preach the abolition of the proletariat. . . . He would be a socialist.[17]

Since Montagnards believed their role was to spread the moral values essential to a truly democratic society, they likened their political mission to the religious quest of Jesus and the apostles: "Apostles of democracy, persecuted by the enemies of our young and beautiful republic, we are like the apostles of Jesus Christ who were persecuted by the Pharisees of their time."[18] If democ-soc activists resembled the apostles, their party's elected parliamentary representatives compared with Jesus himself:

> The parliamentary representatives of socialism have proclaimed a large number of powerful truths. And since these truths are eternal, our response to our leaders has been like the apostles' response to Christ. "We will follow you." . . . We must follow the socialist leaders as the apostles followed the great republican of the Gospels—that is, in propagating the faith.[19]

Laponneraye believed that republican militants, like the apostles, had to transcend their middle-class interests to embrace a universalist cause. In the first issue of *La Voix du peuple* the Montagnard leader declared that the best republicans were those

N. 1.   Prix : 5 centimes.   Jeudi 8 Juin.

LE CHRIST RÉPUBLICAIN

Journal du citoyen DELCLERGUES, administré par le citoyen RIDEL.

Et paraissant le Dimanche et le Jeudi,

À PARIS, RUE DU PETIT-LION-SAINT-SAUVEUR, 40.

2. Jesus as Republican Hero

whose "hearts burn with the holy flame of devotion and sacrifice, and who forget entirely their personal interests to concern themselves solely with the well-being of all men."[20] Before fifteen hundred members of the Club démocratique de Castellane, Laponneraye added: "Republicans were not born to taste the pleasures and luxuries of life; they were born for struggle, for sacrifice, and for the apostolate."[21]

That large numbers of démocrates-socialistes were willing to risk jail and even exile for their political work indicates the extent to which French republicans shared Laponneraye's highly religious devotion to the cause.[22] What gave so many republicans the courage to persevere in their revolutionary zeal was the faith that they acted in God's name and in accordance with His will. "God says through our voice," exclaimed *La République*, "give to the people that which belongs to the people, that is to say, popular sovereignty!"[23] Above all, it was the belief that God was on their side that buttressed the democsocs' commitment. *La République* confidently argued:

> God is with those who are ahead of their time [en avant de leur siècle]. He is with us just as He was with Moses . . . just as He was with Jesus who taught human fraternity . . . God is with us just as He was with Luther, Calvin, Christopher Columbus, Galileo, Newton, and all of that noble phalange of sincere republicans who . . . swept away the vestiges of feudalism.[24]

Motivated by such missionary fervor, the democ-socs proved to be indefatigable campaigners and able propagandists. They successfully carried their political message from major provincial cities to cantonal seats and from there to some of the most remote rural communes in the country (see Chapters V and VI).[25]

Despite their preoccupation with early Christianity, the democ-socs did not believe that social change was purely a matter of inculcating or reviving faith in this doctrine. Although they argued that the ideology of democracy and socialism was contained entirely in the Gospels, the Montagnards realized that the nation needed a set of political institutions to put this ideology into practice. Genuine believers, the democ-socs were political beings as well. They argued that the republic—the form of government based on universal suffrage, freedom of the press and assembly, and public education—was the only political system capable of realizing in the material world the Christian moral values of justice, equality, and fraternity. As Dr. A. Guépin, a frequent contributor to democ-soc journals, put it: "Far from seeking to destroy Christianity [as the right argued], we want to develop it and extend it to the material realm."[26] Under the republic, argued philosopher Charles Renouvier, the laws of the land would be drawn up by a parliament motivated by the dictates of Christian fraternity and brotherhood: "The morality taught until now in the churches in the name of Jesus Christ must now enter the assemblies of men that form governments and make laws."[27]

To embody the morality of Jesus, the republic had to be more than simply a political system that operated without monarchical authority. The democ-socs viewed the republic as a system of government, a set of institutions, and a code of morality that contained all the seeds of a future utopia of economic well-being and social justice. According to Laponneraye:

> The republic is not simply the absence of a king. It is the abolition of all privileges, the termination of all abuses. It is the organization of labor through [producers'] associations . . . it is the establishment of a system of credit . . . a more equitable distribution of taxes . . . universal education . . . freedom of the press and assembly. . . . In a word, the republic . . . is a government that functions for the benefit of the masses.[28]

Laponneraye and his colleagues believed that once the republican revolution was accomplished, no further revolution would be necessary. The Great Revolution of 1789 had simply to be carried out to its logical conclusion by using the instrument it had created: universal suffrage.

Democ-soc publicists were unanimous in linking a ban on violent insurrection to the existence of universal suffrage.[29] According to Louis Blanc, there must be "no insurrection as long as universal suffrage remains in force."[30] For those accustomed to a society in which the franchise had been restricted to about 3 percent of the adult male population, the promise of universal manhood suffrage seemed limitless. Political power no longer rested on money and privilege, for under the new republican electoral laws of 1848 the humblest peasant had political rights theoretically equal to those of the wealthiest landowner. The locus of revolution had thus been transferred from the barricade to the ballot box. For Laponneraye:

> Universal suffrage is an arm more efficient than all others. It is more fatal to the bourgeoisie than all the cannons in all the arsenals. The day that the great family of proletarians—those of the cities, but especially those of the countryside—exercises the sacred right of suffrage independent of the oppressive influences of the bourgeoisie, the *droit au travail* will be written into the laws of the land.[31]

Though he viewed universal suffrage as a revolutionary instrument with vast possibilities, Laponneraye indulged in no illusions about its actual operation. The revolutionary potential of universal suffrage would be realized only if a massive campaign of propaganda could detach the peasantry from the notables who continued to influence them.[32] The right to vote, therefore, required as its corollary freedom of the press and assembly.[33]

Firm believers in nonviolence, the democ-socs nevertheless foresaw the possible necessity of using force in political contests. To a man, the Montagnards proclaimed that any government assault against constitutional rights and guarantees not only justified armed rebellion but also made it a duty.[34] The sole purpose, however, of any use of violence against the government would be to restore republican legality. Thus, after Louis Napoleon restricted suffrage in May 1850, left republicans urged disenfranchised Frenchmen to prepare to vote in the election of 1852 with "a ballot in one hand and a gun in the other" or with "the constitution in one hand and a gun in the other."[35] The significance of these statements is clear: violence might be necessary to establish or reestablish republican institutions, but once these political gains were secured, social renovation would occur solely as a result of the democratic expression of popular will. The democ-socs possessed a sophisticated understanding of the dangers of establishing socialism through force. In Louis Blanc's words, "If the triumph of socialism were the product of violent revolution instead of the result of the normal and regular operation of universal suffrage, the country would find itself in a singularly difficult position. Difficult! Why, the situation would be terrible—almost as terrible for the victors as for the vanquished."[36] Socialism could not, then, be instituted as a direct and immediate result of a revolutionary victory. It would have to come about as the logical extension of democracy.

True to their political label, the democ-socs argued that democracy and socialism were inseparable and that "all those who are true democrats are necessarily socialists, for how could democracy be meaningful in France without improving society?"[37] Democracy, moreover, contained the seeds of socialism and created the conditions under which it could grow. Thus, the editors of L'Union républicaine believed that "socialism is to democracy what the oak tree is to the acorn, what the head of wheat is to the seed that man places in the furrow where it must germinate and grow."[38] Socialism was simply the republic with its potential fully realized.

These statements establish the connection between democracy and socialism, but they do not define either term. What did the democ-socs mean by each of the two halves of their hybrid label? Virtually everyone on the republican left agreed on the definition of democracy. Based on universal manhood suffrage, democracy was the political system in which all citizens had both equal political rights and the ability to participate in government. The terms "democracy" and "republic" were synonymous.[39] The word "socialism" was somewhat more ambiguous. Leading democ-soc journalists like Laponneraye defined socialism simply as "the doctrine of those committed to improving society."[40] For most Montagnards, however, the term embraced a series of three related meanings: socialism was at once the science that enabled social ills to be diagnosed, the social reforms necessary to remedy these ills, and the ethic of the future society that would come into being as the result of these reforms. According to Dr. Guépin, socialism was both the "improved social body which will replace the present one . . . [and] the very science of social economy. Socialism, therefore, is a twofold phenomenon. . . . The near future of humanity and the science that should lead us to that future: the goal and the means of attaining it."[41] Similarly, a group of republican-socialist journalists from Macon defined socialism as

> the act of concerning oneself with society, with its vices, its afflictions and its suffering. It represents at the same time the improvements that society has the right to expect, the reform of abuses that have been a part of all institutions. . . . [In addition] socialism . . . is the union of the weak and oppressed against their oppressors. It is the extinction of poverty . . . it is the science of society.[42]

Socialism, therefore, was the science of social reform, a doctrine whose precise analysis of society's problems permitted a clear-cut understanding of the solutions that were required. The worker-edited *L'Atelier* argued that "socialism was the science by which the economic state of society would be modified in order that all those who are able to work would find work, and that the product of their work would be substantial enough to guarantee the subsistence of the worker and his family."[43] For *L'Atelier*'s editors, as for most others in the democ-soc camp, the greatest evils of French society were the forced idleness of unemployment and the worker's inability to reap the full fruit of his labor. One of the strengths of democ-soc ideology lay in its capacity both to provide a plausible explanation of the reasons for these problems and to propose radical and seemingly practical solutions.

Just as the democ-socs fashioned their vision of a progressive republican government out of the moral imperatives of early Christianity, so they also transformed the ethic of the Gospels into a socialist critique of mid-century economic reality. Unlike the republicans of the Provisional Government, the Montagnard coalition formed in the wake of June 1848 understood that the institutions of political democracy alone could not put an end to economic inequality and social injustice. The social question had to be addressed directly. Thus *La République* argued that the idées généreuses of early 1848 had degenerated into despair and insurrection instead of producing a better society precisely because they ignored the central economic reality of the time, namely, the domination of labor by capital:

> It [the Provisional Government] did not understand that to grant universal suffrage without at the same time requiring universal instruction and, above all, without providing for the material independence of the worker is to consecrate a reign of illusion and falsehood. To overthrow Louis Philippe while allowing capital to retain the right to dominate labor is to abandon the quarry in exchange for its shadow.[44]

The essential task the democ-socs set for themselves, a task dictated by the Christian imperative of fraternal cooperation, was to abolish what they called the "privileges of capital." The socialist republic, argued *La République du peuple*, would "realize the promises of Christianity in the material world by associating the mass of proletarians still subjected to the collective slavery of capital."[45] To this end, they formulated a critique of the economy of mid-nineteenth-century France that focused on the role of financial capital and on the distribution of credit. In their view, the widespread unemployment and misery among industrial workers and the poverty and dependence of peasant cultivators stemmed from a virtual monopoly on capital held by a small group of men whom they labeled "capitalists." According to the democ-socs, the capitalist class did not consist of those who directed industrial enterprises (excepting the "barons" who owned France's largest factories); rather, it comprised those who controlled the nation's purse strings. In making their lending decisions on the basis of private interest rather than public need, the barons of the Bank of France and other capitalists subjected the prosperity of the nation's productive citizens to the requirements of their own self-serving greed. "Credit is monopolized," said Aristide Olivier, editor of *Le Suffrage uni-*

versel (Montpellier), "by a few high-placed barons who dispense it according to their own desires and their own caprice."[46]

Democ-socs unanimously believed that an economy in which a small group of privileged individuals possessed the power to decide who received credit contradicted the very idea of a republic. For Eugène Bareste, editor of *La République*, a republic was a system "based on fraternity among citizens . . . and the abolition of the privileges of capital."[47] The prevailing economic system resembled the social and political setting of the ancien régime. According to Laponneraye, the *hauts barons de la finance* occupied in 1849 the same position relative to the proletariat that the *hauts barons feodaux* occupied with respect to the Third Estate in the late eighteenth century.[48] Similarly, *Le Républicain de Lyon* argued that whereas the Great Revolution had abolished the aristocracy of birth, the July Monarchy promoted a new aristocracy of finance capital: "Formerly a class of warriors, it [the aristocracy] has become a powerful coterie of bankers."[49] As *Le Peuple souverain* (Bordeaux) put it: "Just as the concepts of monarchy and divine right bound us to the aristocracy during the Old Regime, so the power of capital binds us today to the bourgeoisie."[50]

The democ-socs saw France as divided into two classes: those who possessed capital and those who did not. Thus, according to the *L'Union républicaine*, France was composed on the one hand of an exploited class of "travailleurs, petits propriétaires, industriels" and on the other of a powerful, dominant class of "gens de loisirs, de grands propriétaires et de puissants capitalistes."[51] Similarly, the democ-soc *Almanach des associations ouvrières de 1850* maintained that society's fundamental cleavage was between travailleurs and capitalistes—that is, between masters and workers on the one hand, and "bankers and all others who lend money" on the other.[52] Diverse as the exploited group of travailleurs might seem, its members had common interests, argued the democ-socs, because they all suffered from the financial monopoly of capitalists.[53] Montagnards considered this class division irreconcilable and embedded in the very laws of Christianity, for one could not, according to Pierre-Léon

Salin, democ-soc publicist from the Nièvre, "simultaneously serve God and Capital, worldly interests and the Gospels."[54]

According to the Montagnards, the economic dominance of the hauts barons de la finance meant that industry, labor, and agriculture "were at the mercy of capital, that is to say, at the mercy . . . of bankers and usurers."[55] Private capital, in the words of the Montagnard electoral platform of December 1848, "causes . . . periodic disasters and incessant iniquities." An end to this narrow monopoly over capital, the platform continued, "would deliver labor from the exigencies and timidities of capital, the two great obstacles to industrial progress." It would also save agriculture "from the exploitation of the usury that ruins it."[56] The capitalists' autocratic control over the economy not only caused misery and suffering, but it blocked industrial and agricultural development as well.

The democ-socs' critique of capital was not simply or even primarily a defense of small manufacturers against the power of banking and finance. Rather, it constituted an indictment of an economy that compromised peasants' independence by burdening them with debt and deprived workers of the full fruit of their labor. The democ-socs took up the cause of small manufacturers because they counted them among the exploited. Like workers and peasants, small entrepreneurs faced a market economy ruled by those who possessed liquid capital. What the republican left wanted, argued Le Républicain des Ardennes, "was that all those who labor and produce, whether members of the working or the middle class, unite to defend their *common* interests against the tyranny of capital."[57]

Above all, Montagnards concerned themselves with workers and peasants, the groups that suffered most from the domination of capital. Without access to capital, the worker, according to Alphonse Esquiros, "was forced to lend his strength and his intelligence to the machines of another." As a result, "those who perform all the work do not have the right to enjoy its fruits."[58] The peasantry suffered a similar kind of injustice. Le Républicain du Gard argued that peasant debts to usurers transferred the small profits gained from agricultural work into the hands of others. L'Union républicaine charged that the peasants' lack of capital forced them to sell their products at abnormally low prices to merchant capitalists, who then resold the products at an enormous profit. Big merchants, deplored *L'Union républicaine*, "benefit from the fact that a huge number of cultivators are forced to sell their wheat for next to nothing in order to meet the daily expenses of their farms and their families."[59] As a result, the paper contended, the peasants who perform all the work reap almost none of the benefits: "Capital, that idle and luxuriant parasite, absorbs the lion's share . . . of the profits of an agricultural holding."[60]

Although their economic analysis was far from complete, the democ-socs did recognize the fundamental importance of the merchant capitalist in mid-nineteenth-century France. They also understood that commercial peasants, artisans, and small entrepreneurs often shared a common relationship to the market, a common lack of credit, and a common independence in the workplace combined with a subservience to merchant capitalists. According to one democ-soc publicist, "Small industrialists, shopkeepers, cultivators, medium and small landowners, tenant farmers, proletarians of city and countryside, our interests, our needs, are exactly the same."[61] To be sure, this statement contains an element of wishful thinking, and the democ-socs often underestimated the differences among all of these groups. But the Montagnards' analysis must be seen in light of the industrial structure of the time. That the vast majority of French enterprises possessed little capital and employed fewer than five workers testifies to the extremely modest economic position of most master artisans and small entrepreneurs and thus to their weak standing in the marketplace.[62] Even if these small producers fared somewhat better than their workers, their conditions much more closely resembled the circumstances of labor than those of capital.

Had the democ-socs identified solely with the entrepreneurs, they would have sought economic changes designed to improve the manufacturers' position without regard to the workers. Such changes might have included low-interest loans to small businessmen, longer working days for salaried labor, and restrictions on workers' associations. Instead, the democ-socs proposed a radical alternative to the prevailing economic system, an alternative that sought to abolish all distinctions between bosses and workers: existing enterprises in which bosses were exploited by financiers and in which workers were forced to sell their labor for wages would ultimately give way to collectively owned producers' cooperatives. In the democ-socs' view, establishment of producers' cooperatives would not only represent a moral and cultural revolution based on Christian fraternity, but it would embody an economic revolution as well. "Workers' associations," according to Le Peuple (Nevers), "are the instruments of social transformation which will . . . establish the ties of fraternity within the working class."[63] Producers' cooperatives, in Laponneraye's view, would both "conciliate the interests of master and worker . . . [and] abolish all distinctions between them."[64] The democ-socs' proposed solution to the economic injustice of their time, a solution they believed could be effected peacefully, formed the most radical part of their doctrine, for in advocating producers' cooperatives, the democ-socs aimed at nothing less than the abolition of the wage system itself.

Prominent democ-socs unanimously called for an end to the wage system, for the abolition of the proletariat. At the banquet commemorating the first anniversary of February 1848, Ledru-Rollin demanded "an end to the last remaining form of servitude, the proletariat."[65] Louis Blanc repeatedly argued that socialism's goal was to "destroy the proletariat [and thus] to liberate labor."[66] For the editors of L'Union républicaine, "the goal of the revolution of 1848 . . . was none other . . . than the suppression of the wage system [salariat]."[67] And Laponneraye proclaimed that "the social republic means the abolition of the proletariat." "What we want," wrote the editor of La Voix du peuple, "is for the proletariat, that is, the exploitation of man by his fellow man, to give way to associations between bosses and workers."[68] Even L'Atelier, the reputedly moderate workers' journal that did not declare allegiance to the democ-soc cause until 1850, argued two years earlier that the fight to shorten the workday was not enough. The principle of equality "requires that we put an end to the wage system itself."[69]

The roots of the Montagnards' hostility to the wage system lay in the Christian-moral critique of capitalism advanced by July Monarchy socialists. Reproducing virtually verbatim part of an editorial from the *Démocratie pacifique* of 1843, *La République* declared five years later that "the work of Christ remains incomplete, for the wage system, the last remnant of ancient slavery, still stands in the midst of our own civilization."[70] Atop this moral foundation, the democ-socs added a superstructure of Lockean natural right theory and another concept drawn from Fourierism, the droit au travail.[71] In so doing, they sought to elevate employment and the ability to possess the product of one's labor to the status of natural rights. The Montagnards even tried—unsuccessfully—to have the right to employment written into the constitution of 1848.

The democ-socs based their effort to raise employment to a natural right on a synthesis of Jacobinism and July Monarchy socialism. As William H. Sewell has shown, the Jacobins followed Locke in maintaining that property could be legitimate only if created by labor.[72] Since property, for Locke, was a natural right, it antedated the rise of monarchy and the state and therefore could not have been created by these institutions. Property existed solely as the result of an individual's active efforts to shape nature. Forms of property characteristic of the ancien régime, such as hereditary titles and venal offices were illegitimate because they stemmed from conferred privileges and not from accomplished work.

The Jacobin view of property as a natural right based on labor helped to eliminate certain longstanding privileges, but at the same time it produced some troubling ambiguities. Although labor and labor alone gave man the right to property, it was evident that a lifetime of labor on the part of some men gained them no property.[73] Indeed, their labor often contributed to extending the private property of those who did not work.

If the Jacobins could live with the contradictions of the new definition of property they institutionalized, the socialists of the July Monarchy could not. In his *Théorie du droit de propriété et du droit au travail* (1839), Fourierist leader Victor Considérant agreed that property was a natural right based on labor and that as a natural right it was inviolable. But he went on to argue that those whose labor created no property for themselves were denied a fundamental natural right and thus deserved compensation. That compensation would be the right to employment, a guaranteed job for everyone. If a wage worker could obtain no property, the droit au travail would at least give him proprietary rights over his job.[74]

In the mid-1840s *La Réforme* introduced Considérant's concept of the droit au travail to its progressive middle-class readership, but his notion did not become an integral part of the left-republican program until after June 1848.[75] The workers' movement, represented by the revolutionary clubs and Luxembourg Commission, adopted the droit au travail as one of its primary demands in March 1848.[76] In the aftermath of June 1848 the democ-socs combined the Jacobin conception of property with Considérant's droit au travail to develop their own radical version of the right to employment.[77] Accepting the Jacobin notion that the only legitimate property was that which was created by labor, the democ-socs argued in the words of Esquiros, that "if property is a right, and if the roots of all property are in labor, labor must therefore constitute a right equivalent to that of property."[78] This view of labor as a natural right figured prominently in the Montagnard electoral platform of 10 December 1848:

> We believe that labor is just as sacred as property. The latter is simply the motive and the reward for the former. In its essence, property is an absolute right . . . [but] labor . . . is the most inviolable of all rights. The right to employment is the right to life itself. The right to employment comes before the right to property, which is nothing more than the result of the former. . . . Property simply represents accomplished work.[79]

The democ-socs saw no contradiction between the droit au travail and their ultimate goal of creating a society in which everyone possessed property.[80] On the contrary, the droit au travail would be the mechanism by which everyone could acquire property. Firm believers in the sanctity of private holdings, the democ-socs soundly rejected the idea of redistributing existing domains as a means of turning all citizens into proprietors. Instead, they argued that even though the democratic and social republic could not give property to all its citizens, it could at least guarantee them the possibility of achieving it. Since all property was created through work, guaranteeing work for all would universalize the condition that was necessary, if not sufficient, for obtaining property. In the democ-socs' view, all citizens could exercise their natural right to employment without violating the natural rights of any of their fellows. Esquiros summed up the Montagnard position:

> We socialists do not want to destroy property. On the contrary, we want to establish on earth a new kind of property, the ownership of labor. This is the property of all those who possess neither land nor capital. All we want is for this new property, which after all is the source of all other property and is the mother of all production, to be given the same rights that you so profusely accord to established wealth.[81]

Though the democ-socs drew heavily on Considérant's theory of the droit au travail, their concept had far more radical implications than his. Considérant had posited the droit au travail simply as a means of compensating workers for the deprivation of their natural right to property.[82] The Montagnards, on the other hand, viewed the right to employment as a stepping stone to the achievement of property, as the means by which to transcend the inherently dependent status of wage labor. Considérant wanted to guarantee the workers' condition; the democ-socs sought to abolish it.

The democ-socs realized that for the droit au travail to make possible the achievement of property, it would have to ensure the worker's ability to own the product of his labor. In this way, an individual's labor would generate personal property. This result could occur only if the wage system were abolished. So long as wage labor governed the conditions of employment, the product of a worker's labor would go to others. The droit au travail, therefore, was incompatible with the wage system and implied its abolition. According to Esquiros, the worker "is forced by the hard necessities of life to lend his strength and his intelligence to others. Today's socialists seek to eliminate this remaining form of slavery by imposing the droit au travail . . . what we want is for the worker to become the owner of his work . . . to reap the fruit of his labor."[83] After joining the democ-soc camp in early 1850, L'Atelier took precisely the same stand. Editor A. Corbon argued that "what is without fail at the root of all our demands, whether realized by the force of arms or through peaceful petitioning, is our belief in the right to the fruit of our labor."[84] Ironically, then, the democ-socs' attempt to extend private property rights to all led to an attack on one of the keystones of modern capitalism—the system of wage labor.

How did the democ-socs propose to abolish wage labor? Unanimously, movement spokesmen argued that producers' co-operatives would gradually undermine wage labor. By raising workers to the status of associated owners, cooperatives would form the foundation of an economic system in which all those who worked for a particular enterprise would share the expenses of production as well as the value of the total output. Under a system of universal producers' cooperatives, all workers would be owners and thus all labor would be performed both for oneself and for an entrepreneurial collectivity. No one would toil for the pure benefit of others, and everyone would receive the full value of his labor.

Unlike the Fourierists of the July Monarchy, the democ-socs were fully aware that the successful development of an economic system based on producers' cooperatives could take place only under the aegis of a government committed to the ideals of the democratic and social republic—that is, to economic as well as political democracy. In practical terms, this meant substantial state intervention in the economy. The establishment of producers' cooperatives required credits, and since the Bank of France refused to provide them, it was up to the state to democratize industrial opportunity by advancing money to humble citizens. To mobilize credit on the behalf of workers and peasants, the democ-socs proposed to set up state-owned-and-operated banking institutions that would have branches in every cantonal seat in the country. According to the Montagnard platform of December 1848:

> It is through good institutions of credit that the state can assure the droit au travail and realize the promises of the February revolution . . . the state must intervene in the relationship of capital and labor and make itself the regulator of credit.
>
> Private credit, which causes . . . periodic disasters and unending iniquity, must be controlled and completed by a vast social credit, a credit that would exist not to serve the interests of the few, but rather for the benefit of all.
>
> A network of cantonal banks linked to departmental banks, which in turn would be linked to a central bank, all operating under the surveillance and control of the state, would distribute credit to workers and peasants.[85]

These banks would lend at 2.5 to 3 percent interest, as opposed to the going rate of 8 to 10 percent (usurers, of course, charged far more) and allow twenty years for payment of the principal.

The goal of this vast proposal to liberate the flow of credit was twofold: to encourage the establishment of producers' cooperatives and to permit peasants to free themselves from the hold of usury, expand their holdings, and become fully independent owners of property. In a statement typical of the democ-soc press, the editors of L'Union républicaine urged that "the state make possible the liberation of industrial labor by favoring the spirit of association through credits to workers' cooperatives." The paper argued furthermore for the "establishment of state-owned agricultural banks in order that the proprietors and simple cultivators who today are the victims of usury and serfs of the barons of finance can obtain the funds required for all aspects of their agricultural exploitations."[86]

How would a democratic and social republic procure the enormous financial resources necessary for such an ambitious effort? The démocrates-socialistes sought to provide the state with two means of amassing revenue: progressive taxation and the nationalization of vital industries and services.[87] Progressive taxation of incomes would be more equitable than the archaic tax system of the mid-nineteenth century, and it would also sharply increase the government's revenue. Nationalization of railroads, canals, mines, insurance companies, and all forms of communication would enable the republican state both to expand its income and to ensure more economic equity.[88]

The logic of the Montagnards' desire to make private property accessible to all produced a set of proposals with highly radical implications. By the end of 1848 a nascent democratic-socialist party advocated a system of industrial production based on small-scale collectivized workshops. Agricultural production was to be accomplished by independent peasant proprietors who relied on state aid for the production and marketing of their goods. The transformation to this system would be achieved through large-scale state intervention in the economy. State-owned banks would encourage producers' associations and peasant advancement by distributing low-interest loans to all those previously denied credit. The revenue for these loans would be obtained through progressive taxation and a program of nationalization ambitious even for the twentieth century.

Some historians have sought to explain away the radical character of democ-soc ideology by dismissing it as either petty-bourgeois Proudhonianism or utopian reverie.[89] A glance at Proudhon's writings of the period, however, suffices to show how fundamentally his views differed from what he considered the "statist" character of the Montagnard program.[90] Furthermore, analysis of France's economy in the mid-nineteenth century demonstrates that the democ-soc alternative to the prevailing form of economic organization was an appropriate, if highly radical, response to the existing state of affairs. The lone utopian element in the democ-socs' position was perhaps their vast underestimation of the conservatives' ability to resist change.[91]

Since the overwhelming majority of French enterprises at the mid-century were very small, and since French industry relied on highly skilled labor and not on heavy capital investment (see Chapter I), the idea of transforming the French economy through the establishment of producers' cooperatives was, at least in theory, not unfeasible. Only a small amount of capital was needed to set up a cooperative enterprise capable of competing with existing capitalist ateliers. And since most French workers were skilled and accustomed to working independently, a group of artisans surely possessed the ability to run their own business.

During the Second Republic associated workers managed to establish in Paris alone more than three hundred cooperatives representing 120 different trades. Some of these ventures, such as the tailors' cooperative of Clichy, proved immensely successful.[92] After mid-1849, however, government hostility hindered the new worker-owned enterprises, and in the aftermath of Louis Napoleon's 1851 coup d'état police closed down virtually all cooperatives still in business.

The democ-socs' rural program, which sought to combine private ownership of the land with a collectivized commercial structure, was no less radical in its implications than the project for industrial "collectivization from below." The Montagnards intended to free peasants from the burden of debt and regressive taxation that weighed so heavily on their meager livelihoods.[93] The institution of progressive taxation and the abolition of imposts on wine, salt, doors and windows, goods entering towns, and the like would improve peasant income significantly. Most important, the ability to obtain state-guaranteed credit at 2-3 percent interest repayable over a long term would allow peasants to settle outstanding debts and permit both the purchase of new land and the improvement of existing holdings. The purpose of low-interest agricultural loans was to encourage peasant land purchases from large owners and thus to promote a more equitable distribution of rural property. As was demonstrated in Chapter I, peasants had already been able to buy significant amounts of land from large- and medium-sized holders between 1815 and 1848. Peasants thus extended their domains at the expense not of other peasants but of rural notables. Further encouraged by the Montagnards' ambitious program of rural credit, the peasantry could well have made substantial inroads into large domains and thereby transformed property relations in the countryside. Small peasant property was in no way doomed to extinction in 1850, and had small cultivators been relieved of debt and the burden of taxation, as the Montagnards proposed, a large segment of the French peasantry, especially those who marketed cash crops, could have derived a more than adequate income from the land.

In terms of the future of French agriculture, the attempt to encourage small-scale, independently owned peasant holdings was by no means necessarily retrograde. The hilly and rocky nature of much of southern France rendered land consolidation uneconomic. Moreover, land subdivision, as indicated in Chapter I, often provoked agricultural progress. Finally, the production of such cash crops as wine and silkworms benefited from the kind of intensive cultivation that only small holdings could permit. Montagnard doctrine, therefore, proposed a plan for rural transformation that responded to the actual conditions of France's mid-century agricultural economy.

The great political strength of the democ-socs' economic analysis lay in its ability to appeal at the same time and in the same language to both workers and peasants. Since producers' cooperatives promised to turn all workers into owners, Montagnard ideologues could propose "collectivization from below" in the name of private property. In so doing, they pledged to fulfill the workers' central demand—abolition of the capitalist wage system through collective ownership—without in any way appearing to challenge the peasantry's fervent attachment to private property. Unlike later French socialists, who alienated the peasantry over the question of private property, the democ-socs developed an ideology that without any internal inconsistency, could satisfy both workers' demands for cooperatist collectivization and peasant longing for privately owned plots. It was this dual-edged economic thrust, combined with the democ-socs' populist religious outlook, that made their ideology so attractive to both peasant and working-class Frenchmen.

Perhaps the weakest part of democ-soc doctrine was its overestimation of the ease with which market forces could be harnessed for the benefit of humble peasants and workers. Montagnard spokesmen never explained very clearly how the cooperatives established with the aid of government loans would ultimately outcompete capitalist industry in the free market-place.[94] To be sure, they promised that the government would award work contracts exclusively to associative enterprises, but the needs of government were clearly not great enough for this sort of favored treatment to be applied to all industries. More-over, it is certainly conceivable that capitalist ateliers would be able to produce goods more cheaply than cooperative ones. In order to drive their capitalist competitors out of business, the members of a cooperative firm would have to agree to work for minimal compensation. Thus, at least in the early stages of the transition to a regime of universal cooperation, workers would be burdened by the same market forces that kept down wages in traditional enterprises.

The pages of *L'Atelier* demonstrate that more than a few workers were indeed willing to make sacrifices in the interest of cooperation.[95] At mid-century, much of the French working class sought a sense of dignity as skilled and independent work-ers at least as much as they desired higher wages. Above all else, they yearned for freedom from the wage system and for the self-esteem that comes from working on one's own ac-count.[96] The editors of *L'Atelier* argued that the producers' cooperative "is the exact replica in the economic realm of the revolution that took place in the political realm."[97] Writing in the *Almanach de l'Association ouvrière industrielle et agricole* (1850), Henry Feugueray presented even more explicitly the parallel between the political liberty of republican government and the economic liberty of cooperative industry. For Feu-gueray, the producers' association was "la république dans l'a-telier."[98] Democ-soc publicist Gabriel Mortillet agreed with these two working-class pronouncements. In his view the droit au travail guaranteed by producers' cooperatives formed "the in-dispensable complement to universal suffrage. Single-handedly it [the cooperative] is capable of freeing the workers from the powerful grip of their bosses; single-handedly, it can render the workers truly free. It is the principle that can assure for all time the triumph of democracy."[99] The democ-socs understood the workers' longing for independence, and much of their confidence in the ability of cooperatives to outcompete capitalist enterprises rested on the realization that skilled workers might make short-run economic sacrifices in the interests of long-term economic transformation.

In the agricultural realm, democ-soc doctrine addressed not only the peasants' desire for independent status as property holders but also their frustration over their impotence in the face of market realities. The Montagnards' response to the latter question, however, was much less convincing than its response to the former. The democ-socs identified the power of merchant capitalists and the erratic nature of demand as the primary obstacles to improved peasant livelihoods. But their proposed solutions to the problem of supply and demand for agricultural products made no more sense than those of most other revolutionaries.

The democ-socs conceived of a novel, if impractical, means by which to circumvent the laws of the marketplace and free peasants from their dependence on commercial middlemen. They planned to establish a nationwide system of agricultural bazaars, which would assign peasant produce a value independent of its market price.[100] Each commune would establish a *comptoir communal* where all farmers would deposit their produce. An expert would then assign the goods a value. In exchange, the depositor would receive coupons whose face value equaled the assigned value of the deposited goods. These coupons could be retained by the farmer or negotiated like bank notes. If retained, the coupons would represent savings; if negotiated, they would act as a kind of instant credit based on the worth of agricultural produce. The goods exchanged for coupons at the comptoirs communaux would be taken to a public bazaar where they would be put up for sale. Consumers could then buy the products for the assigned value plus transport and administrative charges, both of which would be fixed by the state and uniform for the whole country. When goods were sold at the bazaar, the holder of the coupon corresponding to them could then claim cash for the face value of the coupon. The various local bazaars would communicate among themselves, and those with a surplus of one kind of good would transfer their excess to bazaars where that product was in short supply.

This democ-soc proposal for a nationwide network of agricultural bazaars represented nothing less than an attempt to replace the prevailing capitalist market system with a socialized, state-run commercial structure. Under this new system all produce would be sold at a "just price," and there would be no middlemen to profit from the peasants' inability to market their own products. In theory, therefore, the agricultural bazaar addressed two of the principal obstacles to peasant well-being at the mid-century: the persistent inability to sell their goods at a price high enough to cover the costs of production, and their dependence on merchant capitalists (see Chapter I). As a practical alternative to the capitalist marketplace, however, this scheme suffered from insurmountable problems. For example, during a year in which vintners produced a nationwide surplus of wine, many of the coupons in circulation would represent the assigned value of wine that could never be sold at the government-fixed price. The holders of these coupons thus would not be able to exchange them for cash, and they would become worthless scraps of paper. No one would accept them as bank notes, and the whole system would collapse. If the government decided to redeem coupons before the goods they represented were sold, it would somehow have to find huge sums of cash. Such an effort would require enormous tax revenues and highly inflationary currency creation or both. Furthermore, the potential for black-market subversion of the government bazaars would be enormous. Finally, the democ-soc commercial alternative would work only for nonperishable agricultural products. Grain can be stored until buyers are found, but fruits, vegetables, flowers, table wine, meat, dairy products, and the like must be sold and consumed immediately. A government bazaar that bought excess milk, for example, would find itself subsidizing unneeded products. Such a collectivized commercial system could never be put into practice without carefully planned production quotas and a well-organized, sophisticated bureaucracy to administer it.

Despite their naiveté in commercial matters, the democ-socs

cannot be accused of subscribing to backward-looking economics. Much of their outlook was innovative, and many of their proposed solutions to contemporary economic problems represented appropriate responses to the conditions of their era.

Commercial inexperience does not, of course, account for all the inadequacies of democ-soc ideology. In many cases their acute perceptions of the economic and social disorders of their time engendered a desire for change so intense that they were blinded to the shortcomings of the alternatives they proposed. Their moral outrage over the way in which unrestricted industrial competition squeezed workers' incomes and reduced their status produced a revulsion against competitive capitalism that prevented full objectivity with regard to their cooperatist alternative. Similarly, their understanding of the way in which market pressures undermined peasant livelihoods gave rise to a plan for agricultural bazaars whose shortcomings were outlined above. Furthermore, the democ-socs' disgust with the unending violent conflict that had characterized the whole of their century provoked a longing for harmony and cooperation that blurred their perceptions of the tensions inherent in the proposed Montagnard alliance of workers, small entrepreneurs, master artisans, peasants, and liberal professionals.

In evaluating the strengths and weaknesses of democ-soc ideology, the particular historical circumstances in which it was elaborated as well as the underlying mentality of those who framed it must be taken into account. It is absolutely crucial, therefore, to remember that as path breakers in the art of mass politics, the Montagnards were not, and could not have been, seasoned politicians in the twentieth-century sense of the term. Though their revolutionary predecessors inaugurated democratic practice, the démocrates-socialistes became the first French politicians to engage seriously in mass politics. That is, they were the first to campaign nationwide, to prepare a series of national elections under universal suffrage, to establish the outlines of a political party, and to undertake the political education of the peasantry. Pioneers in the technique of mass propaganda and in the politics of universal suffrage, they had no prior experience—either their own or that of others—from which to draw lessons. They saw only promise in universal suffrage, for they lacked examples of its potential pitfalls. Similarly, they considered their newly acquired legal right to conduct electoral campaigns a virtually limitless opportunity to disseminate truth and lift the curtain of ignorance that had for so long prevented the masses from discovering their own interests. Buoyed by a self-identification with the apostles, the democ-socs had great confidence in their ability to communicate in its entirety a doctrine that claimed to embody the fundamental precepts of Christianity. They saw no need to alter or dilute parts of their ideology for mass consumption. For the Montagnards, propaganda literally meant propagating the faith.[101] The democ-socs' appeal was in essence a straightforward presentation of their views, and their statements can be taken as such.

CHAPTER V
CHANNELS OF
RURAL COMMUNICATION

As the democ-socs formulated their new republican ideology in late 1848 and 1849, they endeavored at the same time to devise a political strategy for putting their ideas into practice. It was a strategy that sought to realize the potential of universal suffrage through a massive effort to propagate Montagnard doctrine. Not only therefore did the democ-socs construct a vision of a socialist future; they also elaborated a political means by which to transform that vision into reality. This attempt to devise a politics of transformation through democratic means distinguished the democ-socs from earlier socialists and foreshadowed the efforts of French socialists in the twentieth century.

The actual process by which the democ-socs transmitted their ideas to the peasantry paralleled the earlier development of Montagnard ideology itself. That is, the republican left rejuvenated longstanding cultural forms with new ideas and new methods. Just as Montagnard leaders fashioned an innovative ideology out of existing religiosity, so they built their pathbreaking propaganda technique on the bedrock of familiar institutions and established patterns of rural communication and social interaction. Thus movement publicists used such fixtures of rural communication and social life as colportage, the village café, and Mediterranean social clubs (*cercles* and *chambrées*) to diffuse a set of doctrines that contained much that twentieth-century observers associate with modernity. Yet, even when democ-socs employed the newest means of communication and political organization, their methods respected prevailing cultural norms.

A similar mixture of established cultural patterns and new ideas can be seen in the propaganda literature itself. In format and style, the democ-socs' nonperiodical propaganda (the press will be discussed in Chapter VI) was nearly identical to the religious literature and popular almanacs that had flooded the countryside earlier in the century. The content of Montagnard literature, however, embodied the democ-socs' distinctive synthesis of unorthodox religiosity and socialist democracy. Thus, the democ-socs began their effort to politicize the countryside by harnessing "traditional" culture for new political ends.[1]

Unfortunately for the republican left, the government was quick to catch on to their propaganda techniques. By mid 1849 officials undertook to prevent the insertion of democ-soc propaganda into traditional channels of communication and social interaction. As the heavy hand of police repression descended on the professional colporteur and the village cabaret, Montagnards had to look elsewhere for ways of diffusing their doctrine. Increasingly denied longstanding circuits of communication, the democ-socs turned to France's new and expanding commercial infrastructure. The railroads, a streamlined postal service, and the multitude of sales agents who traveled for a living (successors to the colporteurs) were to provide the democ-socs new ways to circulate their ideas. France's legal code enabled the government to destroy colportage and repress with ease institutions that were expressly political, but Louis Napoleon was much less successful in preventing the left from using commercial networks to spread its doctrine.[2] That the Montagnards learned to adapt the nation's growing commercial network to their own subversive ends testifies to the extraordinary resourcefulness of the republican left.

In their efforts to establish a national political party, the leaders of both La Solidarité républicaine and La Propagande démocratique et sociale européenne sought to use colportage as one of their principal mechanisms of propaganda diffusion. La Propagande intended to send colporteurs out from Paris, and La Solidarité hoped to employ them both locally and nationally.[3] Though La Solidarité was disbanded in early 1849 and La Propagande lacked the organizational strength to conduct a nationwide propaganda campaign, these two national organizations provided the initial impulse and laid the groundwork for the intensive propaganda effort of spring 1849. As police records demonstrate, local democ-soc organizations relied heavily on colporteurs in the early months of the 1849 effort to propagate their ideology nationally.

In February 1849 police arrested a small-wares peddler (*marchand mercier*) named Launay for selling democ-soc literature along with his habitual goods. Launay had long exercised the profession of colporteur in the rural communes surrounding Rennes, and in early 1849 he was recruited for the democ-soc cause. He may or may not have believed in that cause, but he certainly hoped to earn a profit from it. Launay received his literature from one Dagaret, a Rennes tailor who seems to have been a local leader of the Montagnard left. Police found in Launay's home multiple copies of brochures, newspapers, and almanacs authored by Cabet, and they seized from Dagaret a huge stockpile of literature, all of which had been distributed by La Propagande démocratique et sociale européenne.[4] This literature included many of the principal writings of democ-soc ideologues and organizers, and it demonstrates that La Propagande démocratique et sociale européenne succeeded in disseminating these works to a rural audience. Police found Eugène Sue's "Entretiens démocratiques et socialistes," written for a popular readership, as well as many of the fundamental pieces analyzed in Chapter IV. These included the crucial ideological statement of the Conseil central des républicains démocrates et socialistes, which appeared on the eve of the presidential election, and transcripts of banquet toasts advocating unity on the left (cited in Chapter III). There were songs by Pierre Dupont, copies of Greppo's *Catéchisme social*, Gustave Briand's highly religious "Le Socialisme dévoilé," the important "Almanach démocratique et social," writings by Raspail and Cabet, and publications of Parisian producers' organizations. Stored in Dagaret's home, therefore, were many of the central documents of the democ-soc left, and all of these writings were destined for distribution via colportage in rural France. The police report on the Launay affair not only testifies to the rural penetration of democ-soc ideology, but it also provides insight into the lines of communication that enabled Parisian publicists to reach village readers. La Propagande sent literature to major provincial cities—probably through the mails or via rail, stagecoach, or canal boat (see below)—and from there local Montagnard leaders inserted it into an already existing system of colportage. French archives are filled with reports on colporteurs arrested during the spring and summer of 1849 for selling democ-soc literature. In late February 1849 police picked up a professional colporteur near Riom for selling Malardier's religious ode to the democratic and social republic, "L'Evangile de la République." A few months later police near Clermont detained a colporteur for peddling "Republican Prayers" and an issue of L'Eclaireur républicain that severely criticized government action during the Parisian demonstration of 13 June.[5] In May gendarmes from the Rennes region netted colporteurs for selling Lammenais's "Le Peuple" and Pyat's "Toast aux paysans," and in August they caught three colporteurs with "Le Catéchisme démocratique et social," the "Almanach démocratique et social," and Proudhon's "Les Malthusiens." Two months later Rennes police arrested peddlers for selling lithographed images of Montagnard leaders (similar to those of saints sold earlier in the century).[6]

Why did democ-soc leaders initially embrace colportage as the means by which to disseminate their ideology? According to historian Jules Michelet, an early advocate of colportage in service of the republic, "The masses don't know how to read and don't want to read because reading is extremely tiresome for those not used to it."[7] Republicans could not expect them to achieve enlightenment on their own. Without an active effort to disseminate republican propaganda, continued the historian, the people—both peasants and workers—would inevitably become Bonapartists. Immediate steps to begin the political education of the masses had to be taken, and colportage, a mechanism of rural communication long familiar to France's peasantry, was a logical choice.

In his history of colportage Charles Nisard, the Second Empire's foremost authority on the subject, agreed that colportage provided an ideal means by which to reach the peasantry. He argued that the colporteur was enormously successful in selling his wares to the peasantry* and that villagers almost always received him with open arms:

> The colporteurs knew how to read and write, but no more. They made up for their inadequate education through highly pronounced mercantile instincts that were seconded by a sort of good-natured persuasiveness capable of seducing even the most suspicious buyer. . . . Except for times of extreme misery, they [the colporteurs] were always highly considered and well-received by the peasants . . . [and] being so highly regarded in the countryside—peasants often fed and housed colporteurs for free—the peddlers have always had—and still retain—an influence among the rurals that must be taken into account.[8]

Joseph Benoît, reminiscing about the propaganda effort of the democ-socs, also pointed to the peasant's favorable view of the colporteur: "propaganda through colportage is the most efficient method because it enables thoughts themselves to knock on the door of the citizen. The literature of colportage presents itself to him as a kind of hope or a consolation that is always well-received."[9]

The colporteur was indeed a welcome visitor to village communities in the eighteenth and early nineteenth centuries, for this roving merchant represented a break in the routine of the rural cultivator. The peasant, moreover, attached almost magical power to the colporteur's stock; semiliterate at best, he felt a sense of awe for the printed word.[10] Familiar with rural society, democ-soc activists like Benoît and republican intellectuals like Michelet understood the political potential of colportage. Unfortunately for the left, so did members of Louis Napoleon's government. Having tolerated political colportage to some extent during the electoral campaign of spring 1849, the government succeeded in virtually wiping it out in the aftermath of the abortive 13 June uprising.

---

* As we have seen, colporteurs sold some ten million pieces of literature and lithographed images per year at the end of the July Monarchy (see p. 69 above).

By requiring prefectoral authorization for all writings sold by colporteurs, the antipress legislation of 27 July 1849 effectively prevented the democ-socs from employing professional colporteurs to disseminate their literature. Clearly, no democ-soc materials were likely to enjoy such authorization. Moreover, colporteurs were constantly searched for contraband propaganda after July 1849, and it became extremely risky for professional peddlers to carry democ-soc literature. By the end of 1849 the colportage of oppositionist writings was on the decline everywhere. In December 1849 the subprefect at Tonnerre (Yonne) wrote that "the enemies of the government [have] renounced the use of professional colporteurs, for they are the object of close surveillance. Instead, they endeavor to exploit and corrupt the countryside by sending out emissaries . . . who find numerous ways of hiding their merchandise."[11] Similarly, the procureur général at Metz wrote in January 1850 that, "as a result of the strict application of the law of 27 July which regulates the colportage of literature, it has become extremely difficult to propagate socialist and anarchist doctrines."[12] Not that this new state of affairs allowed the procureurs to rest easy. Though cheered by the success of the law of 27 July, they recognized the extent to which the democ-socs had cleverly adapted to the new situation.

By the time the government succeeded in enacting legislation designed to halt political colportage, the Montagnards had erected an elaborate network of propaganda diffusion that dispensed with the need for professional colporteurs. During the summer and fall of 1849 Montagnard activists assumed for themselves the propaganda functions of the colporteur and began to imitate his methods. Their propaganda network was a pyramidal structure organized on three levels—national, regional, and local. On the national level, the most important democ-soc leaders traveled constantly to France's provincial capitals to give speeches, preside over political banquets, and defend those accused of political offenses. In addition, salesmen, railroad employees, insurance agents, and others who traveled for a living distributed written propaganda and passed instructions to local leaders during the normal course of their professional activities. This is precisely what the colporteur had done, but the new propagandists did it much less conspicuously. At the regional level, the staffs of democ-soc newspapers were responsible for spreading material received from Paris as well as their own news sheets into the towns and villages of their jurisdiction (see Chapter VI). At the local level, small-town doctors, lawyers, innkeepers, and literate artisans transmitted democ-soc ideology to the peasantry. In most of rural France, the village café served as the focal point of the democ-soc propaganda effort. Here propagandists who often called themselves republican apostles transformed ordinary social gatherings into ad hoc political meetings. Before an assembled café clientele, democ-soc apostles read aloud from republican literature whose democratic-socialist message was steeped in the ideals and language of the Gospels.

By late 1849 government officials were fully aware of the extension of the democ-socs' propaganda network, and they recognized that in conquering colportage, they had by no means stifled the Montagnard message. In March 1850 the procureur général at Bourges wrote: "Colportage, having been severely repressed by the courts, seems to be disappearing. It has been more than replaced, however, by oral propaganda conducted in cafés and markets. It is in these locales that the unfortunate peasants are indoctrinated."[13] Officials in eastern France found democ-soc propaganda "highly active, but very secret. Indoctrination takes place in cabarets whose numbers grow from one day to the next."[14] The Bordeaux region had "fewer colporteurs, but dangerous brochures are diffused by ordinary travelers who escape police surveillance."[15] Near Toulouse, "socialist theories have ravaged the region. This situation is less the result of colportage . . . than of journalism and of the political preaching that takes place in cafés, fairs, and public markets."[16] Police could keep track of professional colporteurs, whose numbers were relatively small and who, as merchants, had to make their presence known. But gendarmes could not survey everyone who traveled for a living, and these anonymous voyagers forged crucial links in the Montagnards' nationwide propaganda network much more efficiently than the colporteurs ever could have done. The democ-socs, therefore, relied on professional colporteurs only in the initial stages of their propaganda campaign. As political repression stymied the efforts of these professionals, Montagnard activists assumed their role. In so doing, they were able to gain entrance to and maintain contact with rural society.

The French courts' narrow interpretation of the anti-colportage law of July 1849 facilitated the transfer of the colporteur's propaganda functions to traveling democ-soc sympathizers. Judges ruled that this law applied only to professional colporteurs and that occasional and nonprofessional distribution of printed matter did not constitute a violation of its provisions. The tribunal at Dreux (Eure-et-Loire) argued, for example, that the law of 27 July "was designed uniquely to regulate the conduct of professional colporteurs and of all those who made a living from the distribution of books, writings, brochures, engravings, and lithographs."[17] French prosecutors therefore found it difficult to indict the insurance agents, postal and railroad employees, stagecoach drivers, and road construction engineers (*conducteurs des ponts et chaussées*) who actively spread democ-soc literature, songs, and lithographs after mid-1849.

Insurance agents were particularly prominent among the roving apostles of democratic socialism. Because insurance companies sought to protect ordinary people from natural disaster, and because they espoused a mutualist ideology in which most advanced republicans believed, the directors and employees of France's early insurance companies tended to sympathize with oppositionist politics—carbonarism in the 1820s, republican socialism in the 1830s, and democratic socialism during the Second Republic.*[18] The agents, whose job was to make contact with ordinary people throughout rural and small-town France, made excellent propagandists. They enjoyed virtual immunity from repression, for police found it extremely difficult to prove that agents who doubled as democ-soc apostles were doing anything more than selling policies. An insurance agent named Augustin

* The founder of *La Voix du peuple*, Marseille's influential democ-soc paper, had been a director of an insurance company in southern France (see below p. 181).

Gueneau, accused after the coup d'état of propagating democratic socialism in the countryside, protested that "I am an insurance agent and must traverse the countryside in the interests of my company. I am much more concerned with business than with politics. If my conversations occasionally turn to politics it is to encourage moderation and condemn violence."[19] Gueneau could not completely deny his political role, especially since others identified him as an important local propagandist. In the arrondissement of Limoux (Aude), police accused one Vidal of propagating Montagnard ideology. Gendarmes described Vidal as an "agent of a fire insurance company. As such he criss-crossed the countryside . . . and made numerous converts to his doctrines. He was remarkably clever and knew how to avoid compromising himself."[20] One of the defendants in the Second Republic's political show trial, an event known as the "complot de Lyon," was an insurance salesman named Alexandre Dupont. The prosecution claimed that he used his job as a cover for political travels.[21] An overzealous Dijon mailman discovered another example of an insurance agent who mixed business and politics. By illegally opening a letter written by one Tessier, agent for a fire insurance company called La Paternelle, the nosy mailman discovered that Tessier planned to peddle subscriptions to Joigneaux's *La Feuille du village* while selling insurance policies in the Dijon region.[22] Only in instances like the Tessier case could police muster firm proof against these insurance agent propagandists. In general, those whose business activity required extensive travel could spread democ-soc ideology with relative safety. This was one of the principal ways in which the Montagnards retained a measure of immunity from intensifying government repression.

Indeed, the growing French system of commerce and communication as a whole provided a cover under which Montagnard doctrines could spread. Just as road and canal construction, railroad building, and postal reform stimulated French economic growth, so these developments also facilitated ideological diffusion. Reduced postal rates aided propaganda efforts as much as they contributed to business profits, and rails and roads moved oppositionist literature while they extended commercial markets. In the political conjuncture of 1848, any attempt to cut off the flow of subversive ideas into the countryside would have required nothing less than an authoritarian state on the one hand or strict controls on technological and commercial growth on the other. The government of Louis Napoleon Bonaparte was to choose the former solution.

Government reports from the Yonne portray admirably the ambiguous effect of railroad extension. On the one hand, "the creation of a railroad line [through the Yonne] has had the happy effect of increasing the circulation of travelers and merchandise in the region." But on the other, "the three thousand railroad workers present in the department are all very bad subjects who have infected . . . [the district] with socialist propaganda!"[23] The embryonic French railroad system indeed played a crucial role in the politicization of the French countryside; not only did railroad employees secretly move contraband literature over the completed lines, but those who worked on the construction of new ones brought democ-soc ideology into the rural regions in which they labored.

It was the foremen who supervised the laying of track and the building of roads and waterways who led the propaganda effort. The procureur général at Toulouse described the ways in which foremen acted to politicize hitherto untouched rural regions:

> The canton of Valème has until now been absolutely closed to socialism. But now the region is being invaded by construction foremen [conducteurs des ponts et chaussées] who work on the canal lateral to the Garonne River. They consider themselves apostles of these maxims [i.e., democ-soc doctrine], and they do more than just preach. They use their authority to make converts.[24]

Everywhere they went during the Second Republic, conducteurs des ponts et chaussées seem to have become leaders of the democ-soc left. Police reports from Joigny (Yonne) repeatedly singled out two Paris-Lyon conducteurs named Petit and Billard for their attempts to politicize workers and peasants who lived near the route of the new rail line.[25] An innkeeper from Narcy in the Nièvre told police that one Baron, a conducteur des ponts et chaussées, regularly read propaganda and led republican songs in his auberge.[26] In Bourges, the prefect of the Cher wrote that "a huge number of low-level agents of the department of *ponts et chaussées* made themselves the instruments of the anarchist party [i.e., the democ-socs] in the elections of this department [in 1849]. Some took charge of diffusing throughout the region the most abominable of writings and others did their best to entice the opinion of the popular classes. . . ."[27] The government found the conducteurs des ponts et chaussées so troublesome that in July 1849 the Minister of the Interior directed the Minister of Public Works "to put a stop to the spirit of indiscipline and to the demagogic propaganda of many government employees . . . especially those who belong to the department of *ponts et chaussées* [part of the Ministry of Public Works]."[28]

Thus, as workmen moved into a new region to extend rails and canals they brought new and often subversive political ideas. And once the rail lines were in place, conductors, engineers, station managers, and other railroad employees formed the skeleton of a regional network for the circulation of propaganda. In January 1850 a Rouen court convicted M. Duchesne, an employee of the Rouen–Le Havre railroad, for using his position to send illegally some one thousand copies of the democ-soc *L'Union démocratique* along the line.[29] Joigny's commissioner of police complained that "all the employees of the rail line [between Joigny and Tonnerre] with but one exception are full-blooded Reds."[30] Station managers received democ-soc writings and other propaganda and transmitted political information from Paris to local sympathizers. Those who worked on the trains themselves moved democ-soc documents and served as go-betweens linking Parisian leaders to democ-socs in the Yonne, both in major towns like Joigny and in small villages near the rail line. Police singled out railroad employees in particular, for they "were men who could speak of nothing else besides politics. They attempt to spread socialist propaganda when they come into contact with the least educated class [i.e., the peasants]."[31] Port workers performed a similar function for the democ-socs. A Monsieur Chétrier who worked for Auxerre's wine entrepôt "received propaganda brochures from Paris and distributed them to the peasants."[32]

Since the French railroad network was still in its infancy in 1850, Montagnards turned to the newly reformed postal system for aid in propelling their propoganda throughout the country. Courts ruled that the anticolportage law of 27 July 1849 did not apply to literature sent through the mails. Thus, senders did not need the prior authorization of the prefect of the departments to which they mailed their literature.[33] Moreover, the Minister of Finance, who directed the postal system, prohibited prefects from seizing in post offices newspapers that the government was suing.[34] The democ-socs quickly took advantage of this relatively favorable state of affairs, and after July 1849 they relied heavily on the postal system for the distribution of their propaganda. In launching his *Feuille du village* at the end of October 1849, Pierre Joigneaux declared that the law against colportage made him abandon writing brochures in favor of publishing a newspaper, for only the mail system remained as a means of reaching the peasantry:

> Thanks to a new law, it is no longer possible to peddle republican brochures. Colportage is now subjected to the political whims of the prefects. . . . Our enemies can make use of colportage to harm us, but we are not permitted to use colportage to nurse our wounds. . . .
>
> Deprived of the possibility of using colportage in the service of our ideas, we will make use of the mails to send them to each domicile. The goal that the brochures can no longer attain, the newspaper, we hope, will. This is why we founded *La Feuille du village*.[35]

Joigneaux's eight-page weekly, written expressly for a peasant audience, did indeed manage to reach rural readers through the postal system. Since peasants normally banded together in groups of three or four to share Joigneux's journal, the subscription fee of six francs a year (as opposed to twenty-five to forty francs for most daily democ-soc papers) burdened one's budget only slightly. Government officials throughout central France, where the paper seems to have penetrated most successfully, reported that peasants received *La Feuille* in the mail. Thus, a procureur based in the Aube complained of the "disturbing influence that the corrupt press exercises over the countryside. Perhaps the most influential is Joigneaux's newspaper, distributed in large numbers through the mails."[36]

Joigneaux's use of the mail to foster his propaganda effort set a trend for the democ-soc left. In late November 1849 the Minister of the Interior reported that "colportage is no longer the primary means of disseminating subversive literature. Now the mails are used."[37] Similarly, the procureur général at Douai reported that "the revolutionaries, suffering from the active surveillance of the police and the gendarmes, no longer can use colportage to disseminate among their brothers and friends the incendiary writings that provoke people to rebel. The postal system now seems to them less complicated and more secure."[38] That this second letter was written in mid-1850, when repression had reached new heights, indicates that the postal system remained a haven for democ-soc propaganda. The mails were perhaps too important to France's expanding commercial economy to be subjected to tight government-imposed restraints.

The democ-socs found encouragement in the relative freedom of the mails, but for good measure they took care to enlist rural postmen, post office employees, and telegraph operators to serve the cause of propaganda. Police constantly accused rural mailmen of delivering democ-soc propaganda not just to regular subscribers of newspapers but to others as well. These postmen would receive packages of brochures from Paris or another major city and then sell or give them to rural dwellers during the course of their regular mail rounds. Gendarmes from Joigny, for example, reported that a local postman named Frossard was "an agent of demagogic propaganda who peddled socialist newspapers clandestinely."[39] Police found it difficult to repress this postal propaganda, for much of it was legal, and gendarmes could hardly inspect the sacks of every rural mailman every day to separate legal from illegal propaganda. Moreover, many post office and telegraph employees sympathized with the democ-socs, hampering police action even more.[40]

One final way in which democ-socs used France's expanding

network of transport and communications was to infiltrate the horsedrawn parcel delivery service and the stagecoach lines. These older forms of transport took up where the rails left off. Coach drivers would collect literature that arrived by train and then distribute it at each stop on their regular runs. "A stagecoach driver on the line between Joigny and Toucy," reported the prefect of the Yonne, "carried hidden in his coach newspapers and other socialist literature given to him at the train station in Joigny. He normally hides this literature in a small compartment just to the right of the driver's seat."[41] Gendarmes in the arrondissement of Vienne (Isère) found "in a coach belonging to the national parcel post a bundle of socialist brochures addressed to M. Joubart, clerk of the justice of the peace at Bordeaux [Drôme]." The booty included numerous copies of Louis Blanc's *Nouveau monde* and forty-eight copies of the *Catéchisme des socialistes* by the same author.[42] Charles Tisserandot, a Dijonnais democ-soc leader, made use of his position as an inspector for a local parcel delivery service to spread propaganda throughout the Burgundy region. In addition, Tisserandot's "parcel delivery coaches facilitated the transmission of his party's orders and communications between Dijon, Besançon, and Geneva."[43] In Sens (Yonne) the director of the national parcel delivery service served as correspondent for *La Feuille du peuple*, and he spread the paper's democ-soc message in the course of his work. Elsewhere local drivers carried secret correspondence between democ-soc leaders of the various provincial towns in their region.[44]

By infiltrating the nation's insurance companies, railways, mail system, parcel delivery service, and coach lines, the democsocs more than made up for the government's repression of colportage. The colporteurs of time-honored tradition had introduced rural Frenchmen to democ-soc propaganda. Once that introduction had been made, however, repression forced the Montagnards to refine their methods. Having begun by inserting their ideas into longstanding circuits of rural communication, the democ-socs endeavored after mid-1849 to use newer channels of communication in the countryside. This change of tactics neither disrupted the flow of democ-soc literature nor inhibited its influence, for those who transmitted Montagnard propaganda on a village level were well-known to the local peasantry, and the literature itself remained in a form familiar and understandable to them. As will be shown below, both the form and the content of a substantial part of Montagnard propaganda resembled the popular religious literature widely circulated in rural France earlier in the century.

How did Montagnard materials and the political ideology they carried actually reach the rural artisanat and peasantry? Two local institutions, the democ-soc press and the secret Montagnard societies, played the pivotal role in this process, and they will be examined in Chapter VI. The remaining discussion of this chapter will be concerned with the informal mechanisms of diffusion at the village level. The traveling salesmen, insurance agents, coach drivers, railroad employees, and post office workers who brought democ-soc literature into a small town or village would deliver it to one or more local sympathizers of the Montagnard party. These village agents tended to be café proprietors, booksellers, literate artisans, members of the liberal professions, and minor functionaries, and they completed the chain of propaganda that linked urban publicists to a vast rural constituency.[45] Their job was to make sure that Montagnard ideas and propaganda reached the peasantry. And it was the local café that served as the primary nexus of ideological transmission at the village level.

Country doctors figured prominently among these local agents of democratic socialism, and the records of the Mixed Commissions testify to their importance at the village level.*[46] In the commune of Prémery (Nièvre), for example, a highly respected doctor named Basset served as the local leader of Montagnard sympathizers. Basset subscribed to Montagnard journals and read them to artisans and peasants in the café run by his friend Bailly. While making his rural rounds, he discussed politics with patients, and when the Nièvre's democ-soc move-

---

* Composed of both military and civilian officials, the Mixed Commissions were quasi-judicial tribunals that prosecuted individuals arrested for rebellion in December 1851.

ment went underground after May 1850, Basset was elected *decurion* (section leader) of his commune's secret society.[47] A doctor named Lachamp played a similar role in the town of Thiers (Puy-de-Dôme). Lachamp's peasant parents had envisaged for their mentally alert son (born in 1806) one of the few paths of social ascension available to the peasantry: the priesthood. Thus, like so many other country doctors of peasant stock, Lachamp began his studies in religious institutions. He took his secondary schooling with the Jesuits, but immediately after graduation Lachamp renounced the ecclesiastical life and decided to become a doctor. Poverty prevented him from undertaking full-time medical study, and he went to work in a high school while he slowly pursued his degree. Upon receiving his diploma, he married into a middle-class family and set up practice in Thiers. Town officials described Dr. Lachamp as anticlerical but not irreligious. As happened with democ-socs throughout France, his religious education had produced an animosity to priests but not to Catholicism. After 24 February 1848 Lachamp led charivaris against the curé of Thiers and established a club in which he expressed "the most advanced democratic ideas." At the same time, he undertook actively to propagate democ-soc doctrine. Lachamp "fraternized with the people, and converted them to democracy." He made a habit of attending political trials and always treated coreligionists newly released from prison to a round of drinks at the local left-wing café. In mid-1850 Lachamp became the leader of Thiers's secret society, and he used the organization to continue his effort to propagate democ-soc ideology. He was fined for yelling "Vive la république démocratique et sociale" inside the town church, and in December 1851 the Mixed Commission deported him for having helped to organize the December insurrection.[48]

A fascinating little book, *Un Medecin de campagne d'autrefois*, provides yet another portrait of a country doctor turned Montagnard leader. Writing in 1905, Léon Guyon recorded the life of his father, whom he considered one of the last true country doctors.[49] In the early and mid-nineteenth century, wrote Guyon, rural doctors were men of the people who shared their patients' interests and understood their problems. Of peasant stock himself, Guyon *père* was regarded by the peasants as one of them, and they trusted him fully. In the early years of his career Dr. Guyon found himself perpetually engaged in a two-front battle with the curé on the one hand and the sub-prefect on the other. The priest envied Guyon's prestige among the people, and the subprefect cared little for his liberal views. Early in the 1830s Guyon was elected municipal councilor of his native Bonnetable (Sarthe), and, despite the opposition of local notables, he became mayor in 1846. Influenced by Raspail, Guyon believed there was a tie between poverty and ill health, and he viewed politics in medical terms. The doctor compared the new republic of 1848 with an organism that had undergone a difficult operation. It needed healthy stimulation and good nourishment. Both would be provided by democ-soc propaganda, the political medicine that would abolish ignorance and bolster the republic. To this end, Dr. Guyon became local correspondent of the *Bonhomme Manceau*, a journal founded in February 1849 and devoted to a rural audience. Each month Guyon sold between 150 and 200 copies to the peasants of Bonnetable: "Always every bit as prudent as he was cautious, the peasant would ring Dr. Guyon's doorbell on the pretext of a medical visit. But as soon as he stepped inside, he asked if the *Bonhomme* had arrived. Upon receiving an affirmative response, he often took two or three copies for himself and his neighbors."[50]

In addition to selling the *Bonhomme Manceau*, Dr. Guyon would respond to the political queries of his peasant patients during his medical rounds and in so doing spread democ-soc ideas. When elections approached, peasants sought his advice on whom to vote for, and Léon remembered his father's customary response: " 'Do you have confidence in me,' he would begin. 'You have known me long enough to realize that I would not lead you astray. Well then, I'm voting for the republican list which features the names of Ledru-Rollin, Granges, Démontry, and Joigneaux. . . .' "[51]

In describing his father, Léon Guyon provided important insights into the mentality of village democ-soc leaders. These local activists, sympathetic to the plight of common people, possessed an unshakable optimism about the future of their society as well as a religious faith in the legitimacy of their cause. Such sentiments enabled them to persevere in their political work, often at great personal cost. How different they were, lamented Guyon, from the self-seeking professional politicians of the Third Republic. Léon's portrait of his father, albeit nostalgic and somewhat sentimental, was not without justice: "During the two years and some months of reaction that preceded the coup d'état, how many martyrs there were who sacrificed their tranquility, their fortune, their family, and even their life rather than renounce their political faith! The men of that era [the Second Republic] did not view politics as a means of getting ahead."[52]

Small-town lawyers played a role in rural France similar to that of country doctors. Local branches of La Solidarité républicaine often counted lawyers among their officers, and lawyers profited from their professional contacts with lower-class Frenchmen to spread propaganda and make converts to democratic socialism.[53] The role of notaries proved more ambiguous, for they were just as likely to aid the rural moneylender as to support the Montagnard cause. The notary's clerks, however, tended to side with the republican left. The procureur général at Bourges complained that small-town clerks who assisted lawyers, notaries, and judges "were perpetually in contact with the people of the countryside . . . and have caused us and will continue to cause us much harm."[54] Other important focuses of small-town propaganda diffusion included small retailers whose shops were frequented by common people and village booksellers who corresponded with La Propagande démocratique et sociale européenne. In the village of Aubenas (Ardèche), for example, the bookstore of a Monsieur Planches served as the local entrepôt of democ-soc literature.[55] The Minister of the Interior found booksellers so important to the democ-soc propaganda network that he felt it necessary in August 1850 to alert his judicial counterpart to the magnitude of the problem.[56]

In many regions of rural France, this powerful effort to propagate democ-soc ideology bore its first fruit among France's large numbers of village and rural artisans. A pair of fascinating documents permits a glimpse at the nature of the relationship between middle-class démocrates-socialistes and their artisan protégés. Two democ-socs imprisoned for their political activity, Emile Dussoubes and Alfred Erlarassain, had maintained a correspondence with a worker named Laruelle from near Limoges. Dussoubes was the brother of a Montagnard Representative of the People. Erlarassain belonged to "one of the most honorable families of the region."[57] Two letters confiscated by police demonstrate the extent to which the middle-class writers served as intellectual and political tutors for their working-class pupil. Both letters begin with critiques of Laruelle's grammar and handwriting and then go on to analyze the political situation. The tone of Erlarassain's opening paragraph resembles that of a schoolmaster disappointed in the work of his star pupil:

Dussoube's criticisms of your handwriting are, I must say, all too justified. Given all that you have learned, it would be a shame if instead of making progress you forget what you have learned (the great authors, for example). I told you once before to ask my sister for a French grammar book, and I repeat the suggestion. If you copy and study the verbs, I'm sure that before too long we will have the satisfaction of complimenting your progress. If you need any help in these matters, my sister will take great pleasure in giving it to you.[58]

In the latter sections of the letters, points of grammar give way to political education. The tone becomes slightly less paternalistic and even betrays a certain dependence on the views and knowledge of their working-class comrade. Erlarassain asks for details about the government's prosecution of their local democ-soc paper and seeks Laruelle's assessment of the likelihood of winning the case. Dussoube's letter shows a similar reliance on the independent judgment of his ex-disciple, though the schoolmaster tone is still there: "What you have told us about the Haute-Vienne and about the progress of social ideas in the countryside fills us with joy. If Jacques bonhomme [i.e., the peasantry] could finally see the light, the revolution would be three-quarters accomplished. It is he, oppressed, robbed, and beaten, who holds the key to the republic."[59]

These two letters suggest that middle-class democ-socs viewed intellectual training and political education as necessary complements. For them, political enlightenment was simply one component of the overall intellectual advancement of the working class. Education in the formal sense was one of the preconditions of political awakening. It is difficult to know precisely how artisans felt about their relationship with middle-class democ-socs, but there is evidence that they looked to middle-class coreligionists for intellectual and political guidance, even as the actual experience of the Second Republic contributed to their political independence. A railroad worker (*piqueur des ponts et chaussées*) from Joigny referred to the democ-soc Dr. Grenet as "the father of the workers" and expressed the wish that Grenet be elected mayor.[60] Similarly, a Troyes artisan addressed a local democ-soc notary named Lefebvre as "an unalienable friend of the people" and asked him to "come once again to us to tell us that the cause of the people is your cause, that our interests are not forever annihilated, that the struggles of which we are witnesses and victims prepare the alliance of fraternity and politics."[61] The "alliance of fraternity and politics" most likely refers to the religious-based ideals of democratic socialism and thus reflects the penetration of Montagnard ideology.

Though it is impossible to know how representative the above statements are, they do suggest that working-class democ-socs continued to look to middle-class Montagnards for political inspiration. They indicate, moreover, that the conflicts that were to surface within the republican movement in the late 1860s remained for the most part foreign to the democratic-socialist coalition of 1849-1851. Once the republican left separated itself from the moderates of the Provisional Government to join socialists in a left-wing alliance, a republican movement was able to develop the capacity to appeal to the aspirations of peasants, artisans, and modest members of the middle class.

Once converted to democratic socialism, newly politicized artisans took the Montagnard message to peasant cultivators. Artisans and peasants often lived in close proximity, and since both groups tended to sell their products to each other, especially in central and southern France, peasants and artisans were in constant contact. This contact facilitated the transmission of political ideas. Detailed studies of the Côte-d'Or, the Saône-et-Loire, the Gard, and the Yonne show that artisans played a major—perhaps *the* major—role in transmitting democ-soc ideas at the village level.[62] Archival sources from other departments confirm the importance of their role. In the canton of Cosne (Nièvre), for example, artisans engaged actively in democ-soc propaganda. C. Lamy, a stonecutter from Pouilly-sur-Loire, shared a subscription to *La Feuille du village* with three colleagues, and he admitted to police that "a number of local people would come regularly to my place to hear me read the newspaper."[63] A search of Lamy's dwelling uncovered numerous political song sheets, copies of a brochure entitled "Le Petit manuel du paysan électeur," Pyat's "Toast aux paysans," as well as copies of *La Feuille du village*. Lamy undoubtedly used all these documents in his efforts to propagate democ-soc ideology among the peasantry.[64] In the Hérault, reports from justices of the peace throughout the department testify to the central political role of village artisans. Asked in December 1851 to indicate who were the most influential democ-soc leaders in each commune, the justices overwhelmingly pointed to the artisans. Of the twenty-five leaders mentioned in the town of Sette, seventeen were artisans. Other leaders included a conducteur des ponts et chaussées, a doctor, a wine seller, and a clerk. In the commune of Ganges, eleven of the thirty-one leaders were artisans; in Béziers the proportion was twenty-one of thirty-two; in St. Pons, nine of twenty-seven; in Lodève, forty-three of seventy-six. As in the Nièvre and elsewhere, these Hérault artisans sought to convert the peasantry. A clockmaker from Béziers named Relin propagated democ-soc ideology among "the villagers [who] streamed into his shop on the pretext of having their watches fixed."[65]

In addition to spreading propaganda on the village level, members of the artisanat were known to travel around the country as emissaries of national Montagnard leaders. Democ-soc newspapers hired ex-artisans to sell subscriptions in the provinces and to establish links between urban leaders and their country constituencies (see Chapter VI). Other urban leaders charged artisans with propaganda and organizational missions that involved extensive travel through rural France. In September 1850 police in Valence detained two typesetters suspected of subversive activity. The two artisans, natives of Dunkerque and Lille, were carrying a bundle of republican song sheets, and they surrendered to police a notebook listing their itinerary in detail. Their journey had been elaborately planned by unnamed democ-soc leaders; they were to pay visits to local Montagnard leaders in Bergerac (Dordogne), Périgueux (Dordogne), Angoulême (Charente), Chabonais (Dordogne), St. Julien (Haute-Vienne), Limoges (Haute-Vienne), Thiviers (Dordogne), Excideuil (Dordogne), Montignac (Dordogne), and Cahors (Lot). The *amis de la Montagne* that the two emissaries were to see at each stopping point exercised the now-familiar professions of France's small-town democ-soc leaders: doctor, ex-schoolteachers, *cabaretier* (café keeper), notary, and even stagecoach driver.[66]

At the village level, then, doctors, notaries, lawyers, booksellers, and literate artisans transmitted democ-soc ideas to the peasantry during the normal course of their professional activity. Thus the structure of work and the nature of commercial and business relations in themselves facilitated politicization in the villages of mid-nineteenth-century France. But perhaps even more important to the transmission of Montagnard ideology at the village level was the café, hub of rural sociability. In the familiar surroundings of the modest local inn, democ-soc politics found its rural home. Pierre Joigneaux, who spent countless hours in the village cafés of the Côte-d'Or, provides a detailed description of a typical country cabaret:

> On the wall was a mirror worth no more than thirty sous [a sou equals five centimes] with a branch of boxwood above it. The café tables were made of ordinary wood and the chairs fashioned out of straw or reeds. Our images [pasted to the walls] are no more costly. They include portraits of the four seasons, a few battles of the Empire worth five

sous a piece, and two or three rascals of the Red Party likewise stuck to the walls with a bit of yeast.[67]

After a day's labor in the fields or workshops, peasants and artisans would head for "their" café—rural Frenchmen tended to choose a particular café and stick with it as if it were a private club—to enjoy an evening drink. As the clientele of a given café relaxed in the company of familiar faces, a village democsoc would begin to read from the latest issue of the Montagnard newspaper to which the cabaretier subscribed.[68] The reader spiced his articles with liberal doses of commentary and explanation, while questions and interjections constantly interrupted his progress. In this way, a public reading turned into wide-ranging political discussion. Having digested the newspaper or other democ-soc writing, the café's clientele would then break into song—"Charlotte La Républicaine," Durrand's "Chant du vigneron," Pierre Dupont's "Chant aux paysans," or any one of the hundreds of other Montagnard songs composed during the Second Republic. Thus in the canton of Bléneau (Yonne) the regular clients of the "red" café gathered nightly to listen to readings of *La Réforme* and to sing democ-soc songs.[69] "Every night without exception," wrote the police commissioner of Toucy (also in the Yonne), "a meeting is held in the café run by one Lallemand during which his clients sing the most anarchistic [i.e., democ-soc] songs."[70]

Democ-socs and conservatives alike were intensely aware of the village café's political importance during the Second Republic, and this mutual awareness gave rise to a violent polemic over the "morality" of the cabaret. For the Party of Order, the café was the locus of debauchery and decadence, a place that encouraged drunkenness, threatened family life, and facilitated intellectual degeneration, one form of which was socialist politics:

The close surveillance of cafés, cabarets, and other public establishments is one of our most important duties. In carrying out this duty with just severity, we act in the interests of a moral code that rejects debauchery and protects family life. . . . Moreover, in surveying cafés we properly enforce the law which prohibits political meetings. In so doing we prevent the secret meetings in which the most subversive doctrines are discussed and propagated.[71]

Cafés brought together bad morals and bad politics in an unseemly whole. The one bred the other in the minds of the men of order, and by policing the café, the government believed it could put an end to moral and political degeneration with a single blow. For democ-socs, on the other hand, the rural café symbolized the democratic right of even the humblest Frenchman to enjoy rest and relaxation among peers and to maintain a measure of political and intellectual independence. In a sharply worded defense of the rural café, Pierre Joigneaux argued that this modest institution provided one of the very few, perhaps the only, means of escape for a peasantry subjected to the drudgery and isolation of agricultural life:

> When one has performed unremitting back-breaking labor for a whole week without having anyone else on the same field to chat with, it is perfectly natural and understandable that he would take great pleasure in spending Sunday afternoon talking with his neighbors. . . . Since no one person can afford to serve wine and food to all his comrades, peasants have chosen the café as their meeting place. For it is only there that they can sit down at the same table, drink together, and say what's on their minds. It is only in the café that peasants can discuss their budding wheat or their ripening ears, that they can learn from each other. Only in the café can peasants build the Republic and read the week's newspapers. We have no other distractions but these.
>
> And, that's not all, Messieurs les moralistes, for without cafés there would be no more commerce, no more business, no more money and thus no more people. Often our business begins at the fair and concludes in the cabaret. . . . How rare it is that men who have drunk together do not do business together. And finally . . . the cabaret . . . is not simply the stock exchange of the peasant world, but it

is also the notary's sales office. . . . You [the moralists] must admit that these places are more respectable than your own upper-class clubs and that they are, without a doubt, more useful and less boring.[72]

Joigneaux's portrait, albeit romanticized, of the village café ennobles a simple village institution that, far from being a den of immorality, is simply a focal point of peasant life. As a center of personal contact, the café fulfilled the purely utilitarian role of facilitating business transactions. More important, it provided a forum for the exchange of practical information, for intellectual growth, and for political education. To be sure, Joigneaux glossed over the drunkenness that the cabaret could encourage, just as he refused to admit its potential drain on the meager resources of a peasant family. But what he emphasized about the café was precisely what most aroused the conservatives' fears—its role in fostering peasant independence from the moral and ideological hegemony of the rural notability.[73]

The village café was one of the very few institutions of rural life open to the external world. It was in the café that peasants encountered travelers from the outside who brought new ideas and tales of novel adventures. Here politicized villagers from the middle ranks of rural society exposed peasants to advanced political ideas, and here democ-soc organizers and propagandists diffused their ideology. By early 1850 procureurs généreaux and prefects throughout the country had identified the rural café as a central staging ground of the democ-soc challenge.[74] In February 1850 the procureur at Nancy exclaimed:"Cafés! There is the plague!" Cafés "have more than replaced the clubs."[75] And in the words of the procureur at Lyon:

At this moment [January 1850] we must beware of the influence that the cabarets exert on the political beliefs of the rural population. Earlier the cafés were nothing more than meeting places for drinking. But ever since the newspaper penetrated its walls, the café has been transformed almost everywhere. It has become a circle whose purpose is to develop political news. Cabarets have become schools of demoralization for the inhabitants of the countryside.[76]

Lyon's procureur emphasized the crucial role of the newspaper in the politicization of the rural population (a point that will be taken up in detail in the next chapter), and, like other conservatives, he linked the development of new political ideas to moral degradation. This conservative belief that socialist politics was just one aspect of an overall moral decay encouraged by the proliferation of rural cabarets found blunt expression in a report from the Minister of Justice: "Rural cafés have become centers of homicide, prostitution, and thievery . . . [and] from a political point of view, the multiplicity of cafés and cabarets has become a real danger. Socialist propaganda has developed there as a result of the public reading of newspapers, of seditious speechmaking, and of the affiliations to secret societies that take place there."[77]

Much of the political matter disseminated through the elaborate network outlined above was intended specifically for a rural audience. Like the more theoretical writings discussed in Chapter IV, peasant-oriented propaganda expressed the ideals of democratic socialism in the idiom of populist religiosity. But these popular genres differed significantly in style and format from the democ-socs' more sophisticated literature. Propaganda directed to the countryside often took the form of brochures, catechisms, political almanacs, lithographs, and song sheets, and as such it bore a striking resemblance to the religious materials widely circulated earlier in the century.[78] After 1848 lithographs of Catholic saints gave way to lithographs of republican saints. Religious song sheets were replaced by republican songsheets that looked just like their religious predecessors. Pocket-sized catechisms and other popular religious brochures gave way to identical-looking republican catechisms and political pamphlets. Thus both content and format of democ-soc propaganda were familiar and understandable to country dwellers accustomed to the kinds of popular literature analyzed in Chapter II. It is unclear whether the left's use of existing cultural forms to transmit a new political ideology was conscious or unconscious. But the democ-socs unquestionably facilitated their task by grounding their efforts in rural religious culture.

So alarming did conservatives find the populist religiosity of democ-soc rural propaganda that the Minister of the Interior himself was moved to analyze the religious content of this literature. In a letter advising the prefect of the Bouches-du-Rhône that Marseillais democ-socs were distributing large quantities of "dangerous literature in the countryside," the minister described the tone of this material: "At the same time as they accuse the priests of abusing Catholicism, these materials show no disrespect for the peasants' religious beliefs nor do they deny the importance of Jesus Christ and the Gospels."[79] One could hardly ask for a more apt description of populist religiosity, and it was precisely this unorthodox religious tone that made the minister view these writings as "contrary to both religion and social order."[80] This official clearly recognized one of the great strengths of democ-soc ideology: its ability to build a social and political critique on the basis of the anticlerical religiosity to which so many French peasants subscribed.

Religious leaders, too, recognized the danger to conservative order represented by Montagnard propaganda. In an 1849 pamphlet remarkable for its insights into the reasons for democ-soc successes in the countryside, Abbé Bernard, director of the Bibliothèque catholique et populaire, confirmed among other things the unorthodox religiosity of the democ-soc appeal:

> Today, unbelief is no longer the province of the rich and well-born. It has descended into the street, the atelier, and the café; it has invaded the peasant cottage. In short, unbelief has erupted everywhere. Renouncing all literary pretensions and philosophical abstractions, and abdicating its deluxe format, unbelief has acquired a popular style. It has transformed itself into feuilletons, little books, pamphlets, songs, and tracts. With a diabolical genius, unbelief has even assumed a *pious mask.* . . . Those who have lived among the people understand the esteem with which it holds printed literature, and know how much these printed materials can affect its ideas and beliefs.[81]

In describing with great accuracy the democ-socs' methods of propaganda, the Abbé Bernard referred to the content of the

SAINTE PÉTRONILLE.

CANTIQUE

Air : Laissé-moi donc.

Célébrons la victoire
D'un Dieu mort sur la croix,
Et pour chanter sa gloire
Réunissons nos voix :
De son amour extrême
Cédons aux traits vainqueurs ;
Pour le Dieu qui nous aime
Réunissons nos cœurs.

Sa croix, heureux symbole
De son amour pour nous,
Jadis du Capitole
Chassa les dieux jaloux :
Alors, dans l'esclavage,
L'homme, à d'infâmes dieux,
Payait par son hommage
Le droit d'être comme eux.

Grand Dieu, seul adorable,
Seul digne de nos chants,
Seul, de l'homme coupable,
Vous n'avez point d'encens ;
Mais que votre tonnerre
Fasse entendre sa voix,
Et force enfin la terre
A respecter vos lois.

Mais son cœur m'oppose
A ses foudres vengeurs,
Par l'amour se propose
De conquérir les cœurs :
Pour expier nos crimes,
Notre sang est trop peu ;
Il faut d'autres victimes
Pour désarmer un Dieu.

« Son Fils, Verbe adorable,
Doit tomber sous ses coups ;
Son sang seul est capable
De calmer son courroux ;
Pour ma grâce il sompire,
Il exige en mourant ;
Sur la croix il expire,
Et l'univers se rend.

Tel qu'après les orages,
Le soleil radieux
Dissipe les nuages,
Rend leur éclat aux cieux ;
Tel le Dieu que j'adore,
Trop long-temps ignoré,
Du couchant à l'aurore
Voit son nom adoré.

La croix, heureux asile
De l'univers soumis,
Brave l'orgueil stérile
De ses fiers ennemis ;
On s'empresse à lui rendre
Des hommages parfaits ;
Sa gloire va s'étendre
Autant que ses bienfaits.

Quel éclat l'environne !
Elle voit à ses pieds
Le sceptre et la couronne
Des rois humiliés ;
Rome cherche à lui plaire,
Tout suit ses étendards,
Et le Dieu du Calvaire
Est le Dieu des Césars.

Que le ciel applaudisse
Aux chants de son amour,
Et que l'enfer frémisse
Du bonheur de ce jour !
Chantons la victoire
Du Maître des vainqueurs !
Consacrons à sa gloire
Et nos voix et nos cœurs.

FIN.

CANTIQUE.

Air de la l'Enfant de Saint-Gaul.

Cesse tes concerts funèbres ;
Le jour qu'attendait ta foi,
Du sombre sein des ténèbres,
O Sion, paraît pour toi !
Ton Dieu, maître des miracles,
Par un prodige nouveau,
Pour accomplir ses oracles,
Sort vainqueur de son tombeau.

Il a fait trembler la terre,
Et libre parmi les morts,
Il a renversé la pierre
Et les gardes de son corps.
Il sortit, ô Vierge heureuse !
De votre sein pour souffrir ;
De sa tombe glorieuse
Il sert pour ne plus mourir.

Allez, apôtres timides,
De Jésus ressuscité ;
Devant ces juges perfides
Prêcher la divinité.
Parlez !... qu'aujourd'hui les traîtres
Apprennent en frémissant,
Que le Dieu de leurs ancêtres
Est le seul Dieu tout-puissant.

Sa gloire était moins brillante,
Et jetait bien moins d'éclat
Sur la montagne brûlante
Où sa main grava sa loi.
La victoire le couronne ;
La croix élevée en prix ;
D'un bras vengeur, à son trône,
Il enchaîne le trépas.

Est-ce une force étrangère,
Sensible à notre douleur,
Qui rend le fils à son père,
A la terre son Sauveur ?
Non, de ses mains invincibles,
Lui-même, et sans nul effort,
Brave les portes terribles
De l'enfer et de la mort.

En vain, peuple déicide,
Tu fais sceller son tombeau ;
De ta présence stupide
Il rit et brise ton sceau.
Étendu sur la poussière,
Ton satellite cruel,
Attend qu'un coup de tonnerre,
L'écrase et venge le ciel.

Enfin, rentrez en vous-mêmes,
Cœurs barbares et jaloux !
Craignez les rigueurs extrêmes
D'un juge armé contre vous ;
Changez... Tout pécheur qui change,
Sans retour, n'est pas proscrit ;
Ce Dieu juste qui se venge,
Est un Dieu qui s'attendrit.

Loin de consommer tes crimes
Par l'horreur du désespoir,
Gémi... ingrate Solyme...
Un soupir peut t'émouvoir :
Bien plus doux qu'il n'est à craindre,
Pécheurs, s'il tonne sur vous,
Une larme peut éteindre
Tous les feux de son courroux.

FIN.

ORAISON.

Seigneur, sanctifiez et gardez votre peuple, et faites qu'étant aidé par l'assistance de cette grande Sainte, il vous soit agréable par le règlement de sa vie, et qu'il vous serve dans la tranquillité d'une sainte confiance. Ainsi soit-il.

Fabrique de PELLERIN, Imprimeur-Libraire, à ÉPINAL.

3. Early-Nineteenth-Century Cantique

RESPECT AU SUFFRAGE UNIVERSEL

OU

QUI S'Y FROTTE S'Y PIQUE.

AIR : *Vive Paris, ou des Trois Couleurs.*

Entendez-vous ces rhéteurs, vrais corsaires,
Qui du combat sonnent le branle-bas?
« La République à nos goûts ne va guères :
« Vite un bâillon! vite, enchaînons son bras! »
C'est au progrès que vous faites la guerre;
Mais le progrès n'est-il pas éternel?
Vous ne pourrez étouffer la lumière,
Respect, messieurs, au *vote universel!*

Ne vendez pas (croyez-en le proverbe)
La peau de l'ours avant qu'il ne soit mort.
Baissez d'un ton votre courroux superbe;
Criez, messieurs, du moins criez moins, fort.
Vous conspirez; mais nous sommes sans crainte,
Le peuple peut braver votre cartel;
Ne touchez pas du peuple l'arche sainte,
Oui, respectez le vote universel!

Quand le volcan gronde; de sa colère,
Qui donc de vous étoufferait sa voix?
Comment toucher au foudre populaire
Sans risquer fort de vous brûler les doigts?
Ce problème est difficile à résoudre :
La Liberté c'est la fille du ciel;
Gardez-vous donc de toucher à sa foudre;
Oui, respectez le vote universel!

Le peuple est roi; mais souverain modeste,
S'est-il jamais enrichi de votre or?
Qu'espère-t-il de la bonté céleste?
De voir enfin s'améliorer son sort!
Place au soleil : que la terre fertile
De tous ses fils puisse entendre l'appel!
Le peuple est roi; mais sa liste civile,
Songez-y, c'est le vote universel!

Le peuple est roi; laissez sa pauvre blouse
S'enorgueillir sous son royal blason;
Votre fierté se rebelle jalouse,
Comme un coursier qu'irrite l'éperon.
Pourquoi jaloux, quand le pouvoir suprême
S'étend sur tous comme un lien fraternel?
Ne touchez pas à notre diadème;
Oui, respectez le vote universel!

Quels sont nos vœux quand notre voix réclame
Du pain pour tous, pour tous l'égalité?
Nous désirons que chaque cœur s'enflamme
A tes rayons, soleil de liberté!
Liberté sainte, astre démocratique,
Marche toujours... n'es-tu pas immortel?
Songez-y bien, qui s'y frotte s'y pique,
Respectez donc le vote universel!

DÉPÔT : Rue des Gravilliers, 25.

Par l'Auteur de : *Du Pain, cri du Peuple* (10e *édition*).

Paris.—Impr. BEAULÉ et MAIGNAND, r. Jacques de Brosse, 8.

4. Typical Democ-Soc Song Sheet

literature as covering unbelief with a "pious mask"—that is, as embodying an unorthodox religiosity.

In addition to almanacs, catechisms, and brochures, Montagnard propagandists used songs to transmit their views in rural France. Printed on single sheets of low-grade paper, democ-soc songs resembled the religious *cantiques* disseminated in the countryside by colporteurs earlier in the century. Like the cantiques, the republican song sheets almost always featured a large drawing placed atop or between the text of the song. Compare the cantique printed early in the nineteenth century (fig. 3) with the democ-soc song disseminated in 1849 (fig. 4). During the first half of the nineteenth century peasants had become familiar with the format and tone of the cantique, and when the democ-socs adopted the cantique's format for their own propaganda songs—themselves often religiously inspired—rural dwellers could accept them quite naturally.

Not only were these song sheets familiar and inexpensive (a few centimes apiece),[82] but one did not have to be literate to enjoy them. A peasant who could not read the words of a republican song sheet could nevertheless "read" the meaning of the picture and in so doing develop a sense of the song. The same was true with democ-soc almanacs. Like the popular almanacs to which peasants had been exposed earlier in the century (see Chapter II), Montagnard almanacs were filled with signs and symbols that formed a sort of hieroglyphic that illiterate peasants could decipher. This ability to "read" almanacs and songs gave the peasantry a sense of accomplishment that helped to strengthen their attachment to the content of this material.[83] Local democ-soc leaders, of course, wanted peasants to have more than just a vague understanding of the content of their songs, and the café provided the forum in which Montagnard propagandists taught the words of their songs and assisted the assembled clientele in singing them.

How does the message of these songs compare with that of the other forms of democ-soc propaganda discussed above? Thanks to a two-volume anthology of democratic and social songs entitled *La Voix du peuple* (1848 and 1849), from which Montagnards drew most of the songs sold in the countryside and sung in the cafés,* it is possible to analyze the ideological content of democ-soc songs.[84] Pierre Dupont, the best-known songster of the period, wrote a series of republican airs that were disseminated through the nationwide network of La Propagande démocratique et sociale européenne. In 1849 Pierre Joigneaux asked Dupont to write a song for the peasantry, and the resulting "Chant des paysans" was sung in cafés around the country.[85] Dupont's song was a plea for peasant allegiance to a new republic, a republic different from that of the 45 Centimes.** The new and "belle république" would be a "république des paysans" in which tyrants and usurers would no longer hold sway over peasants and workers:

> Down with the liars and the traitors
> The tyrants and the usurers!
> The peasants will be the masters
> United with the workers.*[86]

Dupont's plea resembled that of Pyat, Joigneaux, Laponneraye, and many others who sought in 1849 to enlist the peasantry in the democ-soc cause.

In "Le Chant du vote" (1850), another of Dupont's most popular songs, the poet expresses many of the central themes of Montagnard ideology. The song's chorus salutes the republic for its ability to realize heavenly ideals on earth:

> O guardian Republic
> Never go back up to heaven

---

* In April 1850 the procureur général at Amiens wrote: "At the moment, socialist propaganda is spread through popular songs that leaders sing in the cabarets. *These songs are extracted, for the most part, from an anthology published by Durand, rue de Rambuteau, Paris and entitled, Voix du peuple, Chansons de 1848.*" AN BB[30] 368, April 1850.

** In spring 1848 the Provisional Government imposed a 45 percent surtax, known as the 45 Centimes, on the high imposts the peasants already paid.

> * A bas les menteurs et les traîtres
> Les tyrans et les usuriers!
> Les Paysans seront les maîtres
> Unis avec les ouvriers.

Your ideal is incarnated on earth
By the universal vote.**

Like the democ-soc press and pamphlets, Dupont's "Chant du vote" exalts universal suffrage and gives it a religious character:

From that day when, with independence,
Each person can express his desires,
Influenced only by his conscience,
The election is the voice of God.†

Why does the universal vote reveal the voice of God? Because Dupont, like other Montagnard spokesmen, as well as the peasants and artisans themselves, identified the common people with Jesus Christ. For Dupont, "Le Peuple" is the "true son of God."[87]

After Pierre Dupont, the next most influential songwriter of the Second Republic was perhaps Gustave Leroy. The collection *La Voix du peuple* contains most of Leroy's songs from the 1848 period, and his odes could be heard throughout urban as well as rural France.[88] Like Dupont and his Montagnard colleagues, Leroy identified a martyred people with Jesus Christ, the working-class hero. In "Le Bal et la guillotine," an angry and bitterly ironic song condemning the execution of two June insurgents, Leroy's metaphor is the crucifixion: "Priest and executioner follow them [the insurgents] to Calvary."[89] Thus, the two working-class martyrs face the guillotine at the site of Jesus' crucifixion. Leroy's most moving song of the period is a hymn dedicated to the victims of the June Days. Entitled "Les Soldats du désespoir" ("The Soldiers of Despair"), it elegizes the insurgents and ends with a prayer:

God, accept our protestation
You have only to wish it,

** O République tutelaire
Ne remonte jamais au ciel.
Idéal incarné sur terre
Par le suffrage universel.
†Du jour qu'avec indépendance
Chacun peut exprimer son voeu,
En face de sa conscience,
Le scrutin est la Voix de Dieu.

> Protect the holy cause
> Of the soldiers of despair!*[90]

Leroy ardently supported Ledru-Rollin and his Montagnard coalition of 1849, and many of his songs were written expressly for democ-soc electoral campaigns.[91] One of them, "La Course aux élections," did little more than list conditions to avoid and candidates to support:

> Ledru-Rollin, Deville, Baune
> Bac, Jolly, Leroux, Stourm, Madier
> Olivier (of Bouches-du-Rhône)
> Gent, Pyat, Proudhon, Perdiguier
> And all those by whom the people gain
> Rights that are solid and important:
> Glory to the men of the Mountain
> Who will be our Representatives.**[92]

In "Les Députés de la Montagne," written during the electoral contest of 1849, Leroy prays to the left's leaders as if they were saints:

> Representatives of the people, occupy the Mountain
> Turn into reality the abstract rights of February
> Liberate our political prisoners,
> Give employment to the worker:
> Education for everyone, equal and free,
> Bread and shelter for the elderly poor,
> Inaugurate the social republic.

> *Dieu, recevez notre plainte
> Vous n'avez qu'à le vouloir,
> Protégez la cause sainte
> Des soldats du désespoir!
> **Ledru-Rollin, Deville, Baune
> Bac, Jolly, Leroux, Stourm, Madier
> Olivier (des Bouches-du-Rhône)
> Gent, Pyat, Proudhon, Perdiguier
> Tous ceux par qui le peuple gagne
> Des droits solides importants:
> Gloire aux hommes de la Montagne
> Qui furent nos Représentants.

Give us the right to employment . . .
For misfortune overwhelms us,
And this right must at long last be bestowed on us;
The speculator believes himself invulnerable
Protected by his silver-plated armor;
The workers dissipate their health and their youth,
While the lazy pocket billions.
Let us break the machine of riches.†[93]

The verses of obscure poets that composed the bulk of *La Voix du peuple* also embodied most of the main themes of Montagnard ideology. Rural communities had expressed their longing for material improvement through the worship of popular saints. And in large part the songs collected in the anthology represented a Montagnard attempt to reorient the religious energy once devoted to saints, processions, and celebrations toward a republic that possessed religious qualities and promised worldly improvement. To this end, a song entitled "La Couronne de Saint Février" ("The Crown of Saint February") simultaneously personified and deified the February revolution by turning it into a popular saint:

Saint February, saint whom they persecute,
On the calendar, the people have placed your name;
But contrary to the popular will, there are those,
Who, degrading your Church, already try to erase your pediment!

† Elus du peuple, occupez la Montagne
Faîtes valoir nos droits de Février
Que les proscrits quittent enfin le bagne,
Que le travail echoie à l'ouvrier:
Instruction pour tous, gratuite, égale,
Du pain, du feu pour nos pauvres vieillards,
Inaugurez la France sociale.

Droit au travail . . . le malheur nous accable,
Ce droit enfin doit nous être octroyé;
L'agioteur se croit invulnérable
Sous sa cuirasse en argent monnoyé;
Les travailleurs usent santé, jeunesse,
Les paresseux entassent les milliards,
Veulent briser la machine à richesse.

To whitewash it, they paint you over
Ha! how they wish they could uproot your cross!
Holy February, defend well your crown
Let all those who touch it burn their fingers!
. . . .
Everyone says: You are a people's saint.*[94]

Similarly, "Prière à la Sainte République" ("Prayer to the
Holy Republic") identified the republic with the Virgin Mary
and linked the people, as children of the Virgin/Republic, with
Jesus Christ: "O Republic, O our holy mother / Republic, pray
for us!"[95] The drawing that accompanied this prayer features a
feminine image of the republic portrayed as patron saint of the
nation's liberty trees (see figs. 5 and 6). She is no secular Goddess of Liberty, but a saint or virgin appropriated for political
purposes. She represents the sacralized republic that promises
to realize the aspirations of popular religiosity. In investing the
republic with religious qualities and in portraying it as a popular
saint, Montagnard songs cast what was a highly abstract concept
in comprehensible and familiar terms.

As a whole, these republican songs demonstrate the extent
to which democ-soc ideology drew on elements of early Christian morality. In a song entitled "Les Socialistes" a Parisian
cabinetmaker who directed the spring 1848 propaganda effort
of the Club des Clubs, evoked the democ-socs' commitment to
the Gospels as well as their identification with Jesus Christ:

It is written in the holy gospels:
Man, help yourself, and then heaven will help you.
From this holy book, all advice is useful;
Yes, it is for us that Christ expired.

> *Saint Février, saint qu'on martyrise,
> Au calendrier le peuple a mis ton nom;
> Et cependant, dégradant ton Eglise,
> Déjà l'on cherche à gratter son fronton!
> Pour le blanchir leur main te badigeonne
> Ha! s'ils pouvaient déraciner ta croix!
> Saint Février, défends bien ta couronne,
> Qu'en y touchant l'on se brûle les doigts!
> . . . .
> On dit de toi: C'est un saint populaire.

PRIÈRE

A

Sainte République

PATRONNE

DES ARBRES DE LIBERTÉ.

PRIX : 10 C.  **PRIX : 10 C.**

Air de : Lionne, défends tes petits.

1

Autour de nous vient mugir la tempête :
Ce vent funèbre est un arrêt de mort.
Frères, il faut, hélas ! 'courber la tête ;
Il faut mourir : Oui, voilà notre sort ?
Et cependant pourquoi tant de colère ?
Nous grandissions... ! ils en furent jaloux !
O république, O notre sainte mère,
République, priez pour nous !

2

Le printemps va, de son haleine pure
Donner l'éveil aux arbres comme aux fleurs;
Tout va chanter, fleurir dans la nature ;
Nous seuls hélas ! nous verserons des pleurs
Arbres martyrs d'un arrêt trop sévère
Faut il, hélas, que nous succombions tous
O république, O notre sainte mère,
République, priez pour nous !

3

Au sol français nous avions pris racine,
Et chaque jour nous devenions plus forts :
Et cependant (le motif s'en devine)
On nous abat comme des arbres morts.
Morts, oh ! non non; c'était tout le contraine ;
Moins vigoureux, on nous aurait absous !
O république! O notre sainte mère !
République, priez pour nous !

4

La liberté nous livre ses insignes ;
Avec orgueil nous portions son drapeau :
D'un meilleur sort nous qu'on avait cru dignes,
Nous descendons tristement au tombeau ;
Ne plus sentir la chaleur printannière
D'un beau soleil, riche en rayons si doux!
O république, O notre sainte mère !
République, priez pour nous :

5

En février nous donnant le baptême,
Un bon curé nous bénit de sa main ;
Pourtant sur nous on lance l'anathème !
Chers la ¡veille, proscrits le lendemain !
Le peuple et nous, c'est l'ormeau, c'est le lière;
Et tous les deux souffrent des même coups.
O république ! O notre sainte mère !
République, priez pour nous

JÉROME, ouvrier.

Paris. Im Bautruche, r. de la Harpe 90

---

5. Prayer to the Holy Republic

6. Feminine Image of the Republic Portrayed as a Patron Saint

Glory to the martyr of the holy light,
All the nonbelievers destroyed his flag,
But his motto remains on our banner;
He digs the tomb of despotism!*⁹⁶

* Il est écrit dans le saint Evangile:
  Homme, aide-toi, puis le ciel t'aidera.
  Du livre saint tout conseil est utile;
  Oui, c'est pour nous que le Christ expira.
  Gloire au martyr de la sainte lumière,
  Tous les Gentils déchirent son drapeau,
  Mais sa devise est sur notre bannière;
  Du despotisme il creusa le tombeau!

August Alais's "Jésus républicain" took up the familiar theme
that depicted Jesus as founder of both parts of the democ-soc
dual heritage—republicanism and Christianity:

> It is Christ who gave birth
> To equality for all.
> . . . .
> I am, he said, put on earth
> To knock down the vain power of the great,
> And to level the ranks of mortals,
> I have founded the principle of association.**[97]

In "La Trinité humaine" a poet named Barrillot portrayed one
of the democ-socs' most common themes—the Christian heritage of the republican motto of Liberty, Equality, and Fraternity:

> This holy motto
> Which comes from Christ, who died for humankind,
> Was illuminated suddenly
> On the church front in February.†[98]

And in Dominique Bessède's "Le Socialisme" the laws of Christ
become the laws of socialism, laws that cannot be instituted
without the republic:

Christ himself was a socialist,
Because he said to all men: love one another!
Fake Christian, you are nothing but an egotist,
You who believe only in yourself, only in your fat billfold.

> **De par le Christ, humains sages et fous,
>   L'égalité vient de naître pour tous.
> . . . .
>   Je suis, dit-il, déligué sur la terre
>   Pour abaisser le vain pouvoir des grands,
>   Et des mortels pour niveler les rangs,
>   Je viens fonder le principe unitaire.
> †Cette Saint Dévise
>   Qui vient du Christ, mort pour le genre humain
>   Sur le front du palais de l'église,
>   En février s'illumina soudain.

The law of Christ is our common faith,
It is that all men have their usefulness;
Yes, we want to abolish misery
With the laws of Fraternity.
. . . .
To establish the laws of harmony,
What do we need? To be republican!
. . . .
And then you will see the Republic blossom
With the laws of Fraternity!‡[99]

These songs portray Christian morality not only as underlying republican socialism but also as forming the basis of the
most prominent planks of the democ-soc platform. A. Porte
conceived of the droit au travail as the realization of the "Sainte
Egalité" and fraternal solidarity preached by Christ. His ode
entitled "Le Droit au travail" proclaims:

Down with corruption! No more ignoble victors
No more victors exploiting the vanquished
Right to employment, respect for the family
Excess for no one so there can be bread for all!
Fraternity! . . .

Reformers, save humanity
by repenting: all men are brothers,

> ‡Le Christ lui-même était socialiste,
>   Puisqu'il disait aux hommes: Aimez-vous!
>   Chrétien menteur, tu n'es qu'un égoïste,
>   Toi qui ne crois qu'en toi, qu'en tes gros sous.
>   La loi du Christ est notre foi commune,
>   C'est que tout homme, a son utilité;
>   Oui, nous voulons détruire l'infortune
>   Avec les lois de la Fraternité.
>   . . . .
>   Pour établir les lois de l'harmonie,
>   Que faut-il donc? Etre républicain!
>   . . . .
>   Et vous verrez fleurir la République
>   Avec les lois de la Fraternité!

Christ died preaching equality
Imitate Him; follow his noble example.*[100]

Not all of the songs sung in village cafés had explicitly religious themes. Some simply paid homage to a particular Montagnard leader, though even these songs identified democ-soc figures with Christ or gave them saintly qualities. A. Bourgeois's "Louis Blanc" (fig. 7) explicitly compares Blanc's martyrdom with that of Jesus:

When you [Louis Blanc] pronounced sublime truths,
I saw Malthus's disciples turn white;
Your virtues, they have called crimes,
Pharisees, crucify Jesus!**[101]

Other Montagnard songs attempted to instill a single democsoc idea. In "La Carte électeur," for example, one Landragin made a plea for universal suffrage:

No, no, no longer must it be a bullet
That strikes your oppressors.
It is an electoral urn that will throw out your oppressors;
Continue on with the political struggle
That you support wholeheartedly,
The Republic awaits you in the public square.†[102]

---

*Guerre aux abus! Plus d'ignobles vainqueurs
Plus de vainqueurs exploitant les vaincus
Droit au travail, respect à la famille
Au pain de tous que nul n'ait triple part!
Fraternité! . . .

Renovateurs, sauvons l'humanité
En répétant: tous les hommes sont frères,
Le Christ est mort prêchant l'Egalité
Imitez-le: suivez ce noble example.
**Quand tu [Louis Blanc] disais ces vérités sublimes,
J'ai vu pâlir les enfants de Malthus;
De tes vertus ils en ont fait des crimes,
Pharisiens, crucifiez Jésus!
†Non, non, ce n'est plus une balle
Qui doit frapper tes oppresseurs
Et c'est une urne électorale

7. Louis Blanc: Republican Apostle

This analysis of Montagnard brochures, pamphlets, and songs makes clear that the literature reaching France's rural population through the left's elaborate and continually adaptive network of propaganda diffusion embodied all the principal themes of democ-soc ideology. Popular democ-soc propaganda, like the party's formal ideology, expressed the transformation of unorthodox religiosity into socialist democracy. In fashioning a new ideology from popular religiosity and in spreading that ideology through old and new circuits of communication and social interaction, the democ-socs took the initial and fundamental step toward committing a largely rural nation to republican government and mass democracy.

Que sortiront tes oppresseurs;
Va, pour la lutte politique
Que tu soutiens avec coeur,
La République
T'attend sur la place publique.

CHAPTER VI

THE PROVINCIAL PRESS AND SECRET SOCIETIES

Just as the democ-socs' efforts to establish a nationwide mass political party succumbed to fierce government repression (see Chapter III), so the Montagnards found themselves unable to assure the longevity of local organizations that were expressly political. Police targeted the republican clubs and electoral committees created in 1848 and early 1849, and, for the most part, these organizations did not survive the wave of antioppositionist legislation that followed the republican uprising of 13 June 1849.[1] The democ-socs did achieve remarkable success, however, in adapting certain existing local institutions for the purpose of propaganda diffusion and electoral politics. Throughout Mediterranean France the democ-socs transformed small-town *cercles* and *chambrées*—the institutions of village sociability unique to the South—into de facto political organizations. Elsewhere, small-town democ-soc newspapers provided the institutional focus for the diffusion of propaganda locally. And after 1850, when stepped-up repression and an antidemocratic "electoral reform" drove local republican politics underground,* secret Montagnard societies became a key institutional mechanism of propaganda diffusion.

The local republican clubs' surrender to the same fate suffered by branch committees of La Solidarité républicaine did not seriously damage the democ-soc effort to republicanize the peasantry. Peasants were unaccustomed to the impersonal meetings and boisterous argumentativeness of political clubs. Even if these institutions had not been destroyed by police and judicial action,

---

* The electoral reform bill of 31 May 1850 disenfranchised about one-third of France's voters—the poorest portion of the electorate—by imposing a strict residency requirement that discriminated against workers.

they would have contributed little to the politicization of the peasantry.[2]

Local electoral organizations fared better against Louis Napoleon's police in 1849 and 1850 than did political clubs, but they achieved little independent success in reaching the peasantry. If an electoral organization exercised influence in the countryside, it was because its membership coincided with the editorial staff of the local democ-soc newspaper. Based most often in department capitals, electoral committees normally limited their propaganda activity to placarding a region's largest communes with short proclamations and the names of candidates.[3] Occasionally their posters featured lengthier statements that tried to convince the peasantry of the extent to which the election of democ-soc candidates served their own interests. An electoral poster advertising the candidates of the Assemblée électorale of the Jura (for a by-election in June 1849) proclaimed: "You must realize that frost on the buds of your vines, that hail on the eve of your harvests, that the destruction by fire of your houses are all less harmful to your families . . . than the nomination of representatives who are not firmly attached to the principles of democracy."[4]

These electoral committees, though they helped bring out the vote in urban centers, nevertheless contributed little to the politicization of the peasantry.[5] Such politicization required close personal contact between democ-soc propagandists and their potential rural constituents. The institutions capable of such contact were the chambrées of Mediterranean France, the provincial left-wing press, and the secret Montagnard societies.

Beginning in the 1820s, peasants and artisans in southern departments like the Var, the Basses-Alpes, and the Gard grouped themselves into social circles called chambrées or chambrettes.[6] These lower-class institutions of sociability mirrored the middle-class cercles formed in the aftermath of the French Revolution as centers of relaxation and male camaraderie. Unique to the South, the chambrées provided a locale—usually a rented room—in which peasant and artisan members could gather to drink wine and play cards. During the 1830s and 1840s, when expanded suffrage on the municipal level, struggles over rights to woodlands, and renewed battles over the tax on wine all kindled lower-class interest in political issues, the chambrées served as centers in which economic grievances could be articulated. Middle-class democrats and socialists as well as politicized artisans brought their ideas into the chambrées and provided the peasants and workers assembled there with the rudiments of an oppositionist mentality. After 1848 these chambrées served as ready-made forums for the communication of démocrate-socialiste ideology. Accustomed to political discussion, the members of chambrées were receptive to the Montagnard propaganda presented to them. As will be shown below, traveling emissaries of democ-soc candidates and of such democ-soc organizations as La Propagande démocratique et sociale européenne and the local Montagnard newspaper gained admittance to the chambrées of southern France and used this institution as a forum in which to spread their ideology. Important as they were, however, the chambrées have only limited usefulness in explaining the rural politicization of the Second Republic, for chambrées did not exist outside the southernmost part of France. By far the most important institutional agency of rural politicization was the huge number of democ-soc newspapers that commenced publication in the aftermath of June 1848.

Not only did the provincial Montagnard press help to articulate democ-soc ideology, but, just as importantly, it served as the organizational focus—at least until late 1850—of Montagnard political activity in the French provinces. Most democ-soc journals were based in department capitals and boasted editorial committees composed of the most prominent Montagnard activists of their regions. What made the newspapers different from electoral committees was the journal editors' conscious effort to contact peasants and rural artisans. To this end, democ-soc newspapers hired subscription salesmen to travel throughout the regions that their papers served. While selling subscriptions in rural communes—an endeavor that remained entirely within the law even during the Second Republic's most intense period of repression—the salesmen doubled as agents of democ-soc propaganda.[7] In addition, most Montagnard journals organized a network of local correspondents composed in general of artisans, small merchants, country doctors, and others whose professions brought them into constant contact with the peasantry. These correspondents were responsible for selling subscriptions, marketing shares of stock in the journal, reporting to the editors on the political events of their localities, and ensuring that the peasants and artisans of their regions were exposed to the newspaper's ideology. Thus, very often it was the local correspondent who read issues of his paper aloud to peasants gathered in a café or chambrée. These well-known members of the community would also introduce traveling emissaries of their papers to the peasants, thus lowering the social barriers that made residents of a rural commune suspicious of strangers. The ability of local representatives to "sponsor" outsiders who shared démocrate-socialiste sympathies facilitated the dissemination of new ideas in the rural provinces and enabled the peasantry to dissociate ideas from the individuals who presented them. So long as a rural community remained closed to outsiders, peasants tended to support a particular position not so much because of the merits of the position itself but because of the personal qualities and standing of those who held it. But when a succession of different strangers all holding similar ideas exposed their views in a given commune, it became possible for peasants to begin to comprehend the merits and meaning of ideas independent of the status and personal qualities of those who held them.

When La Solidarité républicaine was outlawed at the end of January 1849, local democ-soc newspapers often replaced the dissolved branch committees of La Solidarité as organizational centers of regional democ-soc politics. The original tie between the provincial Montagnard press and La Solidarité républicaine has already been pointed out (see Chapter III), and when the more formal political party organization was outlawed, the democ-soc paper simply appropriated its functions. After January 1849, therefore, France's provincial democ-soc press on the one hand helped to formulate and disseminate Montagnard ideology and on the other hand took charge of designating candidates for political office, of bringing out the vote for these candidates, of organizing political gatherings—often under the guise of purely business-oriented stockholders' meetings—and of wooing a rural constituency.

How successful was the democ-soc press in forging local political organizations and in drawing rural support for Montagnard candidates and ideology? The procureurs généraux blamed this press for the strong democ-soc electoral showing in May 1849, and they believed it played a fundamental role in subverting the countryside. The procureur of Riom, for example, wrote that the *Eclaireur républicain* (Clermont) was responsible for driving a wedge between the peasants of Auvergne and the notables to whom they had traditionally shown allegiance. At the same time, the paper acted "skillfully . . . to recommend its own [electoral list] which included nothing but red republicans."[8] As a result, continued the procureur, of the efforts of the *Eclaireur* and of such Paris papers as *La Réforme* and Joigneaux's *La Feuille du village*, "the masses have become sympathetic to socialist doctrine and are the object of incessant and indefatigable proselytism. As each day passes, the diffusion of newspapers that treat political subjects becomes more widespread in the French countryside."[9] Alarmed by the same phenomenon, the procureur of Aix complained that the Toulon-based *Démocrate du Var* "has caused much political damage among the workers and in the countryside."[10] *L'Egalité* had a similar effect in the Gers, and the *Démocrate du Rhin* (Strasbourg), addressed to the peasants of Alsace, "causes harm. . . . It is written to convey the most exalted socialist ideas."[11]

That the judicial officials of the Second Republic considered the press responsible for converting the peasantry to socialism does not of course prove that it in fact did so, though statements made by humble Frenchmen do bolster these claims. J. Laurent, an agricultural day laborer from St. Amand (Nièvre), told government prosecutors that "in 1849, I received the weekly edition of the journal *La Réforme*. I considered true everything I read, and reading the newspaper changed my ideas and turned my head around. I became a socialist."[12] Chapter VII will address in detail the question of the extent to which rural Frenchmen adopted democ-soc ideas. Here I shall show that after 1848 the press played a pivotal role in building democ-soc political organization and in diffusing Montagnard ideology in the French provinces.

In mid-nineteenth-century France no distinction existed between journalism and political activism. Journalism had not yet become a profession, and those who wrote for newspapers—whether of the right, left, or center—believed that their essential functions were political. Since the democ-socs' political views were grounded in religious concepts and expressed in the language of the Gospels, Montagnard journalists quite naturally saw their political role as a religious quest that aimed for nothing less than the political, moral, and economic salvation of France's peasants and workers. For the editors of *L'Eclaireur républicain*, "journalism is an apostolate. . . . Our work is a labor of devotion to the poor and disinherited classes. . . . To teach, to moralize, that is our goal. . . . Bolstered by our conscience, we will march toward our goal, and nothing will make us deviate from the route we have charted for ourselves."[13]

Motivated by religious zeal, democ-soc journalists set out to communicate their ideas to the rural population. Beginning in early 1849, they combined their propaganda role with an active effort to organize for the all-important legislative elections of May. The editors of *L'Union républicaine* told their subscribers in March 1849 to "propagate our journal, make others read it . . . read it aloud and comment on it . . . [soon] we will send you printed electoral ballots containing the names of our candidates."[14] Thus, *L'Union's* editors took the initial steps toward establishing an informal political organization capable of preparing for the elections of mid-May. The paper's core of subscribers—about four hundred[15]—was asked not only to continue buying the journal but also to help propagate its word. Readers were expected, moreover, to solicit support for the Yonne's democ-soc candidates. It went without saying that the editors of *L'Union* would play a major role in choosing those candidates.

The editorial staffs of the democ-soc papers were not content to survey the political scene from their headquarters in departmental capitals. They traveled regularly to the main towns of their departments and made occasional forays into rural communes to spread propaganda and forge organizational links. Louis Auriol, editor of Montpellier's Le Montagnard, "traveled to the rural villages of the Montpellier region. In each commune, he [Auriol] gathered the most politically radical men of the locality at the home or café of one of his coreligionists."[16] In many cases, the coreligionist with whom Auriol stayed was a café proprietor, but the editor was known to have enjoyed the hospitality of simple workers as well.[17] The Montagnard journalist certainly seemed satisfied with the results of his travels. In early January 1850 he told the police chief of Montpellier "that his recent propaganda foray into the countryside was highly fruitful."[18]

Alphonse Esquiros, Laponneraye's successor at the helm of La Voix du peuple, also undertook personal propaganda trips into the countryside. During a journey to the commune of Gardanne (Bouches-du-Rhône) at the end of 1849, Esquiros "spread propaganda in the village's cercles and chambrées." Police believed his visit provoked a demonstration in which villagers paraded through the town crying, "Vive Raspail, vive Proudhon, vive Ledru-Rollin."[19]

Though newspaper editors and journalists liked to maintain direct contact with local sympathizers, they could not single-handedly produce their journals, ensure their diffusion, and sustain organizational links among the democ-soc sympathizers of their departments. To fulfill the latter two functions on a regular basis, Montagnard newspapers employed representatives, both professional and voluntary, whose task was to handle subscription sales and political organizing throughout the newspapers' geographical regions. The professional salesmen tended to be men of working-class origin who worked full-time for their papers—often after having been fired from their jobs for political reasons. They were perhaps France's first full-time paid political activists. The newspapers' voluntary emissaries tended to be small-town members of the liberal professions, café proprietors, booksellers, and literate artisans who agreed to become local correspondents of a journal. Since democ-soc journals could not afford the luxury of more than one or two full-time traveling representatives—if they could afford them at all—they endeavored to establish a network of local unpaid correspondents throughout the regions to which they appealed.

Le Démocrate du Var hired as its principal professional representative Pierre Arambide, a locksmith fired from Toulon's huge military arsenal in 1848 for his vocal support of Ledru-Rollin.[20] Arambide traveled throughout the Var selling subscriptions to Le Démocrate, spreading democ-soc propaganda, and maintaining vital political contacts. The ex-locksmith's commercial function was not simply a pretext for political activity. The journal needed to sell subscriptions to stay alive, and what could be a better way to make such sales than to convince people of the justice of Le Démocrate's cause? A letter confiscated by the police of Béziers (Hérault) from one Lagarde, subscription salesman for Le Vote universel, explained clearly the duties assigned to professional salesman-propagandists:

> This letter will serve to accredit you as our representative of Le Vote universel in the departments of the Gard, the Aude, and the Hérault. . . . Your specific tasks are to explain the goals of our journal, to sell shares of stock in the paper, to sell subscriptions, and to organize in the various central localities of these departments organizations of propaganda capable of coordinating the diffusion of our paper and of keeping the editors informed about all the political events of the region that are of interest to the republican cause.[21]

How did men like Arambide and Lagarde carry out their functions? Before traveling to a given commune, they made contact with a local democ-soc sympathizer likely to be well-known to the villagers. This local contact would then introduce the professional representative to the members of a chambrée or to the habitual clients of a café run by a village activist. In this way, Arambide and Lagarde could allay the small-town hostility toward strangers and be in a position to expose the villagers to new political ideas. In the Var commune of Cuers, a respectable citizen hostile to the democ-socs described an Arambide visit to the chambrées of his locality:

An individual by the name of Arambide . . . was admitted to a number of chambrées. . . . I was there by accident as I am not a member of any such organization. . . . I heard what Arambide had to say. He ardently solicited subscriptions to the newspaper, Le Démocrate du Var, which in his view was the organ of the poor. He told the members that Le Démocrate would enlighten them as to their rights and instruct them about all that might be of interest to them. . . . He spoke as well about the oppression "they" wanted to bring down on the poor people.[22]

A subscription list found in Arambide's possession showed that his visits to village chambrées and cafés were not without success. Fifty of the 124 subscribers on his list (which clearly did not include all of Le Démocrate's subscribers) were collectivities such as chambrées, cercles, cafés, and mutual aid societies.[23] These chambrées and cafés became local links in a growing department-wide democ-soc organization directed by the Montagnard newspaper. At the same time, they provided forums in which the ideology of democ-soc papers like Le Démocrate du Var could be communicated to illiterate peasants (see Chapter V). One of the main events of chambrée meetings was the public reading from a Montagnard journal. The captain of Le Luc's (Var) gendarmes reported that one of the town's chambrées "received Le Démocrate du Var, a paper that is read aloud every night by an oven tender [fournier] to the members of the chambrée who gathered in their meeting place after a day of work either in their ateliers or on the land."[24] According to the mayor of Gardanne (Bouches-du-Rhône), La Voix du peuple, La Réforme, and Le Peuple were read aloud regularly to the peasant and artisan members of the town's chambrées.[25] The same was true of cafés in Lodève and Floreniac in the Hérault and of those in the canton of Bléneau in the Yonne.[26]

The success of democ-soc journals in using chambrées and cafés as centers of political organization and propaganda diffusion was widespread enough to elicit a worried report from the Minister of Justice in April 1850. Arguing that democ-soc newspapers had turned selected cafés into veritable branch offices, the minister called for legislation to prohibit both the sale and the reading aloud of papers in cafés and cabarets:

> It cannot be denied that the sale and reading of newspapers in certain establishments—notably in cafés—is a perpetual cause of all sorts of disputes [i.e., political discussion]. This occurs especially in the countryside, where the cabaret so often becomes a veritable political club. One of the best ways of maintaining order in such locales would be to outlaw the sale and even the collective reading of newspapers.[27]

The Montagnard's relative success in the legislative election of 13 May 1849 spurred Louis Napoleon's government to intensify the apparatus of repression installed in the aftermath of the June Days. France's rulers recognized the importance of the press in diffusing democ-soc propaganda after 1848, and they attacked oppositionist journalism on two fronts. The government passed ambiguously worded laws that gave judicial officials broad license to prosecute newspapers for articles the government found offensive.[28] And perhaps more important, the Bonapartist regime sought after May 1849 to prevent the democ-soc press from using established institutions of rural sociability, including chambrées and cafés, to facilitate political organization and ideological transmission. Laws against clubs and other organizations that could be construed as political harmed the left-wing press at least as much as legislation aimed directly at the newspapers themselves.[29] Beginning in the summer of 1849, the government began to close down chambrées considered too political and to prosecute café proprietors for allowing political meetings. Judicial officials also pursued with a vengeance newspaper representatives like Arambide. In this climate of intensified repression, the democ-soc press found its freedom of movement seriously hampered.[30]

At this point, a number of democ-soc newspapers devised an innovative response to the problem of political repression. Influenced perhaps by the Paris-based Propagande démocratique et sociale européenne, a political organization that remained afloat by maintaining an impeccable commercial alibi (see Chapter III), provincial Montagnard newspapers decided to circumvent political repression by transforming themselves into joint-stock companies in accordance with prevailing business law. In so doing, they hoped to transmit propaganda and forge organizational links under the perfectly legal cover of selling shares of stock in newspaper enterprises. Periodic stockholders' meetings—permissible under business law—would provide a means by which to hold political meetings. And the establishment of business headquarters and permanent staffs of directors for joint-stock newspapers in each region would give the democ-socs numerous central offices from which to coordinate political activity. This effort demonstrates once again the left's resourcefulness in using the structures of capitalism to diffuse a subversive ideology.

Louis Napoleon's judicial officials were quick to comprehend the implications of this democ-soc innovation, and they lamented their lack of legal weapons against it. When *Le Démocrate du Var* announced its intention to sell twenty thousand shares of stock at one franc each, the procureur général at Aix immediately understood the political implications. Such a sale provided "an ideal means for this party [the democ-socs] to organize itself and to count its members. It enables them to correspond amongst themselves, to have an organizational center and a group of leaders all set for action."[31] Responding to an October 1849 proposal by *Le Démocrate de la Loire* (St.-Etienne) to establish itself as a joint-stock company, the procureur général of Lyon wrote:

> These socialist conspirators have found a way to take advantage of the perfectly legal forms of commercial and civil enterprise that presently exist, to circumvent the laws concerning political associations. Whereas in the recent past, they [the Montagnards] succeeded in disguising a secret society behind a club, now they are ingenious enough to disguise a political association behind a newspaper.[32]

The attempt by Lyonnais republicans to establish a new journal financed by twenty-five thousand one-franc shares of stock demonstrates the importance that provincial democ-socs, like the Parisian founders of La Solidarité républicaine before them, gave to the creation of structured political organizations. In a highly detailed set of statutes designed to govern their journalistic commercial enterprise, these Lyonnais democ-socs outlined an elaborate plan for a sort of combination political party–labor union–mutual aid society with ambitious goals. The purposes of this commercially based journalistic venture were to be threefold: to discuss and popularize social questions; to sell the newspaper at the lowest possible price; and to provide association members the means to exercise their political rights. In addition to backing the newspaper, funds collected from the sale of stock would pay fines levied against the journal for political offenses, finance electoral campaigns, pay the salaries of members assigned to jury duty, support those who become sick, disabled, or unemployed, and subsidize the subscriptions of the poorest affiliates. The political implications of this proposed journalistic association are clear, and the group's statutes demonstrate the extent to which the democ-socs counted on their press as a three-tiered medium of ideological diffusion, social support, and political organization.

Louis Napoleon's government showed understandable concern over the threat that such an enterprise posed to its political and social legitimacy. As Lyon's procureur général put it:

[Such a journalistic endeavor] would represent in reality a vast association devoted to the development of socialism. The central committee of twenty-one delegates would exercise a sovereign authority; the movement would have a newspaper as its instrument of propaganda and official record of its resolutions; it would dispose of substantial funds destined for political uses; it would turn the enterprise's office into headquarters of oppositionist politics . . . and, given the state of our legislation, only the enterprise's managers would be vulnerable to legal action. Both the editors of the paper and the members of the central committee would be immune from legal penalties.[33]

This Lyonnais organization and others like it were highly innovative institutions appropriate to a nation experimenting with mass democratic politics in an era that antedated the rise of large-scale industry and labor movements. The democ-socs were groping for institutions that could accomplish simultaneously two fundamental goals; to protect a growing constituency of peasants and artisans from the hazards of mid-nineteenth-century French capitalism and to contend seriously for political power.

The institutional role of the democ-soc press as a medium of ideological diffusion and political organization can be illuminated in detail through a case study of Marseille's *La Voix du peuple*, the Second Republic's most important provincial democ-soc paper. With a circulation that topped four thousand and a geographical reach that extended from Marseille to the rest of the Bouches-du-Rhône and into the Var and the Basses-Alpes, *La Voix du peuple* became the major left-wing ideological and political force in southeastern France.[34] Founded in October 1848 by Charles Poumicon, an ex-director of a southern French insurance company, and H. Bondilh, a radical journalist from Marseille, *La Voix du peuple* was a four-page news sheet that addressed itself to the French *peuple*—modest members of the middle class, artisans, and peasants.[35] Page one presented a political editorial written by the paper's editor-in-chief, Albert Laponneraye, and a *feuilleton* written by Laponneraye or by a Marseillais democ-soc with literary pretensions. Page two featured political news from Paris and summaries of parliamentary proceedings, and three carried transcripts of the most recent Legislative Assembly sessions, as well as additional philosophical and political articles. Page four was reserved for *petites annonces* that advertised employment opportunities, rooms for rent, popular medicines, items for sale, ship sailings, commodity prices, and the like. Every day during election campaigns the paper's front page advertised the democ-soc list of candidates for the Bouches-du-Rhône, a list chosen by *La Voix*'s editorial staff and ratified by other Marseillais Montagnard organizations. Prominently displayed as well were all the places in Marseille where issues of the paper could be bought. These locales included six cafés, four liquor distillers, two tobacco dealers, two paper-goods sellers, one barbershop, and one *salon de décrottage*—a shop that specialized in removing mud from customers' shoes. All, of course, were places where common people congregated regularly and often stayed around to chat.

As noted earlier, Laponneraye was quick to recognize the need to reach the peasantry.[36] In order to expose the rural populace to *La Voix*'s ideology, he hired professional propagandists–subscription salesmen and proceeded to create a network of local correspondents. Laponneraye engaged as his principal roving representative one Louis Langomazino, a blacksmith who had been fired from Toulon's arsenal in 1845 for having helped to lead the important strike of that year. Langomazino traveled extensively in the Basses- and Hautes-Alpes and occasionally contributed a column devoted to the political events of this region.[37] His work for *La Voix* made him one of southeastern France's leading left-wing figures. Articulating a religious-based democratic socialism, Langomazino helped to engineer the Basses-Alpes' overwhelming rural vote for the democ-socs in May 1849.[38]

After Langomazino was jailed in late 1850 for his role in the so-called "complot de Lyon,"[39] *La Voix du peuple*—now edited by Pierre Dubosc and Camille Dutheil and called simply *Le Peuple**— engaged M. Leverny, an unemployed schoolteacher who had been fired from his post for expressing democ-soc convictions. Leverny traveled throughout the Var and the Bouches-du-Rhône hawking subscriptions and maintaining ties between the paper's editorial staff and its rural democ-soc audience. Like Langomazino and Arambide of *Le Démocrate du Var*, Leverny used chambrées and village cafés as forums in which to present *La Voix*'s message to the peasantry.[40]

In addition to these professional propagandists, *La Voix du peuple* possessed a network of local correspondents spread

---

* Laponneraye died in September 1849, and his successor, Alphonse Esquiros, quit *La Voix du peuple* when he was elected to the Legislative Assembly in April 1850. For the sake of simplicity, I shall continue to refer to the paper as *La Voix du peuple*.

throughout the rural regions of the Var and the Bouches-du-Rhône. A list of the journal's Var correspondents, surviving from a police raid on La Voix's offices, has made it possible to obtain detailed information about the professions and activities of many of those who served Marseille's democ-soc newspaper.[41] The professions of twenty-six of the twenty-nine correspondents on this list can be determined: ten artisans, three café proprietors, three peasant cultivators, four merchants, one notary, two proprietors (those who made a living from ownership of property), one schoolteacher, one pharmacist, and one assistant mayor. Virtually all of these professions would have placed their practitioners in constant contact with the peasantry. The artisan correspondents included two agricultural toolmakers, a shoemaker, a hat maker, and a leather dresser. Café proprietors in small villages of the Var normally had large peasant clienteles, and the notary, pharmacist, small merchants, and schoolteacher undoubtedly had frequent business dealings with the members of the peasant community. Like the professional traveling representatives of the democ-soc press, the local correspondents of La Voix du peuple exercised a dual role. As one of Marseille's chief magistrates put it: "They both propagated socialist doctrine and handled the commercial affairs of the journal. All can be distinguished by their extremist political views."[42]

The editors of La Voix du peuple chose their correspondents carefully, for not only did most of them have constant professional relations with the peasantry, but virtually all served as communal leaders of the democ-soc party. In most cases, the correspondent became the head of a secret society in 1850 or 1851 and then helped to direct the Var's massive rebellion against Louis Napoleon's coup d'état. Table 5 portrays the social characteristics and precise political roles of La Voix's correspondents. All of these men were well placed to solicit subscriptions to La Voix and to forge department-wide organizational links for the embryonic political party that this democ-soc journal represented.

Most of La Voix's Var correspondents were arrested for their role in the insurrection of December 1851, and a number of them confessed in detail to their work as propagandists and

TABLE 5
Local Correspondents for *La Voix du peuple* in the Var

Name	Age	Place of Residence	Marital Status	No. of Children	Profession	Political Role in Democ-Soc Movement	Position in Secret Society	Role in Insurrection
Arambide	34	Cogolon			locksmith	municipal council, Toulon		leader
Betiancourt	24	Pierrefeu	single		cork maker			
Bonnasse	35	Gonssaron	married	3	café proprietor			rank-and-file
Casimir	44	Mazaugue	married	3	well-off peasant	principal leader	member	
Cigales		St. Maxime						
Constant		Brignoles	married		property owner	leader		head, provisional municipal council
Desoye	33	Toulon			typesetter	propagandist		
Dupont		Hyères						
Fabre	23	Ollières	single		peasant	propagandist	president	provisional mayor
Flayols	38	Bras	married		merchant	leader	president	leader
Fournier		Cuers			pharmacist			
Gariel	37	Salernes	single		notary	principal leader	member	leader
Gautier		St. Macherie			schoolteacher			head, provisional municipal council

						propaganist	section leader	member, insurrectionary municipal council rank-and-file
Giraud	38	St. Maxime	married		barber			
Guien	26	Vins	single		horse dealer			
Hugues	26	Cuers	single		property owner			
Jassand	38	Cabasse	married	1	café proprietor	organized democ-soc cercles	member	*
Labrit		Flassans			asst. mayor			
Long	40	Cotignac	widower	1	leather dresser	leader	president	column leader
Louche, A.	32	Barjols	married	1	toolmaker	propagandist	leader	*
Louche, J.-F.	34	Barjols	single		toolmaker	propagandist	leader	*
Martel, E.	39	Pignans	married	2	wood dealer	principal leader	president	insurrectionary mayor
Martel, L.	41	St. Tropez	married	6	locksmith			leader
Nicolas		Le Luc	married	0	hat maker	leader	member	column leader
Nivière		Nans	married		peasant			
Noullet	52	St. Maxime			merchant		section leader	
Requier	35	Tourves	married	2	shoemaker	principal leader	president	provisional mayor
Roux		Roquebruse			café proprietor			
Senes		Hyères						

* Invaded town hall and constituted the insurrectionary municipal council of Brignoles.

NOTE: Blank space indicates unknown information.

SOURCES: AD Var 4M 19/1-3; AN F⁷ 2588-2595; *DBMOF.*

party organizers for their paper. André Louche acknowledged membership in Barjols's secret society and admitted "to having helped propagate democratic newspapers." How did he accomplish his charge of spreading *La Voix du peuple* and its ideas to the peasantry? "I limited my propaganda activity to the town of Barjols and to its surrounding villages. And I did this propaganda work in the course of my trips to these places."[43] As an agricultural toolmaker, Louche traveled regularly in order to sell his wares to the local peasantry. Like many artisan-propagandists of the Second Republic, Louche successfully combined the requirements of his profession with the demands of his political commitment. Louche was well-known to the peasants of the Barjols region, and this familiarity greatly facilitated his political work. Moreover, in marrying his propaganda role to his professional duties, Louche was virtually immune from police repression, and this immunity protected one of the democsocs' most important modes of contact with the peasantry.

How successful were these correspondents in presenting *La Voix*'s message to rural Frenchmen? Unfortunately, there exists no master subscription list that might provide precise information about who received the paper regularly. But a few scattered subscription registers and other kinds of information do give some idea of who was exposed to *La Voix du peuple*. An 1849 subscription list for Draguignan, probably representing the new sales of one correspondent, shows nineteen names.[44] Of these nineteen, only six were individuals. The rest of the subscriptions went to collectivities—six chambrées and cercles, six cafés and auberges, and one liquor distiller. That is, thirteen of the nineteen subscriptions were taken by café proprietors for the benefit of their clientele or by the members of a chambrée or cercle for their collective use. Unfortunately, no information exists concerning the social composition of the chambrées' membership or of the cafés' clientele. But since large numbers of artisans and cultivators resided in and around Draguignan, many of the institutions that subscribed to *La Voix* undoubtedly had lower-class patrons.[45] Another incomplete subscription list for Manosque (Basses-Alpes) has seven entries: five individuals, one café, and one chambrée.[46] A list of twenty-five Marseille subscribers shows twelve individuals and thirteen collectivities, mostly cafés.[47] It is, of course, likely that those who frequented these Marseille cafés were artisans and not cultivators. Other indications concerning the success of La Voix's correspondents in distributing their paper come from scattered reports of police and judicial officials. The mayor of Gardanne reported that La Voix was read aloud regularly in the town's many chambrées, and officials in the Hérault listed numerous chambrées and cafés that subscribed to it.[48] In addition, the paper reached cafés and chambrées throughout the Basses-Alpes as a result of the tireless efforts of Louis Langomazino.[49] These incomplete subscription figures mirror what is known about the subscribers of Le Démocrate du Var. A list confiscated from Arambide showed 50 collectivities among 124 subscribers.[50]

What sorts of relationships did La Voix du peuple maintain with its readers, and how did its audience—both those who actually read the paper and those who heard it read aloud— react to it as an ideological force and as a political institution? The seized correspondence of La Voix du peuple includes hundreds of letters from the journal's regular correspondents and from many others who took it upon themselves to write the editors in Marseille. A large number of writers volunteered information about the political situation in their localities, offered to sell subscriptions to the paper, made suggestions for changes in the journal's content, and gave unsolicited legal advice concerning La Voix's judicial battles with the government. A democ-soc sympathizer named Dymes from the village of Cornillon (Bouches-du-Rhône) accompanied his request for a subscription with an expression of confidence: "Desiring to spread the democratic word [la parole démocratique] in our humble commune, I have decided to take a three-month subscription to your patriotic publication . . . I am counting on your exactitude in order to reinforce my political views."[51] An ex-schoolteacher turned café keeper from Grans sent a similar note with his subscription request:

After seventeen months of unemployment to which the reaction condemned me, I have finally been able to open a café in this commune . . . while I await more favorable times . . . I am taking a three-month subscription to your patriotic paper in order that your republican verve can make the hearts of our villagers vibrate once again when they come to my café for refreshment.[52]

These two letters provide perfect examples of the way in which a democ-soc newspaper could forge political unity among a multitude of sympathizers who lived isolated from each other in different rural communes. It was crucial for village démocrates-socialistes to feel linked to a wider community of similarly committed people through an institution like *La Voix du peuple*. That linkage both reinforced the political views of each individual Montagnard and gave him the courage to act on his commitment. In many ways, the unifying role of the democ-soc press equaled its ideological message in importance.

Just as local democ-socs benefited from their contact with *La Voix*, so the paper's editors profited from their ties to rural readers. *La Voix* received stacks of letters suggesting names of individuals who might make good local correspondents, not to mention information about the ideological coloring of juries that would be hearing political cases.[53] Correspondence from readers also gave needed encouragement to an editorial staff that had to face almost daily harassment from government officials and whose members continually risked fines and jail for their writings. As a result of the contacts they maintained with readers, *La Voix*'s editors could be assured that their labor of self-sacrifice was achieving something and that their voice was being heard. The members of Aix's Cercle du débris de la concorde (an appropriately pessimistic name for a cercle founded late in the Second Republic) sent what must have been a heartwarming message of appreciation to the newspaper that provided them political sustenance. The awkward wording and misspelled words of the original French text indicate that the members of this cercle were not middle class: "Since we are moved by no other sentiment besides our republican ardor, we are honored to be able to profit from your teaching. For your teaching will forever be our sole and unique motto . . . you can count on us to defend you just as you defend us."[54] Another correspondent from the provinces told *La Voix du peuple* that, as a result of its efforts, "the democratic spirit has made immense progress among our agricultural population. Everything makes me believe we will have a great majority in the event that the elections of 1852 are actually held."[55] *La Voix du peuple* also received numerous letters of support from democ-socs imprisoned for their political activity,[56] as well as letters from café proprietors explaining how important the journal was to their clientele. In May 1851 the owner of Aix's Café d'Europe wrote: "I have been a subscriber of your worthy journal for many years, and I have never ceased to read it with much pleasure, and I have always done my best to make it indispensable to my establishment. The result [of these efforts] has been so good that my clientele never ceases to complain—with good reason—when the paper fails to arrive in the mail. . . ."[57]

The correspondence of *La Voix* shows that it received more than just moral support from its readers. Letters list the number of subscriptions sold by village correspondents and report the results of campaigns to solicit donations to the journal's ever-empty treasury. A writer from Arles proudly sent the 283 francs he had collected for the paper. Someone from Trets reported he could come up with only ten centimes in donations: it was all the poor peasants of his region could afford, he added apologetically.[58]

Letters from *La Voix*'s more plebian readers reveal that the paper served as a source of intellectual stimulation and educational advancement and as an institution capable of providing a measure of relief from the rigors of lower-class existence. Sending a text he hoped *La Voix* would print, a self-described worker named Millaud asked the editors to excuse his bad handwriting and to correct his poor grammar: "I am a worker and I have only received the limited education that the poor classes receive in our day. If you find the enclosed article acceptable, please make the necessary corrections and print it soon."[59] Democ-soc papers produced by journalists sympathetic to France's humble citizens gave Millaud and others like him the inspiration to write, for they set a standard of prose modest enough to seem attainable to semiliterate workers. It is not clear whether *La Voix*'s editors did in fact correct Millaud's article (the manuscript of the text, unfortunately, has been lost), but, as suggested in Chapter V, middle-class democ-soc leaders sought to contribute simultaneously to the political and literary education of their lower-class sympathizers.

In addition to its perceived role as a political and educational institution, *La Voix du peuple* was also seen—especially by its most disadvantaged readers—as a kind of institutional haven to which individuals who suffered for their political opinions or from poverty and injustice could appeal for help. Readers expected it to be a center of social service as well as a vehicle of political organization and propaganda diffusion. Numerous letters requested that *La Voix* organize a system of relief for the poor of their region, and others sought aid for specific individuals.[60] One worker, for example, wrote on behalf of a friend who got caught stealing wood—he was too poor to buy it—and wanted to know if *La Voix* could help him. In many cases individuals wrote seeking help for themselves. A Monsieur Barthelemy lost his job as a paper maker and asked if *La Voix* could give him a position.[61] Other readers wrote to relate their sad life stories and to explain how they were converted to the democ-soc cause.

Many letter writers sought help in resisting government efforts to repress their political expression or simply wanted sympathy for their political martyrdom. The proprietor of a St.-Chamas (Bouches-du-Rhône) locale called Le Café du peuple complained that police had forbidden the singing of political songs in his establishment. This is not fair, he adds, for "in the Café Flamen which is every bit as 'white' as the Café du peuple is 'red,' people sing political songs without any interference from anybody."[62] In another complaint about political repression, one Biard wrote from prison to recount the incident that had landed him and a comrade in jail. Passing by the mayor's house one afternoon, Biard and a friend were accosted by His Honor's barking dog. When Biard smacked the mutt with his cane, the mayor came charging out of the house with his tri-colored sash hastily thrown over his undershirt. Enraged, the good mayor summoned a pair of gendarmes who promptly hauled the two dog beaters off to jail. With the culprits safely behind bars, the mayor triumphantly declared that now there were two more demagogues in prison where they belonged.[63]

All of these complaints and requests for aid suggest that by the end of the Second Republic, many rural Frenchmen had ceased to rely on the old notables and the Church for charitable service. In many regions the notables and the clergy no longer possessed the power to provide certain services in exchange for allegiance to their authority, for the democ-socs had convinced rural dwellers that it was the Montagnards who held the key to material betterment. Since the state had not yet established its own institutions of social service, poor Frenchmen looked to the democ-soc press as the organ of an ideology, steeped in populist Catholicism, that seemed to promise aid and solace.

This is not to argue that the democ-socs simply became the new rural notables. Unlike the old notables, democ-soc journalists never commanded allegiance on the basis of their personal standing in the community. Nor did individual democ-socs possess the resources to provide relief and protection in exchange for acquiescence to their authority. La Voix's readership did not know the paper's editors as individuals. Rather, it was the institution of the journal that Frenchmen knew, and it was the institution that commanded their allegiance. Their devotion derived not from acquiescence to paternalistic authority but rather from two very different phenomena: La Voix's sincerely manifested sympathy for the plight of the lower classes, and the paper's apparent role as the mediator of a democratic and social republic that promised to realize through new political structures the ideals of a populist Christianity.

La Voix du peuple and papers like it became complex institutions called upon to perform a number of roles only marginally related to journalism. During an era in which government repression frustrated the effort to establish a mass political party and in which old mechanisms of rural social welfare had given way to a triumphant market and democratized politics, the democ-socs assumed responsibility for political organization and, to a lesser extent, social welfare. The prestige and recognition it received for these activities did much to facilitate its primary mission—the republicanization of the French provinces.

By late 1850 and 1851, when repression began to obstruct seriously above-ground propaganda activity, the democ-soc press found it increasingly difficult to make contact with the rural population. Chambrées and left-wing cafés found themselves perpetually under police surveillance, and traveling propagandists suffered unrelenting police harassment. It was at this point that the secret society began to take over from the democ-soc press as the primary agency of propaganda diffusion.

The Montagnard left responded to intensified repression and to the May 1850 electoral reform law by going underground. Though many democ-soc newspapers managed to stay alive— often at great personal and financial cost—antioppositionist legislation and growing government arbitrariness meant that democ-socs' efforts to propagate their ideology would henceforth have to proceed in secret. The institutional expression of this new situation was the secret society.[64] Beginning in 1850, local activists built a network of clandestine organizations that, by the eve of the coup d'état, extended throughout central, southeastern, and southwestern France. Montagnard societies devoted themselves to a pair of goals: defense of the republic by arms if necessary, and propagation of democ-soc ideology. Hierarchic in structure, these clandestine bodies were organized by commune; within each commune, society affiliates formed ten-member cells called *décuries*, each with its own elected leader. In communes with enough members, the décuries were grouped by tens into hundred-member formations led by a centurion. In a well-organized department like the Nièvre or the Hérault the secret societies of the various communes corresponded with each other and even held periodic meetings of the department's communal leaders. In the central French departments of the Yonne and the Nièvre, societies were composed mostly of artisans but included some winegrowers. In southern France, secret societies tended to include at least as many peasant cultivators as artisans. Leaders of these organizations came, for the most part, from the ranks of the artisanat and the modest village middle-class. But peasants did play leadership roles, especially in southern departments like the Var and the Hérault.[65]

Though these societies were clandestine organizations theoretically devoted to armed insurrection, they served functions in many ways similar to those of the press, the chambrées and the republican cafés. Indeed, the secret society endeavored above all to keep alive in the countryside the spirit of democratic socialism.[66] Since secret societies arose in the regions that voted most heavily for the democ-socs in May 1849,[67] it is highly likely that most of those who joined had already expressed an electoral commitment to the Montagnard left. The task of the clandestine society was to reinforce and broaden this tie. The allegiance of rural Frenchmen to democratic socialism was new and therefore fragile. In the face of the government's powerful attempt to block the expression of democ-soc ideas, the movement needed a special kind of organizational structure to keep these ideas alive. Paradoxically, repression itself helped to anchor firmly within much of the rural population of central and southern France the ideology of the republican left, for the repression obliged communal democ-soc leaders to establish a political organization well-suited to peasant culture and tradition. Since peasants were accustomed to communities whose members all knew each other, the secret society, like the village café and chambrée, was in many ways an ideal institution for the transmission and reinforcement of new political ideas. It provided an organizational framework in which peasants could feel comfortable and at the same time be exposed to the ideas of its middle-class and artisan members.

Judicial officials discovered the existence of rural networks of secret societies late in the Second Republic and immediately recognized their potential to politicize rural Frenchmen. The procureur général of Lyon complained bitterly of the secret societies' virtual immunity from the government's apparatus of repression. These organizations, lurking incognito throughout much of rural France, could simply vanish into thin air when police came looking for them. This invisibility made the secret society an ideal forum of propaganda diffusion and ideological indoctrination. Thus in creating secret societies, wrote Lyon's procureur général, "the revolutionary party has demonstrated considerable sophistication. For they have reoriented their methods of propaganda and recruitment toward the countryside . . . where the government is least capable of combatting them."[68]

Statements made by society members at the time of their arrest in December 1851 indicate that the ideology and goals of the Montagnard secret societies were virtually identical to those of the above-ground democ-soc organizations. Members viewed the republic as the realization of Christian ideals, and their institutions exhibited many characteristics of the religious confraternities of the eighteenth and early nineteenth centuries.[69] Affiliates sang the same songs and read the same newspapers that earlier had served as mainstays of the democ-soc propaganda effort in the chambrées and popular cafés.

The elaborate initiation ritual of the secret society incorporated the populist religiosity so important to the peasants' receptivity to democ-soc ideology and expressed the people's desire to identify themselves with Jesus Christ. Interestingly enough, society members called this solemn ceremony a baptism. Limion, a cultivator from Brue Auriac in the Var, described the initiation rite performed by André Louche, the *Voix du peuple* correspondent who became prominent in the secret societies of the Brignoles region: "One of the society members touched his [the new recruit's] bared head with a cold instrument which he knew was a weapon even though he was told it was the hand of Christ. At the same time [Louche] said to him, 'I baptise you in the name of the Mountain.' "[70] Although most initiation ceremonies seemed to end with "I baptise you in the name of the Mountain" or "I baptise you Montagnard,"[71] some expressed the popular identification with Jesus even more directly. After swearing allegiance to the society, a mason from Brignoles (Var) received the following response: "In the name of the Christ of the Mountain, I receive you as a Montagnard and as a brother."[72] Virtually all initiates, it should be added, swore allegiance to their societies on two knives or two sticks formed into a cross, and their oath often ended as follows: "I swear [allegiance] three times in the name of Christ our Redeemer."[73]

Just as peasant communities of the first half of the nineteenth century sought to direct religious ritual toward their own ends, so the communal leaders of the secret societies employed the Catholic rite of baptism to their own purposes. In baptizing new recruits, societies consecrated the initiate's identification with Jesus Christ, considered to be the founding father of the Montagnard movement. Once inducted into the society, the new member was wedded by solemn oath to the egalitarian quest that Jesus was said to have begun some eighteen centuries earlier. Whereas rural communities had witnessed strained relations between priests and peasants who wanted clergymen to accept their rather unorthodox conception of religious devotion (see Chapter II), the secret society solved the priest problem by appointing its own "clergy" from within the ranks of the organization. Society members took turns playing the role of priest in the ceremonies of initiation, and since the "priest" was most often a peer of the inductee, the society, in good populist form, abolished the hierarchic distinction of clergyman and parishioner.

Following his "baptism," the new recruit received a set of passwords with which he could identify himself to society members from other communes. Often these passwords were religious. For example, secret society members from the various communes of the Cosne (Nièvre) region established an elaborate duet of recognition:[74]

First Person	Second Person
The Hour	has tolled.
God sees it	from the heights of the Mountain.
The Droit	au travail.

Sometimes the word "Christ" was added to this list of passwords, and in many regions of the country society members were told to yell "Christ! Christ! Christ!" when in danger. Such a cry obliged a fellow brother in Christ to run to the aid of his threatened comrade.[75]

If the rituals and code words of the secret society were steeped
in religious meaning, so were the actual ideas expressed in its
meetings. One member from Brignoles in the Var declared that,
among other things, "the society has as its goal the establishment of the reign of fraternity."[76] Similarly, Valaire Dardenne,
secret society leader from the Nièvre, told his recruits that the
goal of his organization was "to unite in order to pursue the
goal of fraternity."[77] The statement of another Brignoles recruit
shows clearly that the ideology of the secret society incorporated
the effort to transpose Catholic precepts into a project for republican government. He told police that the members of his
society sought to "end tyranny and establish everywhere the
egalitarian and socialist system. . . . In discussing these goals
we always spoke of Christ and the Gospels."[78]

The society's more specific political ideas and short-term goals
demonstrate the thorough penetration of democ-soc ideology
at the local level. In central France, where the membership of
clandestine Montagnard societies included mainly skilled workers,[79] the reported goals of the organizations closely resembled
those of the most prominent democ-soc ideologues. These pre-
dominately working-class societies sought to establish producers' cooperatives, obtain the droit au travail, restore universal
suffrage (by force of arms if necessary), reform the tax system,
win free education—in short to transform the existing bogus
republic into a truly democratic and social republic.[80] Jean-Baptiste Riché, a blacksmith from Joigny, declared that the purpose
of his secret society was to encourage the workers "to vote [as
a group] and to aid each other mutually." In his oath of membership he swore to "support universal suffrage, proportional
taxation, free education, and the droit au travail."[81] Moret, a
miller from Avallon (Yonne), joined a society in the hope that
it would establish "la société républicaine et mutuelle."[82] He
longed, in other words for a republic founded on the forms of
worker cooperation advocated by leading democ-soc ideologues.
For some workers, the primary aim of the Montagnard secret
society was to establish the droit au travail;[83] for others, it was
to restore universal suffrage and defend the republic.[84] In the
words of Alexis Aubertin, a tailor from the commune of Cham-

plèmy (Nièvre): "They had me swear to defend the democratic and social republic in order to restore universal suffrage."[85]

Upon joining Cosne's society, François Delacroix, like most other new recruits, swore "to go and vote in 1852 with a gun in one hand and a ballot in the other if universal suffrage is not restored [before the election]."[86] This oath provides evidence of the extent to which the legalistic and democratic principles of the democ-socs penetrated the clandestine society. It suggests that even these conspiratorial organizations envisaged violence solely as a means of reconquering republican legality. So confident were they of the revolutionary power of universal suffrage that they saw no need to seize power through extra-legal means. Society leaders believed France could be transformed from Bonapartist oligarchy to social republic by democratic means. Because local militants considered democracy a revolutionary instrument, their desire to restore republican legality in no way implied an acceptance of formalistic republicanism. Rather, their identification with a revolutionary Jesus and their demands for the droit au travail and workers' cooperatives demonstrated a commitment to a new kind of republic, a democratic and social republic that promised to transform Christian ideals into everyday reality.

In southern France, where secret societies included at least as many peasant cultivators as skilled workers, the ideology transmitted by communal leaders resembled in most respects that of the societies of central France, where most members belonged to the artisanat. According to Felix Boutes, a peasant from Nezignan-l'Evêque in the Hérault, "They [his initiators] had me promise that if in 1852 the universal vote is not restored, I would carry a gun to the voting booth."[87] Another peasant from the Hérault reported that society leaders told him that members would "ease each others' burdens and that the universal vote would be given back to us. We were supposed to vote for real republicans so that they could have a majority. We were told, in addition, that we should respect property, family, and religion."[88] Similarly, Jean Thibeyrenc, a peasant cultivator from Boujan (Hérault) reported that "the goal of the society was a widespread vote in favor of the candidates designated by the society. There would be an insurrection in May 1852 if we were prevented from voting." Thibeyrenc added that "we were promised higher wages, reduced taxes, state-run mortgage banks . . . and we were told that certain rich people had seized for themselves communal property which belonged to the people. The government which would be substituted for the present one would give these communal goods back to the people.[89] Another Hérault peasant, François Lagarde from the village of Abeilhan, said he was told that the secret society had been formed to "defend the republic and to assure a unanimous vote for the Montagnards."[90] And one of Lagarde's comrades from Abeilhan, a baker named Laussel, was told that "my children's education could be free and workers' wages increased . . . but [for this to happen] the republic had to be defended. If they tried to destroy it, all of us had to vote for true republicans."[91] Thus, like the artisans who joined secret societies in central France, peasant affiliates were exposed to an ideology closely resembling the democ-soc doctrines analyzed in Chapter IV. It was an ideology that inextricably linked the promise of social reform with the necessity of a truly republican—that is, democratic and social—government. The doctrines presented in peasant secret societies differed from those discussed in workers' societies only in that the droit au travail seldom came up. To small peasant proprietors who suffered more from an inability to market crops than from lack of work, the promise of mutual aid meant far more than a pledge to ensure the right to employment.

In addition to providing a portrait of the secret society's ideology, statements of arrested members describe the actual political work of these clandestine organizations. The secret societies of the Second Republic were concerned mainly with reinforcing the democ-soc commitment of their members and with spreading that commitment in hopes of bringing more members into the Montagnard fold. They devoted very little effort to preparing for the eventuality of armed insurrection. Like democ-soc journals, Montagnard secret societies provided an institutional setting in which republican propaganda could be transmitted to peasants and artisans. The testimony of one Louis Bajolet, a society member turned police informer, provides a detailed picture of the inner workings of these clandestine organizations: "In our meetings [of the secret society of Joigny] we alternated reading about and discussing political subjects. The subject that concerned us most often was that of the electoral law. It was said that if universal suffrage were not restored before '52, we would march to the ballot box with weapons in our hands."[92] Bajolet went on to say that members did discuss obtaining weapons and gunpowder, but not for the purpose of staging an uprising. The aim, rather, was to restore universal suffrage by force if necessary.[93] Bajolet cannot justly be accused of playing down the violent intentions of the society members; if anything, as a police informer he would have been inclined to do just the opposite.

Other testimony confirms what Bajolet had to say. During election campaigns, said P. A. Bourgie, a café proprietor from St. Amand (Nièvre), "we were concerned solely with elections. We were all supposed to vote for the same candidates, and the members promised to make as many new affiliations as possible."[94] This hardly sounds like the work of a conspiratorial underground. The society resembles more an ordinary electoral organization.

What else went on in the meetings of secret societies? In the commune of Boujan in the Hérault, according to plaster maker David Azéma:

The society dealt with the question of socialism and with the way in which the government should be put together. The society also dealt with politics* and read newspapers. . . . We discussed *La Presse*, but we didn't accept all of its ideas. When it preached civil war, the secret society didn't approve. It believed that we didn't need anything besides the right to vote and that there was no need to spill blood in order to establish the kind of government that the society wanted, a government based on universal suffrage.[95]

What were the specific political points raised in secret society meetings? Azéma attested that the society hoped to achieve "la démocratie universelle," which was said to mean: popular sov-

* "Politics" here probably means elections.

ereignty and universal suffrage; the abolition of *droits reunis and octrois* (indirect taxes); the lowering of huge salaries; that representatives of the People who failed to keep campaign promises would be exiled and their property confiscated by the state; free and obligatory instruction; abolition of usury; the establishment of state-run banks, lending at 2 percent; the creation of paper money; the elimination of executive power; the droit au travail.[96] This program, of course, mirrors the platform of the democ-soc press and testifies to the extent to which that program gained exposure even in the humblest communes.

It is understandable that the above platform was discussed in secret society meetings, for the democ-soc newspapers that advertised these planks were read aloud regularly to the clandestinely assembled membership. One agricultural laborer from Joigny even believed that the main purpose of the secret society was to provide a forum in which people "could get together to read newspapers."[97] The society at Ragny in the Yonne was led by a clog maker named Dutour, who read *L'Union républicaine* every Friday night to members grouped either in his shop or in a cousin's café.[98] In Cochu in the Hérault one society member was assigned to bring a copy of *La Feuille du village* to each meeting. Jean-Baptiste Fabre, a peasant who served as *La Voix du peuple*'s correspondent in Ollières (Var), declared in his testimony before the Mixed Commission that he "subscribed along with other members of the secret society to the newspaper *Le Peuple* [i.e., *La Voix du peuple*] of Marseille." C.-H. Rhodez, a locksmith from Aillant (Yonne) read and commented on *La République* and *L'Union républicaine* to society members assembled in his workshop.[99] In Perpignan, society members gathered in a field just outside the city gates to listen to a leader named Rolland read from democ-soc papers.[100] And secret society leaders in the Gers "read aloud and commented on articles from *L'Ami du peuple* to peasant members," while leaders in the arrondissement of Provins (near Orléans) "received a large number of copies of the journal *Le Vote universel.*"[101] The role that correspondents of *La Voix du peuple* played in the secret societies of the Var was demonstrated above, and there is evidence that correspondents of the democ-soc press participated in the clandestine organizations of other departments as well. One L. Bonnerat, a secret society leader in the rural commune of Villiers (near Joigny), corresponded regularly with M. Calais, managing editor of Auxerre's *Union républicaine*. Police accused Bonnerat of reading both *L'Union* and Louis Blanc's *Le Nouveau monde* to the local secret society membership.[102]

Thus, like the democ-soc press, the secret society acted perhaps above all else to spread Montagnard propaganda. Not only were society members constantly exposed to the tenets of democratic socialism, but each affiliate swore to propagate these tenets to nonmembers. In the oath of allegiance to the society, new recruits pledged to devote themselves "to the propaganda of democratic and social laws" or to "spread propaganda, political as well as religious."[103] Moreover, like the democ-soc press, some secret societies appointed traveling agents charged with spreading propaganda in rural communes. The society of Boisseion in the Hérault, for example, chose four of its members, two of whom worked as hand-loom weavers, to circulate throughout the canton in an effort to "faire la propagande."[104] Most other societies relied on the normal everyday professional contacts between members and nonmembers to disseminate propaganda and recruit new affiliates.[105]

On a local level, at least, the secret society did not seem terribly secret. In their attempts to attract new members, affiliates openly spoke of their organization and of its ideology. When a prospective recruit balked at the idea of joining, the member proceeded to explain the goals of the society and to describe how the organization could help the ordinary worker or peasant.[106] This relatively open and active method of recruitment provides one more example of the ways in which the secret society acted more as an institution of ideological diffusion than as a network of insurrectionary conspiracy.

Complementing the democ-socs' informal network of propaganda diffusion, then, were two local institutions: the press and the secret society. Both endeavored to deepen and broaden popular commitment to democ-soc ideology. This Montagnard ideology remained largely undiluted as it filtered down from the leading publicists in the democ-soc press to the lower ranks of French society. The secret society appears to have been more concerned with keeping the democ-soc message alive during a period of intense repression than with preparing a violent seizure of power. But once society members did take up arms in response to Bonaparte's coup d'état, they fought for much more than the restoration of the status quo. They fought in the name of a democratic and social republic that embodied the revolutionary aspirations of peasants and artisans who sought to realize the promise of the Gospels.

CHAPTER VII

POPULAR COMMITMENT TO DEMOC-SOC DOCTRINE

We have seen how Montagnard ideologues and organizers at the local level transmitted Christian-based democratic socialism to peasants and rural artisans whose own unorthodox religiosity made them receptive to such a doctrine. What remains is to discuss the results of this process of politicization. An analysis of both the actions and the statements of ordinary Frenchmen will demonstrate that democ-soc ideas did indeed penetrate the consciousness of humble peasants and artisans and that popular religiosity played the crucial role in this process. This rural conversion to a rudimentary form of democratic socialism was revealed in two fundamental ways: popular religious devotion and other forms of popular culture became occasions for political protest and expressions of political allegiance, and rural communities developed a precocious commitment to the institutions and values of republican democracy. By mid-1849 the peasants of central and southern France had abandoned older forms of violent protest to vote in large numbers for the Montagnard left. And even the 1851 insurrection itself expressed an attachment to republican legality. This growth of a popular commitment to democratic values was far from complete by the time of Louis Napoleon's coup d'état. But the short-lived experience of the Second Republic had provided an unprecedented political apprenticeship for rural Frenchmen, and it foreshadowed the more mature democratic allegiance that the peasantry would display during the Third Republic.

The unorthodox religiosity of French peasants and artisans, which identified God, Jesus, and the saints as protectors of the people and harbingers of a renovated moral system, achieved its earliest political expression in Paris. Before 1848 bourgeois leftists and spokesmen of the Parisian working class had articulated their religiosity in the form of a moral critique of the July Monarchy. And it was the revolutionary events of February 1848 that triggered the transformation of this working-class religiosity into an overt commitment to the democratic and social republic.

One of the most striking acts of 24 February 1848, the decisive revolutionary day, was a spontaneous, quasi-religious procession from the royal palace to the Church of St. Roch. In the midst of the popular invasion of Louis Philippe's abandoned Tuileries, a group of insurgents seized a crucifix there and with great fanfare, removed it from the palace. In solemnly carrying the huge and ornate crucifix to the church of St. Roch, the revolutionary crowd symbolically liberated the original Christian spirit—incarnated in Jesus, man of the people—from nearly twenty centuries of captivity in the halls of princely power. Lamennais, Louis Blanc, and others had declared that the true Christian spirit belonged to the popular classes and not to their rulers, and the events of 24 February confirmed the extent to which that message had taken hold of the Parisian crowd. In "liberating" Jesus from the Tuileries, the people proclaimed their belief in revolution as catalyst of a new era in which the original Christian promise of equality and brotherhood would be realized on earth. Most accounts agree on the essentials of the event. The insurgent who grabbed the crucifix lifted it high in the air and shouted: "Do you want to be regenerated, well then, do not forget that it is only Christ who can regenerate you." Then, removing their hats, the insurgents cried: "Vive le Christ."[1]

Was this merely an isolated example of revolutionary fervor, perhaps manipulated by crowd leaders? Other events of 1848 indicate the contrary. Parisian typesetters, for example, celebrated a victorious February night on the barricades by trooping off to the church of Saint-Etienne-du-Mont for a mass of thanksgiving. Moreover, according to socialist worker Benoît Malon, most trade organizations made "Jesus the Carpenter" the symbol of their successful revolution, and their headquarters commonly displayed posters depicting "Jesus of Nazareth, First Representative of the People."[2]

The massive Champs de Mars demonstration of 16 April 1848 poignantly revealed the extent to which the religiosity of the July Monarchy's left-wing opponents underlay the political behavior of Parisian workers after February. Demanding the droit au travail and other social reforms, a revolutionary crowd confronted heavily armed national guardsmen who were determined to defend a moderate conception of the republic. As George Sand described the event: "It was at once a beautiful and sad spectacle to see this proud and discontented people marching in the midst of all those bayonets. The bayonets cried and trumpeted 'Long live the Republic! Long live the Provisional Government, Long live Lamartine!' The workers responded: 'Long live the true republic! *Long live the true republic . . . of Christ.*' "[3] In invoking the image of Jesus Christ, these workers demonstrated the extent to which Jesus symbolized for them the "real" social republic of dignity and material improvement. They thus ratified Louis Blanc's view that only the social republic could be legitimate because it alone had Jesus' blessing. For Parisian workers Jesus represented the democratic and social republic of reform, equal opportunity, and brotherhood; the guard symbolized the conservative republic of order and hierarchy. The bayonets that menaced the demonstrating workers equally threatened the existence of Jesus' republic.

While workers on the street exalted Jesus' republic, their representatives in the Luxembourg Commission drew up hundreds of petitions that articulated demands for social reform in religious language. A team of linguists has recently demonstrated a high correlation between the vocabulary of the workers' commissions and that of the religious-oriented *L'Atelier*.[4] This correlation testifies to the influence of *L'Atelier* among working-class leaders as well as to their continuing identification of Christian precepts and social reform.

After the June Days, when the democ-soc coalition assumed leadership of a newly united left, Parisian workers began to imbibe democ-soc ideology. Increasingly they displayed allegiance to a sacralized republic similar to the Gospels-inspired republic of the Montagnard press. The associated tailors of Clichy, a group of workers who operated one of the most successful producers' cooperatives of the Second Republic, pasted three ill-printed lithographs to the otherwise bare walls of their spartan premises: a portrait of Barbès; a scene featuring Marianne, the republican goddess; and a picture of Jesus Christ portrayed as a revolutionary-republican hero. According to *L'Atelier*, the latter lithograph depicted "Jesus crowned with thorns and supported by two allegorical figures: Liberty and Equality. In this touching scene, the son of God restrains under his bare feet the demon of pride, a beast which appears to be vomiting gold coins. The word 'hope' is inscribed on a banner that radiates above his head. Jesus' face is full of tenderness and good will."[5] With Jesus, representing fraternity, at the center of the republican trinity of liberty, equality, and fraternity, this lithograph captures perfectly the identification of Christian purity and progressive republicanism that underlies the ideology of the Montagnard left. The fusion of symbols is complete: Christian trinity and republican trinity; Christian brotherhood and republican fraternity; Jesus, son of God, and Jesus, the worker-revolutionary hero; Christian hope and republican realization. Commenting on this lithograph, the locksmith-poet Gilland declared that republican workers could do no better "than to seek to imitate [Jesus]. He was born into poverty, just like all of us. He labored, He suffered persecution. He died in the name of justice."[6] The Jesus of the tailors' lithograph was a workers' Jesus. Those threatened by the decline of professional status and the degradation of skill affirmed their dignity as skilled craftsmen by identifying with him.

Like the portrait of Jesus, the lithograph of Marianne also represents a mixture of republican and religious symbols. In the picture, according to *L'Atelier*, "behind the Republic [i.e., Marianne] lie superb cities, fields full of wheat, hills covered with grapes. . . . The Republic points out to a group of studious children gathered at her feet, a hive in which bees are hard at work."[7] Represented by Marianne, the republic points the way to a land of milk and honey where work resembles the cooperative effort of bees in a hive.[8] The republic, therefore, is the gateway to the heavenly city. It promises the earthly realization of the harmony and well-being that Christianity reserved for the afterlife. That the idea of redemption on earth was a key element of both working-class religiosity and democ-soc ideology helps to explain the workers' commitment to the democratic and social republic.[9]

In provincial France, where the July Monarchy had seen less ideological ferment than in Paris, the transformation of popular religiosity into republican commitment occurred more gradually. Outside of Paris the events of February 1848 were not enough to trigger such a transformation. It was up to local Montagnard propagandists to fashion rural allegiance to the democratic and social republic from the raw matter of popular religiosity and economic malaise. One of the best ways to gauge the progress of Montagnard ideas is to observe the religiosity of rural communities. In 1848 peasants still expressed a populist religiosity devoid of political content. By mid-1849, however, rural religiosity began to show signs of the influence of democ-soc ideology. Festivals in honor of patron saints, Mardi gras carnivals preceding Lent, and celebrations of the feast of Corpus Christi increasingly took on a political coloring consistent with Montagnard ideas.

In November 1849 the coopers of Montpellier paid homage to their patron saint, as they did every year at that time. Outwardly, this year's celebration looked like any other. Marching to the cadence of tambourines, flag-carrying coopers promenaded in a solemn procession along their traditional route through the narrow streets of Montpellier. What was novel about the celebration of 1849 was that the coopers used it to express newly adopted political commitments. At regular intervals and in time with the beat of the tambourine they chanted, "Down with the Whites, long live the Reds."[10]

Similarly, in September 1851 townsmen from Castelnaudary (Aude) politicized their annual saint's day. Instead of paying homage to the town's own saint, celebrants took it upon themselves to honor the "saints" of the democ-soc left. Townsmen decorated the annual ball not with customary images of their patrons but rather with portraits of Ledru-Rollin, Barbès, and two Montagnard deputies named Rattier and Boitot.[11] Just as lithographs of republican "saints" replaced those of Catholic saints in the colporteur's sack, so villagers began to shift their religious allegiance from patron saints to Montagnard heroes. Government reports from 1850 to 1851 indicate that the transformation of the traditional *fête patronale* into a demonstration of Montagnard political commitment had become a fairly common occurrence. In a small commune near Grenoble a group of young people paid homage to their patron saint by waving a red flag and wearing red belts, ties, and hats—all symbols of the Montagnard left—during the traditional procession. Similarly, the *fête patronale* of Bastide, a village near St. Pons (Hérault), featured socialist songs, and local democ-soc leaders played a prominent role in the celebration.[12] In September 1851, the procureur at Aix complained that even intense political repression could not prevent village fêtes patronales from sparking "a political effervescence hostile to the government.[13]

The annual carnival of Mardi gras, held on the day before Ash Wednesday, provided another occasion on which popular religious celebration could serve as a vehicle for nascent political expression. Traditionally, the carnival provided a setting in which the people could ignore the constraints of socially acceptable everyday behavior. Villagers indulged in dancing, popular theatrics, processions, drinking, and romance as a way of preparing themselves for the rigors of the Lenten season.[14] In southern France, the carnival's frenzied merrymaking culminated in the ceremonial drowning of a humanlike dummy after a mock trial in which popular "magistrates" sentenced it to death. In some instances, the dummy clearly represented a local personage who had aroused the people's anger, but normally the killing of the dummy simply provided an outlet for a community's frustration.[15] It is possible that this ritual drowning was linked to the popular saint worship of Mediterranean France, for southern Frenchmen customarily "drowned" effigies of saints in an effort to kill the evil forces that created droughts and other natural calamities.[16]

After 1848 the carnival began to show signs of the penetration of democ-soc ideology. Once simply the recipient of generalized popular anger, the dummy now took an overt political meaning. During Capestang's (Hérault) carnival of 1851, for example, townsmen turned the dummy into a symbol of the Party of

Order by dressing it entirely in white. The dummy was then "placed in a hearse drawn by mules. After a promenade through the town," the dummy-symbol of order was drowned by his popular judges.[17] It is significant that the dummy did not represent a particular local personage. Rather, it embodied an abstract political force to be condemned.

A similar event occurred during the 1851 carnival of Brou (Seine-et-Marne). In northern France, carnival justice traditionally condemned the dummy to be burned at the stake rather than drowned, and the highlight of Brou's 1851 festivities was the burning of a dummy representing the men and ideas of the Party of Order. The effigy both resembled the commune's conservative mayor and represented the politics and ideology of the right. Villagers had attached symbols of the mayor's profession to the dummy's white clothes, and a pair of white flags and issues of the conservative *Journal de Chartres* decorated its torso. The newspapers served to kindle the blaze, and as the effigy burst into flames, the crowd cried, "Long live the republic! Down with the Whites. Down with the aristocrats. Down with the mayor!"[18] Not only, therefore, did the carnival enable Brou villagers to attack the town's mayor; it also allowed them to vent their hostility to the conservative ideology he embodied. In burning their dummy, townsmen symbolically reduced mayor, party, and ideology to ashes.

In Mauzé (Deux-Sèvres) the carnival of 1850 provided the occasion for a particularly explicit demonstration of democ-soc commitment. That year the Mardi gras celebration featured a procession led by a young woman dressed as a goddess of liberty. Accompanying her was a nineteen-year-old man sporting a bright red cap and a white shirt fastened with a wide belt. Behind the two republican gods marched a group of men singing Claude Durand's "Chant des vignerons" ("The Winegrowers' Song"), one of the best-known Montagnard songs of the Second Republic:[19]

> Good villagers, vote for the Mountain;
> They are the gods of the poor winegrowers,
> Because it is they, good men of the land,
> Who will wipe out the tax on wine.

Good, good, winegrowers
In the next elections,
We must, fellow farmers,
Elect the Montagnards.

The Montagnards are our light
They represent both rich and poor;
For if the little man has not enough,
The rich will have no peace.

Good, good, winegrowers, etc.
. . . .
When the elections will be democratic,
All of the poor workers' taxes
Will be paid in our Republic,
By the fat cats and the big bankers.

Good, good, winegrowers, etc.

In each and every hamlet agricultural banks,
Will exist for you, good peasant.
Free also will be our schools,
And money will be loaned at two percent.*

*Bons villageois, votez pour la Montagne:
Là sont les Dieux des pauvres vignerons,
Car avec eux, bonnes gens de campagne,
Seront rasés les impôts des boissons.
  Bons, bons, vignerons
  Aux prochaines élections,
  Il faut, campagnards,
  Nommer les Montagnards.
Les Montagnards pour nous sont la lumière
Drapeau du riche et de la pauvreté;
Car si les p'tits n'ont pas le nécessaire,
Pour tous les gros, plus de securité.
  Bons, bons vignerons, etc.
  . . . .
Quand l'élection sera démocratique,
Tous les impôts des pauvres ouvriers
Seront payés dans notre République,
Par les richards et par les gros banquiers.
  Bons, bons, vignerons, etc.

Durand's song expressed most of the main points of the Montagnard program, and it shows in a startling way the extent to which new political content could pervade existing forms of popular religious expression.

French police were terrified of any possible source of "disorder" during the Second Republic, and often their clumsy attempts to prevent carnivals from turning into demonstrations of political opposition produced precisely the results they sought to avoid. In 1849 the carnival of St. Florentin (Yonne) began, as always, with a charivari in which the young men of the village ridiculed those female inhabitants whose morals were less than orthodox. In the words of the town's long-time mayor:

> On January 29 at about seven o'clock in the evening, a large number of young men armed with frying pans, pots, watering cans, and other similar utensils began to run through the streets. They produced a fierce racket, but being used to this sort of thing, the adults were not alarmed. The youths were like a flood that one was powerless to stop but which would eventually subside on its own. Unfortunately, the local gendarmes, without consulting me beforehand, took it upon themselves to arrest two of the young revelers.[20]

The arrests violated the town's longstanding tacit agreement to tolerate such carnival-time outbursts. The gendarmes' action appeared patently unjust, and it provoked an immediate response from youthful villagers enraged by this challenge to what they considered an important prerogative. Upon hearing of the youths' arrest, some two hundred young people gathered in front of the mayor's house to demand their release. Hoping to avoid further trouble, the mayor quickly obliged. The official's action, however, came too late to appease the angry crowd, and once the youths had been freed, the demonstrators marched off to the gendarmes' barracks. Acting quickly, the mayor strictly

---

Dans tout hameau des banques agricoles,
Existeront pour toi, bon paysan.
Gratis aussi on aura des écoles,
Et de l'argent au plus à deux du cent.

confined the town's overzealous guardians of order, and in the absence of a police response, tension ultimately subsided as demonstrators went home to bed. The incident, however, was far from over. The next night, at 7 P.M. sharp, a crowd composed of several hundred villagers of all ages gathered in the town square. This time, the demonstration was overtly political, and it expressed the villagers' attachment to the démocrate-socialiste left. Taking to the streets in a religious-style procession, the crowd struck up the "Marseillaise." At the head of the column a villager carried a huge lantern on which four slogans had been inscribed:

> Long live the Mountain
> Long live general amnesty
> Liberty, Equality, Fraternity, or death
> Long live the democratic and social republic.[21]

What is interesting about this event is not so much that the youths rebelled against the police but that from one day to the next, townsmen of all ages transformed an apparently nonpolitical clash between young villagers and police into a demonstration of republican commitment.

Departmental archives are filled with similar examples of the way in which repression turned the carnival or a similar expression of popular religiosity into a political demonstration.[22] It is important to realize, however, that no necessary relationship exists between repression on the one hand and pro-Montagnard politicization on the other. Hostility to the police or to a repressive state can take any number of political forms, or it can simply be released in a single short-lived burst of popular anger that carries no distinct political meaning. Thus, in early 1848 opposition to the Provisional Government's attempts to collect taxes often erupted into violent protest that was devoid of any political content. And in the Gard, where there was an active White Mountain—an ultraroyalist movement that sought to elect the Bourbon pretender to the French throne through universal suffrage—opposition to government restraints took the form of support for the far right.[23] After 1848 repression turned popular expression into pro-Montagnard demonstrations, thanks to the efforts of Montagnard publicists. Democ-soc ideology provided both a political explanation for the existence of this burden and a means of envisaging a new government based not on repression but on liberty and equality. Like popular religiosity, hostility to repression could be transformed into republican commitment because democ-soc propagandists channeled these sentiments into support for their politics.

During the early decades of the nineteenth century Corpus Christi became the most important and widely celebrated religious festival because it enabled rural dwellers to express their identification with a populist Jesus Christ.[24] But peasant efforts to take the celebration of the Eucharist into their own hands provoked severe conflict with local representatives of the Church. Corpus Christi represented, par excellence, the people's unorthodox religiosity, and after 1848 this annual event was ripe for politicization. It was but a short step from the worship of Jesus as symbol of popular suffering and virtue to an allegiance with "Jesus the Montagnard," symbol of republican liberty and popular equality.

The 1851 procession held in honor of Corpus Christi in a small village near Rennes reveals the way in which democ-soc propaganda injected political content into the existing populist image of Jesus. The procession of 1851 was identical to those of earlier years except that it featured a huge lithograph of Jesus portrayed as a revolutionary hero, with the boldly printed caption, "Jésus le Montagnard." A knife maker named Cracheur nailed the lithograph high above the door to his house, where it hung in full view to his fellow townsmen as they marched by. Attached to the lithograph was a quotation from Lamennais:

When you see a man being taken off to prison or torture, don't be quick to assume that he is an evil man who has committed crimes against his fellows. It is just as likely that he is a man of virtue who wanted only to serve his brothers and who was punished by their oppressors. . . .

Eighteen hundred years ago, in a city of the orient, the popes and kings of that era nailed to a cross . . . a man they considered seditious and unreligious. . . . His name was Jesus.[25]

No longer was Jesus simply a man of the people who had suffered with his fellows. Democ-soc propaganda made him the symbol of resistance to repression and the champion of a new political system devoted to popular well-being.

Emile Zola seems to have been acutely aware of the tie between popular religiosity and peasant political behavior, especially with respect to the feast of Corpus Christi. In *La Fortune des Rougon*, a novel set in the midst of the insurrection of 1851, Zola's heroine Miette explicitly links populist Catholicism and republican politics. In the scene in which Zola introduces the Var's rebel column, Miette grabs the insurgents' flag and, striking the symbolic pose of a republican goddess of Liberty, declares, "I feel as though I'm at the procession of the Corpus Christi and that I'm the one who is carrying the banner of the Virgin."[26] Whatever the shortcomings in his understanding of 1851, Zola did succeed in depicting the transformation of religious processions into republican demonstrations and of populist religious symbols (a peasant Virgin Mary) into republican imagery.

The extent to which the nascent political commitment of rural Frenchmen was inextricably linked to their religious beliefs can be seen perhaps even more clearly in the statements they made to government prosecutors, to middle-class observers, and to Montagnard leaders. Emile Buisson, an agricultural day laborer from St.-Amand-en-Puisaye (Nièvre), seemed to worship the republic as a sort of divine protector. Buisson told prosecutors that he joined Cosne's secret society and later took part in the insurrection "in order to prevent the resurgence of famine. I believe strongly that it was the republic that saved me. Without it, I would have died of hunger."[27] A peasant arrested for rebellion at St. Paul la Roche (Dordogne) explicitly associated the insurrection of 1851 with the traditional carnival that ushered in the Lenten season. At the height of the rebellion he reportedly exclaimed, "Today we are the strongest. What a celebration! The ultimate carnival, our peasant republic, has finally arrived. What a big feast we will have."[28] So apparently intertwined— for this peasant at least—were popular religious devotion and expressions of political sentiment that even the insurrection itself could be viewed as a huge carnival ritual. Indeed, the motley peasant bands that took up arms in central and southern France marched in columns resembling religious processions, and their pitiful military performance against units of the French army suggests that the insurgents were much more prepared for ritualistic expression than for armed combat![29]

Not only did the insurrection take the form of popular religious observance, but it seemed to have quasi-religious aims as well. Just as popular religious expression earlier in the century sought to invoke divine intervention in favor of worldly improvement, there is evidence that peasant insurrectionaries in 1851 viewed their armed ritual as a means of achieving divine intervention on behalf of the democratic and social republic. Peasants from Grane (Drôme) viewed insurrectionary successes as proof of God's favor. "How the good lord is pleased by our revolution," they triumphantly declared.[30]

Numerous other statements from humble Frenchmen eloquently confirm this juncture of populist religion and democratic politics. On the eve of the 13 May election the democ-soc newspaper *La Tribune de la Gironde* received a fifty-centime contribution from an anonymous donor who labeled herself "a young woman who loves God, the Republic and Ledru-Rollin."[31] In 1849 a peasant told the curé of Auxerre that he had been chosen by the local democ-soc leadership to "preach the new dogma to the peasantry and winegrowers of the surrounding villages." He added that he had already begun his effort to "evangelize them."[32] A well-off cultivator from Cosne (Nièvre) defended himself before the Mixed Commission by declaring: "I wanted nothing more than an orderly society, for I was a good republican according to the doctrine of Jesus Christ."[33]

Often, rural Frenchmen who expressed allegiance to the republican left viewed democ-soc leaders in much the same way they pictured Jesus and the saints—that is, as human beings who possessed supernatural qualities. Thus, during the 1849 carnival of Paulhan (Hérault), an agricultural laborer donned red robes and draped around his neck a medallion containing a portrait of Barbès, the great republican martyr. Referring to the medallion, he proclaimed, "I'm carrying God on my chest."[34] Similarly, secret society members in the Yonne often carried to their clandestine meetings portraits of Ledru-Rollin, Barbès, Victor Hugo, and Louis Blanc, whom they referred to as "saints."[35] Finally, in a letter replete with incorrect grammar and misspelled words, a village wheelwright named Philippe Bouché told Joigneaux that *La Feuille du village* was for him "the symbol of truth and justice. For [your newspaper] is none other than the life of Christ." What Bouché went on to say is worth quoting at length:

> From the moment of its birth, it [*La Feuille du village*] was just like Christ. It had its own King Herod to attack it. *La Feuille du village* is like Christ, for it has the power to accomplish prodigious miracles. It enables the blind to see, the deaf to hear, the mute to speak. It can turn tortuous paths into straight ones. . . . Christ was persecuted and he descended into his tomb only to be resurrected on the third day. Victorious, he would live forever. Charitable *Feuille du village*, we invoke your name on behalf of the Republic, our mother. And we ask you to continue your charitable aid toward your grown children who are dangerously sick. It is only with your help that they can obtain a perfect cure. For it is you who possess the remedy for all our ills. We choose you as our protector. It is you alone who can guide us toward a happy future.[36]

One could hardly ask for a clearer expression of the transformation of rural religiosity into an attachment to the democratic and social republic. In the past villagers worshiped saints, Jesus Christ, and the Virgin as a means of securing protection from worldly dangers and the promise of a better life. After 1848 rural Frenchmen began to transfer that devotion to republican saints. Now it was a democ-soc newspaper, a Montagnard editor, or the Mother-Republic herself that, deified by the people, would bring them comfort, progress, and well-being. As Bouché put it to Joigneaux, whom the wheelwright saw as a kind of patron saint: "It is you who possess the remedy for all our ills. We choose you as our protector. . . ."

The political discourse of literate artisans from France's larger provincial towns also demonstrates this interpenetration of democ-soc commitment and populist religiosity. More sophisticated, artisans from places like Clamecy (Nièvre) and Auxerre were less likely than their village brethren to canonize democsoc leaders or to view them as earthly protectors. They tended instead to portray their commitment to democratic socialism as the logical extension of their religious beliefs. In a report attached to the enquête of 1848, a typesetter from Auxerre described his republican commitment and belief in producers' cooperatives as "based entirely on the maxims of Christ, who said 'help one another' and urged that the strong support the weak."[37] An Auxerre carpenter ended his contribution to the same enquête with the statement:

> Ever since the holy evangelical doctrines were disfigured in order to serve the passions of men, ever since rulers disguised the truth under a mask of falsehood, there has been no real faith. The real religion, the religion of Christ, therefore, has long been misunderstood. And that real religion *citoyens représentants*, is none other than socialism, none other than fraternity.[38]

Beyond the ways in which the propagation of democ-soc ideology transformed popular religious expression, what other evidence is there for the penetration of Montagnard ideas into the consciousness of rural Frenchmen? One striking example of this penetration can be seen in the custom of *entraide* among peasant cultivators. Practiced in regions where peasants lived in villages as opposed to dwelling on isolated farms, the entraide dictated that whenever one villager was too sick to harvest his own crops, his neighbors would band together to till his fields collectively. In the columns of *La Feuille du village*, Joigneaux repeatedly likened this tradition to the socialism advocated by the republican left, arguing that, in collectively aiding their neighbors, peasants displayed a commitment to the democratic and social republic.[39] After all, cooperative labor founded on sentiments of Christian fraternity was one of the primary goals of Montagnard ideology. Through this comparison Joigneaux sought to encourage allegiance to the republic by altering the peasants' consciousness about important elements of their own behavior. He endeavored, in other words, to use propaganda to turn existing conduct into a self-conscious act of devotion to the republic. The journalist's effort was simply a corollary to the democ-socs' principal task: the transformation of popular religiosity into republican commitment through the propagation of new ideas.

There is evidence that the attempt on the part of Joigneaux and others to infuse the tradition of entraide with democ-soc ideas achieved some success, especially in regions in which peasants were exposed to *La Feuille du village*. According to *Le Républicain démocrate*, a Montagnard journal from Dijon, villagers from the Burgundy town of Alise-Sainte-Reine gathered periodically during the summer of 1851 to cultivate collectively the vines of a neighbor stricken with an incurable disease. This effort differed from earlier manifestations of entraide in that the assembled villagers vociferously sang the "Marseillaise" as they worked. What could be a better way of demonstrating commitment to the democratic and social republic than to sing a song considered subversive by the pseudo-republic of Louis Napoleon. *Le Républicain démocrate* reported a similar event in the village of Nod-sur-Seine (Côte-d'Or), where "a column of democratic workers gathered last Sunday [in May 1851] at 4 A.M. to finish the work of a comrade [a winegrower] who had fallen ill."[40]

The correspondence of Marseille's *Voix du peuple* provides further evidence of the penetration of democ-soc ideas into the rural practice of entraide. According to a Monsieur Mastroul from the village of Eyragues (Bouches-du-Rhône), "a local republican cultivator who had been sick for a long time" received fraternal aid from 160 of his coreligionists. Early one morning, this small army of peasants gathered on the sick man's property to seed his fields and cut his madder (a plant used for making dye). They accomplished in three hours what would have taken one man fifty days. This *phalange républicaine*, as Mastroul called it, revealed its political commitment by performing its labor to the tune of two democ-soc songs, the "Marseillaise" and Pierre Dupont's "Chant des travailleurs."[41] Once again, intracommunal cooperation had been transformed into an expression of allegiance to democ-soc values.

In addition to accepting the Montagnard idea of cooperative labor, rural Frenchmen demonstrated belief in its fundamental corollary, the droit au travail. When vineyard workers near Béziers found themselves unemployed in May 1850, they staged a violent demonstration to demand, among other things, that proprietors be obliged to give them work. And in the Gard, agricultural laborers imposed a kind of de facto droit au travail by simply going to work without being hired and then demanding pay for their day's labor.[42]

More than simply politicizing popular culture, democ-soc ideology also helped to channel the people's anger and frustration into political actions such as voting and peaceful demonstrations that were consistent with republican legality. In 1850 peasants from the Limousin village of La Celette found that a local proprietor had erected a fence around land on which they had been accustomed to pasture their animals. Before 1848 the peasants might have simply knocked down the fence or taken some other extra-legal action against the landlord. But in 1850, influenced by democ-soc propaganda, they journeyed into town to ask local Montagnard leaders how they should respond. The leaders counseled calm and suggested that a better response than violent demonstration would be to vote for the Montagnard left. The peasants did just that. It is important to note, moreover, that in taking the advice of urban militants, these Limousin cultivators broke with a long tradition of hostility to town-dwelling politicians.[43] Not only, therefore, did Montagnard ideology help to overcome town/country antagonism in this region, but it also served to forge a peasant commitment to republican legality and democratic procedure.

The behavior of these Limousin peasants was not an isolated

phenomenon. After 1848 violence subsided throughout the countryside as rural Frenchmen turned overwhelmingly to the ballot box. In the nationwide legislative election of May 1849 some 70 percent of France's eligible voters—most of them rural—actually cast ballots.[44] This was a remarkable turnout, for during the First Republic—the only other period in which peasants exercised direct suffrage in national elections—less than 10 percent of eligible peasant voters bothered to cast ballots.[45] Since democ-soc propagandists worked very hard to convince peasants of the fundamental importance of the right to vote, it is highly likely that Montagnard ideology played a major role in producing this rural commitment to electoral democracy.

That more than 35 percent of the rural electors in virtually every department of southern and central France voted for the democ-socs in May 1849 provides further evidence for the penetration of Montagnard doctrine. The election of May 1849 was the first electoral contest of the Second Republic in which the ideological positions of the major contenders were clearly distinguished. Thus, a vote for the democ-socs in 1849 was more likely to signify a commitment to political doctrines than was a December 1848 vote cast in favor of Louis Napoleon. This conclusion is reinforced by an examination of the ballot itself: in 1849 voters chose not among individuals competing in local electoral districts but rather among department-wide lists of candidates nominated by party organizations in each department. Since electors personally knew few of the candidates on these lists, they were forced to vote for political tendencies and not for individuals.[46]

Even when the government's electoral reform of 31 May 1850 removed some three million (out of a total electorate of ten million) peasants and workers from the electoral rolls, rural Frenchmen stuck to legal means of protest. They expressed their profound bitterness over the emasculation of the institution that they believed promised them political and social equality by signing petitions against the new law.[47] Though a few Montagnard leaders did believe that insurrection represented the only proper response to this electoral betrayal, the peasants were content to petition for the restoration of universal suffrage.

Those who joined secret societies nevertheless pledged that, if suffrage were not restored by election day 1852, they would employ armed force to reconquer that fundamental democratic right.[48] If all else failed, violence would be used not to seize state power but to resurrect the republican legality that they believed held the key to revolutionary change.

Even during the 1851 insurrection itself, peasants demonstrated a commitment to republican legality and an unwillingness to vent social frustration through violence. Criticizing the hysteria that colored the conservative press's portrayal of the rebellion, the procureur général at Aix wrote: "There have been none of the murders, the pillages, and other horrors that one might justly expect . . . indeed a certain moderation, a certain legality—you will excuse the term—can be seen in the acts and speeches of the leaders."[49] Similarly, M. Correnson, a *juge d'instruction* from the Bouches-du-Rhône, declared that "there is no evidence of even a single assault against individuals, and the attacks against property are, with but two or three exceptions, of minor importance."[50] Even the archconservative journal *Le Courier de la Drôme* admitted that, "incredible as it may seem, this savage horde did not indulge in a single excess."[51]

Though isolated examples of crowd brutality occurred in Béziers and Clamecy, insurrectionaries throughout the country exercised the same restraint evident among those in the jurisdiction of Aix's procureur général. Rural rebels showed much more interest in seizing symbols of political power—city hall, subprefectures, and the like—than in pillaging the rich and avenging social frustration,[52] two phenomena that had characterized earlier peasant rebellions. The insurrection of 1851 differed from the *jacqueries* of the past because the consciousness of its participants had been conditioned by democ-soc ideology. Montagnard publicists had argued throughout the Second Republic that violence was not the key to social renovation and economic equality. Both would result from the normal operation of republican democracy. Insurrection, they maintained, could be justified solely in the event of a violation of the republic's fundamental political institutions. The purpose of such an insurrection would be to restore popular sovereignty and constitutional legality, not to redress social and economic inequity. In sparing persons and property while participating in local seizures of power designed to install a democratic and social republic, the rural rebels of 1851 demonstrated the extent to which they had been influenced by Montagnard ideology. The intervention of democ-soc ideas had helped to transform peasant protest into a means of expressing commitment to an egalitarian republic.

The Montagnards' propaganda against violent outbursts may have helped to condition peasant political commitment, but it did little to prepare Frenchmen for resistance to Louis Napoleon's coup d'état. When insurrectionaries were faced with the reality of armed combat in December 1851, they tended to scatter and run. Jean Thibeyrenc, a cultivator from Boujon, testified that "as soon as we [the rebel columns from Boujon] arrived in front of the town hall [of Béziers] we heard the roar of gunfire coming from the Place de la Sous-Préfecture. Immediately, we disbanded and rushed back home. Along the way, we threw away our [red] belts and got rid of our weapons."[53] Very few rebels had really expected to fight. In the words of Jacques Broit, a potter from St. Sauveur: "We were told that there would be no need to fight, that we were simply to march to defend the republic."[54]

Even when rebels faced no more than token resistance, they still tended to display a certain decorum. Thus, in order to ring the tocsin and thereby announce the insurrection, Amédée Patassan, rebel leader from St. Sauveur, politely asked the curé for keys to the church. He then marched to the mayor's house to procure the keys to town hall.[55] Records of the Mixed Commissions provide further examples of the legalistic scruples of individual rebels. After insurrectionaries captured the town hall of Servian (Hérault), a peasant cultivator named Etienne Gouron cried out: "Because the Constitution was violated, the people have had to recapture their rights and name a provisional commission."[56] In justifying the rebels' actions through references to the constitution, this peasant leader betrayed clearly the influence of democ-soc ideas.

An exchange between Jean Thibeyrenc, who cooperated extensively with his prosecutors, and the Hérault's Mixed Commission provides further insight into the mentality of peasant leaders.

QUESTION: Isn't it true that it was promises of gaining other people's land and revenge against the rich . . . that provoked you to rebel.

RESPONSE: No Monsieur, I never heard those sorts of promises.

QUESTION: How is it that if the secret society had nothing but political goals (as you indicated earlier), affiliates nevertheless rose up to cries of "death to the rich" . . . and during the insurrection they committed assassinations and sought to pillage the rich?

RESPONSE: What explains these disorders is that there were all kinds of people in our societies. In principle, we didn't accept individuals who had ever been convicted of a crime, but in recent months . . . the society discriminated less and less. It began to enroll even the worst subjects of our communes. Many of us were opposed to this policy because we saw that this sort of indiscriminate recruitment would lead to some serious disorders.[57]

Thibeyrenc's testimony can probably be taken at face value because it is consistent with the relative decorum that the rebels actually displayed and because the rest of his responses are unusually candid. He admitted to being both a secret society leader and the chief of an armed band, and he provided details about the clandestine organization and his role in it. Seldom did rebel leaders make such avowals, for such candor tended to result in harsh judicial treatment. Thibeyrenc was deported to Algeria for his role in the insurrection.

What do Thibeyrenc's statements suggest about the morality of peasant leaders? They indicate an aversion to vengeful violence and a desire for institutions dedicated to political change and unencumbered by "bad subjects." The effect of democ-soc ideology and four years of political experience was to forge in at least some peasants a certain degree of political sophistication.

All of this evidence suggests, then, that democ-soc ideas did penetrate the consciousness of humble French peasants and artisans and that these new ideas helped to condition their political behavior from 1849 to the insurrection of 1851. Many rural Frenchmen did not realize—until it was too late—the risks they took in acting in accordance with such a new and roughly formed consciousness. But, perhaps because their new political commitment had been fashioned out of a popular religiosity in which miracles and the supernatural played a large role, these unassuming villagers—like their democ-soc mentors—possessed the faith that they would prevail. The coup d'état and the ensuing cycle of resistance and repression shattered these illusions. Saumur Breton, a shoemaker from St. Sauveur, probably spoke for many of his peers when he told prosecutors: "I cannot explain in an absolutely clear way exactly why I took up arms. I believed it was for the good of France, and because I was inexperienced I acted in accordance with my ideas. . . ."[58]

CHAPTER VIII

THE DÉMOCRATE-SOCIALISTE LEGACY

The preceeding analysis has shown how a nascent republican party transformed economic malaise, political discontent, and populist religiosity into a commitment to socialist democracy. It suggests that 1848 does indeed mark a revolutionary turning point, for this era gave birth to mass democratic politics in France. The new political institutions of the Second Republic converted a monarchical regime that had restricted suffrage to a tiny elite (some 250,000 in 1846) into a system of mass democracy. That this transformation occurred while France remained predominantly rural provided peasantry and republican politicians alike with a precocious initiation to democratic politics. And it stamped French republicanism with a uniquely rural character. The fundamental democ-soc achievement of 1849-1851 was to instill in a large segment of the French rural community a commitment to the ideas, values, and institutions of democratic socialism.

How did the institutions of mass politics and the accompanying politicization of ordinary Frenchmen affect the later development of French republicanism? It has become a commonplace of French electoral geography to consider the legislative contest of 1849 to be the origin of modern French voting patterns. Indeed, the electoral maps of 1877, 1914, and 1936 bear remarkable resemblance to that of 1849. One of the most striking aspects of May 1849 is that it marked the "birth of a left-wing tradition," as one prominent historian put it.[1] Having expressed allegiance to the democ-soc left in 1849 (and during the by-elections of 1850 as well), the largely rural regions of the Alps, Provence, Lower Languedoc, the Limousin, and major sections of Burgundy and the Center tended to vote Radical in the 1870s and 1880s, and they began to turn to the Socialists at the end of the century. Some—the Cher, for example—even voted for the French Communist Party after 1920.[2] Moreover, despite all the changes that have taken place in France since the Second World War, certain traditions have remained. The peasants of the Limousin, who have been "rouge" since 1849, voted in large numbers for the Communists in the legislative election of 1978. The Socialists won a comfortable plurality in 1978 in the Nièvre, Cher, Allier, and the Drôme, as they did consistently between 1898 and 1936. The inhabitants of Lower Languedoc obeyed a tradition more than a century old when they voted left in March 1978.[3] And so the list continues.

To be sure, the correspondence between 1849 and 1936 or 1978 is far from exact. The Ardèche voted for the extreme left in 1849 but turned to the right early in the Third Republic. Just as the French left lost certain departments over the years of the Third Republic, so it gained others. By 1914 industrial expansion and economic crisis had helped to create a left-wing electorate in departments such as the Pas-de-Calais and the Ardennes where there had been little support for the democ-socs in 1849.[4]

How did the left-wing *prise de conscience* of the Second Republic become a political tradition, and why did that tradition last so long? In pointing out the similarity of the electoral maps of 1849, 1885, and 1936 in eastern Burgundy, Pierre Levêque argued that the persistence of voting patterns resulted from the "slow rate at which [French] rural societies evolved. . . . The defeat of the Montagnards [in 1851] in no way abolished the durable objective conditions, social and psychological in nature, which would facilitate the reconquest of these territories in the near future."[5] Thus, Levêque explains the persistence of left-wing commitment by emphasizing the factors that provoked the original awakening in 1849. Raymond Huard, on the other hand, suggests that it was the republicanization of multitudes of "political intermediaries" during the Second Republic that enabled left-wing allegiance to outlast Louis Napoleon's empire:

> Hundreds of individuals in [the Gard] . . . exercised responsibility in political or politicized organizations. No other

movement could count on an equal number of intermediaries for the task of reaching the masses. After the coup
d'état, the vast majority of these men, constrained to political silence, nonetheless remained in intimate contact with
the popular classes. . . . The presence of these hundreds
of militants, many of whom were quick to resume their
political activity during the last years of the empire, put
the republican movement in an infinitely more favorable
position in 1870 than it was in 1848.[6]

Both of these explanations are plausible, and both factors
undoubtedly played a role in creating the French rural tradition
of leftism. But, in addition to these reasons, was there not
something about the democ-socs' ideology—namely its religious intensity—that played a powerful role in rooting left-
wing convictions profoundly and lastingly in the consciousness
of rural Frenchmen? The tenacity of this rural commitment to
the extreme left in certain regions of southern and central France
cannot be fully explained by referring to social and economic
structure or through analysis of political organizations and organizing. Ideological commitment must be taken into account
as well, and this study has tried to demonstrate how the inter-
section of economic conditions, popular religiosity, and democ-
soc propaganda and ideology forged new political allegiances in
rural France.

The democ-socs bequeathed to their republican heirs a complicated legacy, for their ideology underlies the two most influential doctrines of the Third Republic: radicalism and socialism.
The Second Republic's democratic socialism stemmed from a
coalition of political forces and social strata. Democrats who had
been little interested in the social question prior to June 1848
united with socialists who had been more interested in utopian
experiments than mass politics. These once-disparate political
tendencies elaborated a common ideology founded on a shared
Christian morality and attuned both to the social question and
to democratic politics. They endeavored at the same time to
forge a broad-based social coalition that joined peasants, rural

and urban artisans, small tradesmen, and petty entrepreneurs, as well as minor officials and members of the liberal professions. Parallel religious beliefs on the one hand and, on the other, the need for a united front against a common conservative enemy held this coalition together despite the social and cultural differences that divided its component parts. The coalition's center of gravity tended toward its left-most—that is, socialist—flank, for the failure of the Provisional Government and the bloody-mindedness of General Cavaignac had thoroughly discredited moderate republicanism. The effect of this leftward orientation and of the transposition of Christian images of fraternity and brotherhood into political form was to stress socialism and the social question as much as democracy. Democ-socs held that neither socialism nor democracy had any meaning in isolation from one another and that a republic could not be a true republic unless it was democratic and social. Socialism, then, was portrayed as the republic in its purest and most complete form: it was the republic carried out to its logical conclusion. In 1850 middle-class republicans could readily embrace socialism, because that doctrine did not yet stand for the abolition of private property. Socialism would be introduced through a kind of "collectivization from below" in which each enterprise would be the jointly owned private property of all those who composed its work force.

Two additional factors help to explain middle-class support for the radical aspects of Montagnard ideology. There existed as yet no independent working-class movement capable of staking out its own position on the French left. And the most politicized and class-conscious sector of the working class was composed of skilled artisans and not factory proletarians. The radical aspirations of skilled artisans were compatible with those of middle-class democ-socs: both groups accepted republican institutions as the framework for revolutionary change, and both believed that such transformation could come about gradually through the logic of universal suffrage.[7]

It took more than thirty years for this coalition to dissolve into two separate political tendencies—radicalism and socialism—and this dissolution resulted from a number of economic and political factors. Some of the most important of these are the coup d'état, the concentration of industry and the rise of a vocal factory proletariat, the Paris Commune, the depression of the 1880s, and, finally, the failure of the democratic republic, once that regime was definitively established in 1879-1881, to be social, to commit itself to the aspirations of France's least privileged citizens. Despite the dissolution of the Second Republic's Montagnard alliance, the ideology of its two political heirs owes a great deal to that original coalition.

Though the explicitly Christian thrust of the democ-socs' ideology became progressively secularized during the Second Empire and the early 1870s, the Montagnards succeeded nonetheless in transmitting a powerful religiosity to their heirs. For the Radicals of the 1870s and 1880s,* republicanism, rather than being the product of profound Christian belief, became a religion itself. Thus, between 1852 and 1880 republicanism was dechristianized without losing the religious intensity that had helped to create the Montagnards' original doctrine.

Even during the Second Republic certain exiled democ-soc spokesmen anticipated this despiritualization of Montagnard doctrine. Félix Pyat, for example, moved beyond the view that republicanism and socialism amounted to applied Christianity to declare that republicanism itself was the new religion, an innovative dogma that transcended the Christian principles on which it was based. For this Montagnard publicist, republicanism embodied "the religion of Christ enlarged, accomplished, and completed by modern philosophy. . . . It is a real religion . . . that realizes what Jesus did no more than desire. . . . Our own religion, our faith, our law, our dogma, our patrie, our love, our Church, our mother—is none other than the Republic."[8] Whereas for most democ-socs the republic was divine because it rested on Christian principles, Pyat came to believe that divinity resided precisely in the tenets of republicanism. God spoke through the people, Pyat argued, therefore popular

---

* Proper political labeling is somewhat confusing here, for early in the Third Republic the terms "republican" and "opportunist" were given to a political position that throughout most of the 1870-1940 period would be labeled "radical."

sovereignty was sacred. Under the republic *"le peuple* is spiritually sovereign just as it is sovereign in the temporal world. . . . *Le peuple* is the true successor to Christ, the sole worldly representative of God. *Vox populi, vox Dei."*[9] Christ had brought the republican message down to earth, and now that it had landed, it could shed its explicitly Christian garb. Pyat concluded his attempt to deify the republic with words that suggest the intellectual process by which republicans ultimately moved from the religiosity of 1848 to the official atheism of the Third Republic. "France," Pyat proclaimed, "is neither Catholic nor atheist. It is republican. Our own revelation is that liberty, equality, and fraternity are ideas just as absolute, just as eternal and just as divine as the dogma of the Holy Trinity."[10] It was but one more step in the same direction to Jules Ferry's attempt to raise republicanism to the status of secular state religion.

During the final months of the Second Republic certain other democ-soc spokesmen, especially in the realm of education, began to dechristianize Montagnard religiosity by portraying the republic itself as the new religion. In the words of Antony Duvivier, a democ-soc schoolteacher from the Nièvre, it is up to *"maîtres de l'école,* humble apostles of modern democracy, to advertise far and wide our political gospel, and to *republicanize* France. . . . Let us raise our intelligence and our hearts to the level of a sacerdocy."[11] For Duvivier, republicanism was the new Gospel and schoolteachers were its apostles. Taking up the question of education in September 1851, *L'Union républicaine* echoed Duvivier in proposing to elevate schoolteachers to the rank of apostles of a new republican religion. This new apostolate would provide "the pupils of municipal schools with a sort of political catechism in which the constitution would be explained and developed through questions and responses. Traditional religious songs would be replaced by hymns to the patrie, to fraternity, liberty, to all the civic virtues. . . ."[12] The anticipation of Jules Ferry is clear. The religiosity of the democ-socs helped perhaps to create the missionary zeal with which the Radicals set out after 1880 to erect their republican state.

Although Second Republic democratic socialism anticipated the deified republic of 1880, its main contribution was to lay the ideological foundation for French socialism. Analysis of the discourse and programmatic statements of fin-de-siècle socialists, both at the national and at the local level shows remarkable continuity with the moral-spiritual fervor and doctrinal positions of the democ-socs. Like the Montagnards of the Second Republic, socialist leaders of the late century argued that socialism simply translated the humane values of justice and equality into practice. To the question "What is a socialist?" a working-class editorialist from Carmaux replied in December 1889:

> He is a man who . . . wants to transform [society] in a more equitable direction. . . . What does he want? . . . He wants justice for everyone. . . . He wishes that the rich were less selfish . . . and that those who give their strength [and] their health were better paid. . . . It is not fair that those who have worked their whole lives have harvested only misery for their old age, while those who do not work possess everything.[13]

Except for the absence of overtly Christian language, this statement bears striking resemblance to the démocrates-socialistes' definition of socialism as the realization of justice.

Statements by Jean Jaurès, the towering genius of French socialism, reveal even more dramatically, the parallels between mid- and late-century socialist ideology. Jaurès constructed his own political theory and practice out of a moral perspective rooted in Catholic religiosity. He defined socialism as "a regeneration of the moral ideal," and he argued that socialism's strength stemmed in large part from its deep reservoir of spirituality:

> Superficial observers see in the socialist movement only a groundswell of covetousness, just as they saw only the exterior and material side of Christianity, the Reformation, and the French Revolution. More than anything else, socialism contains a spirit, a conscience, an extraordinary need for morality and human perfection. . . . Socialism can be defined as follows: a moral revolution which must be facilitated and expressed by a material revolution. At the same time, *it will be a great religious revolution.*[14]

Jaurès's statement echoes the moralistic socialism of 1848 and suggests that democ-soc religiosity may have profoundly influenced what became the mainstream of French socialism.

Jules Guesde claimed that his religion was Marxism, but he too presented socialism in more classically religious terms. The leader of France's officially Marxist Parti ouvrier français told Emile Zola that socialism promised an "Eden, a means of escape from the capitalist mire."[15] A correspondent for *Le Normand socialiste* described one of Guesde's 1891 lectures as a kind of quasi-religious experience: "The orator, worked up to a frenzy of enthusiasm, painted a sumptuous portrait of the socialist future. There will be justice, he cried. [Socialism] is the messiah, it is redemption. It is the promised land. Won't you enter it?"[16]

Another crucial element of continuity between the democ-socs of 1849 and the socialists of 1890 was the belief that socialism was simply the republic honed to a state of perfection. Far from seeing a contradiction between republicanism and socialism, late nineteenth-century socialists, like their Montagnard ancestors, believed that socialism represented the fulfillment of the republican ideal: it was the republic made social. In December 1891 a meeting of 1,400 Carmaux miners and glassworkers nominated a committee to choose ten working-class candidates to the municipal council. One of those present at the meeting declared that the ten candidates would "hold firm and high in their calloused hands the flag of the social republic."[17] When Carmaux miners crowned their successful strike of 1892 with the election of Jaurès to the Chamber of Deputies and a socialist to the mayoralty, spokesmen declared that the "seed of the social republic" had been planted.[18] And when the town's glassworkers went out on strike in 1895, they issued an appeal to the "workers, socialists, and republicans of France."[19]

After 1890 the belief that the republic contained all the necessary seeds of socialism and that the former alone made the latter possible spanned the entire spectrum of French socialism. The different factions within this spectrum appeared to disagree about nearly everything except this fundamental premise. In his writings and parliamentary speeches Jaurès repeatedly stressed his belief in an organic and necessary relationship between the republic and socialism. Like his democ-soc predecessors, the socialist tribune maintained that the republic sowed the seeds of socialism and that a socialist society represented nothing more than the perfection of the republican order. In an 1893 speech before The Chamber of Deputies Jaurès declared: "Socialism proclaims that the political republic must lead to the social republic . . . and that is why socialism grows out of the republican movement. The republic is the originator, it is the great leader."[20] Five years later his discourse remained unchanged: "Socialism is an integral part of the historical tradition of democracy. It forges a new order without breaking the profound continuity of republicanism. And in political combat it touches the very essence of the republic."[21]

For Jaurès, the republic not only led necessarily to socialism, but it could not long survive without socialism, for a fundamental contradiction existed between the republic's "principle of universal suffrage and the premises of capitalism."[22] This incompatibility between capitalism and the republic meant, Jaurès told France's deputies, that no government could endeavor to preserve the existing economic system "without deserting the principles of republicanism."[23] "Socialism," Jaurès added, "grows so obviously, so powerfully out of our republican institutions . . . that in order to fight socialism, you condemn yourselves to the work of reaction in all realms—political, fiscal, and syndical. . . . Since you abandon the politics of republicanism, it is we socialists who will take it over."[24]

Like the democ-socs, Jaurès criticized capitalism not for being structurally flawed but rather for violating the moral and political principles of the republic. Republican institutions gave workers and peasants full political rights, but the capitalist economic system subverted those rights by depriving common people of power and authority in the economic realm. Jaurès argued that "the worker has the same right to direct the affairs of the nation as the greatest entrepreneur, but he possesses no power in the operation of the factory."[25] Jaurès believed that universal suffrage would ultimately resolve this contradiction, for as a "revolutionary legality," suffrage "served as a constant reminder of equality, as a permanent protest against the state of social minority into which capitalism locks the working class. [Universal suffrage] . . . threatens to shake up the very basis of capitalist society."[26] These statements about capitalism, socialism, and the republic echo those of the democ-socs and provide additional evidence of substantial ideological continuity from the democratic socialism of the 1840s to the mainstream socialism of the fin de siècle.

Since Jaurès owed much of his intellectual formation to the archrepublican Ecole normale supérieure, it is not surprising that allegiance to the republican tradition should have conditioned Jaurèsian socialism. It is somewhat more startling to find evidence of similar republican commitment from France's leading formulaic Marxist, Jules Guesde. Buoyed by the socialist electoral gains of the early 1890s, Guesde and his associates in the Parti ouvrier français (POF) abandoned their opposition to democratic politics and joined Jaurès in the belief that the republic would lead the way to socialism. In 1893 the Marxist leader told Lille workers that "*legally*, by your will turned into law, social transformation will be accomplished."[27] Five years later, Guesde maintained to a working-class audience that the republic was the "necessary instrument of their emancipation."[28] And Guesde's friends on the editorial staff of Le Socialiste (Lille) wrote in 1893 that working-class hopes lay "in the transformation by means of universal suffrage of the corrupt republic [*république panamiste*] of the present day into a social republic."[29]

While Guesde and his supporters from the industrialized North laced their Marxist rhetoric with odes to the transformative power of the social republic, self-proclaimed Guesdists from the Center and South employed a discourse even more in line with the democ-soc heritage. The inaugural issue of Le Petit Montluçonnais, Guesdist organ of the Allier, featured an ideological statement that could have been copied from one of its mid-century democ-soc predecessors: "We are socialist republicans. Republicans because the republic is the complete and definitive form of democracy. Socialists because socialism is the natural and necessary capstone of the Republic."[30] The Socialiste de *l'Allier,* founded in 1895 and endorsed by Guesde, Jaurès, and Karl Marx's Guesdist son-in-law, Paul Lafargue, promised to "support with all its forces the interests of the working class against the propertied class. It will champion labor against capital, and it will back the republican avant-guarde in all political battles."[31] Members of the POF's Vaucluse federation presented themselves as "republicans of good faith" who sought to achieve collectivism by relying exclusively on "universal suffrage, the revolutionary weapon of our century."[32] And in the Gironde the POF's 1898 parliamentary candidate proclaimed: "I am a collectivist socialist, but above all, my allegiance is to the great republican family [*la grande famille républicaine*]."[33]

Fin-de-siècle socialism in the Var shows the same kind of continuity with the Montagnard politics of 1849-1851. Socialist spokesmen from the Var, mainly affiliated with the POF, did not call for a new socialist system to replace the existing republic. They sought rather to fulfill the republican promise by substituting a "social" republic for the prevailing "bourgeois" one.[34] Thus, like their colleagues elsewhere in southern and central France, Var socialists intended no break with the republican tradition. They wanted simply to apply the social ideals of that tradition to the real world.

The political platform of the Var's fin-de-siècle socialists shows a doctrine strikingly similar to that of the mid-century Montagnards. The socialist program presented to the Var peasantry between 1890 and the First World War sought to achieve:

> The establishment of a ministry of labor. Nationalization of banks, mines, railways, canals, insurance companies, large farms, energy sources, and the slate and quarrying industries. Minimun wages for all factory, workshop, and farm workers. . . . Legal maximum limits on the length of the working day. A single progressive income tax. Government-financed credit facilities for farmers. . . . Reduced tariffs for the transportation of fertilizer.[35]

The demands contained in the democ-soc platform of 1849 were remarkably similar:

The right to employment [*droit au travail*]. Nationalization of insurance, banking, railroads, canals, all forms of communication, and mines. Progressive taxation. Tariff reform. State-guaranteed credit facilities for cultivators and workers. State-encouraged producers' cooperatives and other means of association.[36]

Early in 1848 the Provisional Government enacted a legal maximum limit on the length of the working day, and Louis Blanc's attempts to establish a workers' ministry are well known. Though the Montagnard program never mentioned minimum wages and the nationalization of large farms, the prewar socialist platform closely resembled its 1849 predecessor. Both sought a large measure of state intervention to protect the poor and to encourage the economic and political independence of small producers through cooperatives and easy credit.

Not only did both Jaurèsians and Guesdists, Parisians and provincials, extoll the virtues of the democ-socs' social republic; so did the leaders, membership, and sympathizers of the nation's other major socialist and labor organizations. Edouard Vaillant, head of France's neo-Blanquists, believed that socialism could not even be conceived of, let alone realized, without the republic.[37] And Jean Allemane, founder of a small socialist faction allied to anarcho-syndicalism, seconded Jaurès's and Guesde's attachment to the nation's republican institutions.[38] Ordinary workers and trade-union rank-and-filers, less drawn to doctrinal dispute than their leaders, guarded France's republican traditions perhaps even more jealously than did their mentors. As Yves Lequin, one of France's foremost labor historians, put it:

This working class . . . did not really feel separate from the great republican mainstream, which in its different forms had governed France since 1876. And this attachment coexisted, without conflict, with the working class's revolutionary dream; indeed, the workers' feeling of eminent dignity turned into a belief that the working class, itself, served as both the soul and the surest defender of the republic. Instinctively, the working class suspected any political current which might threaten the republic's exist-

ence. . . . The feeling of belonging to the republican community was such that each time a group affirmed an explicit
ideology, everyday political practice obliged it to overlook
principles and immerse itself once again in the dominant
republican tide.[39]

Thus, even workers who claimed to be revolutionary showed
little interest in the doctrines and principles of an explicitly
revolutionary ideology. Their commitment, highly religious in
quality, was to a moralistic and messianic socialist republicanism
that formed part of the legacy of 1848. The religiosity that had
spawned the Second Republic's democratic socialism returned
in secular garb after 1880 as the moral and spiritual underpin-
ning of fin-de-siècle socialism. This moralistic spirituality resonated with the lingering religiosity—albeit dechristianized—
of France's workers and peasants, and it helped to anchor many
of them to the nondoctrinaire socialism exemplified by Jean
Jaurès. This socialist republicanism, then, became a complete
and deeply rooted system of belief that, despite factional conflict
at the national level, undergirded the whole of the French left.
So influential was this eclectic and moralistic socialism that it
succeeded in virtually excluding Marxism from pre-First World
War France.

Most of the nation's socialists viewed Marxism as an alien
and largely inscrutable dogma, and even self-proclaimed Marx-
ian disciples like Jules Guesde and Paul Lafargue understood
little of their master's theory. When the French edition of *Das
Kapital* first appeared in 1875, leftists' responses ranged from
indifference to a vaguely nationalistic hostility characteristic of
the era's anti-German atmosphere.[40] In 1882 Possibilist leader
Paul Brousse manifested this left-wing nationalism by likening
French Marxists to ultramontane Catholics: both belonged to
movements lead by a foreigner. Marxists, Brousse declared, "are
the ultramontanes of socialism. . . . The ultramontanes cannot
obey the laws of their country because their leader is in Rome.
The Marxists cannot obey the decisions of the party and its
congresses because their real leader is in London."[41]

Not only did French socialists resent the efforts of Marx and

Engels to influence their movement from abroad, but they also found Marxism—an ideology inconsistent with the language and traditions of French socialism—difficult to grasp. In 1903 the socialist federation of the Yonne explicitly rejected Marxism in favor of France's "eclectic socialism." Marxist doctrines, the federation objected, were "confusing and intangible."[42]

It seems that even Marx's leading French disciples found their mentor's ideology abstruse. POF leaders claimed that Guesde never studied Marx—he didn't need to, they said—and Guesde himself admitted that Marxism had little to do with his becoming a socialist. When asked in 1893 about his intellectual formation, Guesde responded: "I became a republican during the [Second] Empire by reading *Les Châtiments* by Victor Hugo. I became an atheist by reading Kant's *Critique of Pure Reason*. And it was the Commune that made me a socialist."[43]

Paul Lafargue's Marxist credentials were only slightly stronger. He attempted to popularize his father-in-law's ideas in a work entitled *Course in Social Economy on the Economic Materialism of Karl Marx*, but the book displays only a vague acquaintance with the master's theory. And when Lafargue received volume two of *Das Kapital*, he confessed to an inability to make any sense of it.[44] Marxism played only a minor role in Lafargue's intellectual background; like Guesde, he had come to socialism by way of the Enlightenment and France's tradition of moralistic republicanism.[45] Marx and Engels were painfully aware of their French disciples' doctrinal lapses, and Engels's letters to Lafargue bristle with frustration over the latter's ignorance.[46]

Marxism failed, then, to take hold even among those who claimed to be its principal French champions. To most of France's socialists, Marxism seemed a largely irrelevant and obscure creed, a Germanic import that could not speak to their experience or ring true to their cultural and ideological traditions. These traditions had shaped the religious-based socialism of 1848, producing an ideology so rooted in French religious and political culture that its legacy would help to ensure the lingering weakness of Marxism in France.

APPENDIX

Democ-Soc Publications Still Circulating and Specifically Outlawed in Central France on the Eve of the Coup d'Etat (November 1851) (Source: Archives of the Ministry of War, C8 186-187)

NEWSPAPERS

L'Alliance des peuples
L'Allobrage
L'Ami du peuple
Le Bien-être universel
Le Censeur
Le Démocrate
La Démocratie pacifique
Le Drapeau du peuple
L'Eclaireur républicain
La Feuille du peuple
La Feuille du village de Joigneaux
Le Nouveau Monde (de Louis Blanc)
Le Patriote des Alpes
Le Patriote savoisien
Le Peuple de 1850
Le Peuple souverain
Le Populaire de Cabet
Le Prolétaire
La Propagande
La Réforme
La République
La République universelle
Le Semeur républicain
La Sentinelle républicaine de Saint-Etienne

La Solidarité
La Voix du peuple
La Voix du peuple de Manelli
Le Vote Universel

ALMANACS

L'Almanach de l'ami du peuple
        des associations ouvrières pour 1850
        des Blancs
        du cultivateur et du vigneron
        Démoc-soc
        de l'égalité
        napoléonien
        du nouveau monde
        des opprimés
        phalansterien
        populaire de la France
        des proscrits
        de Raspail
        des réformateurs
        républicain démocratique
        la république du peuple
        du travail par Agricol Perdiguier
        du village par Joigneaux

WRITINGS AND BROCHURES

L'Abolition de l'autorité
Aux paysans de France (Pyat)
Bases futures de l'édifice social
Le Berger de Kravan par Eugène Sue
La Bible des idées nouvelles
Le Catéchisme rouge
Catéchisme social ou exposé succinct de la doctrine
La Constitution de la démocratie
De la république de Chenu et de la Hodde par J. Miot
De la solidarité par Greppo

Deux jours de condamnation à mort par Barbès
Du Gouvernement Provisoire par Deville
L'Evangile du peuple par Esquiros
L'Evangile et la République
Le Guide du peuple dans les élections
L'Histoire de la Convention par Léonard Gallais
L'Histoire de la Révolution par le même
L'Histoire des martyrs de la liberté
L'Histoire des Montagnards par Esquiros
*L'Histoire d'une famille de prolétaires à travers les âges par le
    même*
Instructions pour le peuple
Jésus-Christ devant les conseils de guerre
Jugement dernier du vieux monde social par M. Hess
Loisir d'un proscrit par Félix Pyat
La mort de Jésus, tragédie par Sauriac
Le page au 19ᵉ siècle par Mazzini
Le Pape devant le Christ
Plus de Girondins
Plus d'octroi, plus de droits réunis
Prêtres et socialistes
La propagande, c'est la révolution
Qu'est ce que la propriété
Rèponse à Chenu et à ses complices
Reponse aux deux libelles: les conspirateurs et la naissance
Les revenants
Les Soldats du pape
La Solution ou le gouvernement direct du peuple
La Terreur blanche
Le Vieux monde devant le monde nouveau

LITHOGRAPHS

Jésus le Montagnard
Galerie des républicains socialistes (album)
*Gravures ou lithographies représentant les individus inculpés
    dans le procès de Lyon*

SONGS

"La Chanson des transportés par Dupont"
"Le Chant des soldats par Dupont"
"La Lyonnaise"

ABBREVIATIONS

AD	Archives Départementales
ADBA	Archives Départementales, Basses-Alpes
ADCD	Archives Départementales, Côte-d'Or
ADY	Archives Départementales, Yonne
AHDG	Archives of the Ministry of War (Archives Historiques du Département de la Guerre)
AN	Archives Nationales
APP	Archives de la Préfecture de Police
BN	Bibliothèque Nationale
DBMOF	*Dictionnaire biographique du mouvement ouvrier français*
1848	*La Revolution de 1848* (journal published by the Société d'histoire de la Révolution de 1848)
JM	Justice Militaire (collection in AHDG)
SSC	Sociétés Secrètes, Cosne (in AD Nièvre, Series U)
UR	*L'Union républicaine*
VP	*La Voix du peuple* (Marseille)

NOTES

Introduction

1. Maurice Agulhon, *1848 ou l'apprentissage de la République*, Nouvelle histoire de la France contemporaine, 8 (Paris: Editions du Seuil, 1973), and Agulhon, *Les Quarante-huitards* (Paris: Editions Gallimard/Julliard, 1975).

2. Jacques Bouillon, "Les Démocrates-socialistes aux élections de 1849," *Revue française de sciences politiques*, 6 (1956), 78.

3. Ibid., p. 88.

4. Maurice Agulhon, *La République au village* (Paris: Plon, 1970); André Armengaud, *Les Populations de l'Est aquitain au début de l'époque contemporaine (vers 1845-vers 1871)* (Paris: Mouton, 1961); Georges Dupeux, *Aspects de l'histoire sociale et politique du Loir-et-Cher, 1848-1914* (Paris: Mouton, 1962); Alain Corbin, *Archaïsme et modernité en Limousin au XIXᵉ siècle 1845-1880*, 2 vols. (Paris: Rivière, 1975); Philippe Vigier, *La Seconde République dans la région alpine*, 2 vols. (Paris: Presses Universitaires de France, 1963).

5. Agulhon, *La République au village*; Vigier, *La Seconde République dans la région alpine*.

6. One of these leading prewar republican historians, I. Tchernoff, literally skips over the entire period from July 1848 to December 1851. See Tchernoff's *Le Parti républicain sous la Monarchie de Juillet* (Paris: Pedone, 1901) and *Le Parti républicain au coup d'état et sous le Second Empire* (Paris: Pedone, 1906).

7. Gordon Wright, *France in Modern Times* (Chicago: Rand McNally, 1974), p. 53.

8. Charles Tilly, "How Protest Modernized in France, 1845-1855," in W. Aydelotte, ed., *The Dimensions of Quantitative Research in History* (Princeton: Princeton University Press, 1972), pp. 192-255. See also, Tilly, "Collective Violence in European Perspective," in Hugh Graham and Ted Gurr, eds., *Violence in America* (Washington: Government Printing Office, 1969), pp. 4-44; Charles Tilly and Lynn Lees, "The People of June," in Roger Price, ed., *Revolution and Reaction: 1848 and the Second French Republic* (New York: Barnes & Noble, 1975), pp. 170-209.

9. Ted W. Margadant, *French Peasants in Revolt: The Insurrection of 1851* (Princeton: Princeton University Press, 1979).

10. Ted W. Margadant, "The Insurrection of 1851" (Ph.D. diss., Harvard University, 1972); John M. Merriman, *The Agony of the Republic* (New Haven: Yale University Press, 1978).

11. Maurice Agulhon, "L'Agriculture et la société rurale du Var dans la première moitié du XIXe siècle," in *Etudes d'histoire Provençale* (Paris: Ophrys, 1971), pp. 137-210; Agulhon, *La République au village*. The changes in patterns of social interaction that Agulhon describes had particular meaning in southern France. Midi village life embodied a sociability that facilitated intense social interaction both within and among social classes. This sociability was the product of the peculiar cultural traditions and residence patterns of the South. Because peasants dwelled within the walls of their Mediterranean bourgs and not on isolated farmsteads, they lived in close proximity to other social groups and were sheltered from the domination of landowners.

12. William H. Sewell Jr., "La Classe ouvrière de Marseille sous la Seconde République: Structure sociale et comportement politique," *Le Mouvement social*, 76 (July-September 1971), 27-65; Sewell, "The Structure of the Working Class of Marseille in the Middle of the Nineteenth Century" (Ph.D. diss., University of California, Berkeley, 1971); Sewell, "Social Change and the Rise of Working-Class Politics in Nineteenth-Century Marseille," *Past & Present*, 65 (November 1974), 75-109; Sewell, *Work and Revolution in France: The Language of Labor from the Old Regime to 1848* (Cambridge: Cambridge University Press, 1980).

13. See Eugen Weber, *Peasants into Frenchmen: The Modernization of Rural France, 1870-1914* (Stanford: Stanford University Press, 1976).

14. See the memoirs of both Martin Nadaud and Agricol Perdiguier: Nadaud, *Mémoires de Léonard*, ed. M. Agulhon (Paris: Hachette, 1976); Perdiguier, *Mémoires d'un compagnon* (Paris: Maspero, 1977).

15. For a study of Cavaignac's moderate republican government, see Frederick A. de Luna, *The French Republic under Cavaignac 1848* (Princeton: Princeton University Press, 1969).

CHAPTER I. ECONOMIC ROOTS OF POLITICIZATION

1. Maurice Lévy-Leboyer, "La Croissance économique en France au XIXe siècle," *Annales: Economies, Sociétés, Civilisations*, 23 (December 1968), 788-807; Lévy-Leboyer "Le Processus d'industrialisation: Le cas de l'Angleterre et de la France," *Revue historique*, 239 (1968),

281-298; T. J. Markovitch, "La Révolution industrielle: Le cas de France," *Revue d'histoire économique et sociale*, 52 (1974), 115-125; Markovitch, "L'Industrie française de 1789 à 1964. Conclusions générales," *Cahiers de L'Institut de science économique appliqué*, series AF, no. 7 (November 1966); Markovitch, "Le Revenu industriel et artisanal sous la Monarchie de Juillet et le Second Empire," *Economies et sociétés*, no. 4 (April 1967); J. Toutain, *La Production de l'agriculture française, 1700-1958*, vols. 1-2 of *Histoire quantitative de la France* (Paris: Cahiers de L'Institut de science économique appliqué, 1961).

2. Thanks in large part to J. Marczewski's *Histoire quantitative de la France*, 8 vols. (Paris: Cahiers de L'Institut de science économique appliqué, 1961-1967), recent economic historians have been able to measure the substantial economic growth that earlier economic historians missed. In their vain search for "take-off" points and in their attempts to gauge economic growth by counting steam engines and agricultural consolidations, earlier scholars overlooked the relative dynamism of the French economy between 1815 and 1850. Indeed, both agriculture and industry grew faster between 1800 and 1850 than between 1850 and 1900. In addition to the *Cahiers de L'Institut de science économique appliqué*, see François Crouzet, "French Economic Growth in the Nineteenth Century Reconsidered," *History*, 59 (1974). For a typical older view of French economic history, see J. H. Clapham, *The Economic Development of France and Germany* (Cambridge: Cambridge University Press, 1936).

3. François Crouzet found that industrial production nearly doubled between 1815 and 1854, while agricultural production increased by 47%. Crouzet, "Encore la croissance économique française au XIXe siècle," *Revue du Nord*, 62 (1972), 276. William H. Newell found that agricultural output grew by 47% between 1815 and 1849. Newell, "The Agricultural Revolution in France, an Exchange," *Journal of Economic History*, 36 (1976), 438. For population figures, see Charles H. Pouthas, *La Population française pendant la première moitié du XIXe siècle* (Paris: Presses Universitaires de France, 1956), pp. 34-35; J. Toutain, "La Population de la France, 1700 à 1959," *Cahiers de L'Institut de science économique appliqué*, series AF, no. 3 (January 1963). Pouthas found a population increase of 21.2% between 1806 and 1846, while Toutain observed a 22.8% growth during the same period.

4. Fernand Braudel and Ernest Labrousse, eds., *Histoire économique et sociale de la France*, 3 vols. (Paris: Presses Universitaires de France 1968-1976), 3:291-297. Railroads transported 6.3 million passengers

in 1841 and more than three times as many ten years later. The number of letters doubled between 1830 and 1847 and increased by 459% between 1830 and 1870.

5. Markovitch, "Revenu," pp. 87-88.

6. William H. Newell, "The Agricultural Revolution in Nineteenth-Century France," *Journal of Economic History*, 33 (December 1973), 717.

7. Ibid., p. 725; Maurice Agulhon et al., *Histoire de la France rurale*, vol. 3 (Paris: Editions du Seuil, 1976), pp. 134-138.

8. The paragraph follows Newell, "Agricultural Revolution."

9. Roger Price, "The Onset of Labor Shortage in Nineteenth-Century French Agriculture," *Economic History Review*, ser. 2, 28 (1975), 262.

10. Agulhon et al., *France rurale*, p. 134; Newell, "Agricultural Revolution," p. 721.

11. Margadant, *French Peasants in Revolt*, pp. 85-87. Margadant first formulated the North/South distinction in economics and politics that I use extensively in this chapter.

12. Vigier, *La Seconde République dans la région alpine*, 1:26-34.

13. Ibid. See also Daniel Faucher, *Plaines et bassins du Rhône moyen entre Bas-Dauphiné et Provence* (Paris: A. Colin, 1972), pp. 456-481. Intended for local consumption, potatoes substituted for grains in providing basic nourishment and thus freed former cereal land for the production of cash crops.

14. Vigier, *La Seconde République dans la région alpine*, 1:57, 68-69.

15. Ibid., p.57.

16. Ibid.

17. Ibid.

18. M. Gimel, *La Division de la propriété* (Nancy: 1883), p. 15. It is highly probable that the bulk of these land transfers took place between 1826 and 1851. Since the number of *cotes foncières* (individual landed domains) increased 31.8% between 1826 and 1851, but only 17.9% between 1851 and 1871, land subdivision must have been much more active before 1851 than during the Second Empire. See *Bulletin de statistique et législation comparés*, 12 (1882), 321-325. The question of land subdivision is analyzed in more detail later in this chapter.

19. Vigier, *La Seconde République dans la région alpine*, 1:37.

20. Vigier, *La Seconde République dans la région alpine*, 1:36-40; Agulhon et al., *France rurale*, p. 114. On the average, prices of major agricultural products declined 31 percent between 1817 and 1851. The

wages of agricultural laborers increased 35 percent during the same period.

21. Archives Nationales (hereafter AN) C 946.

22. Agulhon, "L'Agriculture et la société rurale," pp. 163-180. Tax officials estimated that wine production increased by a factor of four between 1815 and 1848.

23. J.-B. Avril, "Response à la commission d'enquête sur la consommation et la production de la viande, 27 avril 1851," cited in André Thuillier, *Economie et société nivernaises au début du XIXe siècle* (Paris: Mouton, 1974), pp. 89-93.

24. O. Delafond, *Progrès agricole et amélioration du gros bétail de la Nièvre* (Paris: 1849), p. 97.

25. Newell, "Agricultural Revolution," pp. 707, 725; Guy Thuillier, *Aspects de l'économie nivernaise au XIXe siècle* (Paris: A. Colin, 1966), pp. 89-93.

26. G. Thuillier, *Aspects de l'économie nivernaise,* p. 89.

27. Ibid., pp. 89-95.

28. Pierre Levêque, "La Bourgogne, 1830-1851" (Doctorat d'Etat, Université de Paris IV, 1977), pp. 265-285.

29. Ibid., vol. 6, pp. 114-116; Pierre Gougon, "Le vignoble du Saône-et-Loire au XIXe siècle (1815-1870)" (Doctorat du 3e Cycle, University of Lyon, 1968), p. 132.

30. Agulhon et al., *France rurale,* p. 85; Toutain, "Population," p. 56.

31. Jean Duplex, *Atlas de la France rurale* (Paris: A. Colin, 1968), pp. 83-163; Toutain, "Population," p. 56. Most rural departments reached their population peaks in the 1840s and 1850s.

32. Goujon, "Vignoble du Saône-et-Loire," pp. 117-118. See also Levêque, "La Bourgogne," vol. 6, pp. 91-92, 114-116.

33. Agulhon et al., *France rurale,* p. 113.

34. Vigier, *La Seconde République dans la région alpine,* 1:87.

35. Ibid., p. 58.

36. Ibid., p. 91.

37. Agulhon, "L'Agriculture et la société rurale," p. 163.

38. Ibid., p. 167.

39. Ibid., p. 173.

40. Levêque, "La Bourgogne," p. 373, and vol. 6, p. 173. Tax figures refer to the Côte-d'Or alone.

41. Ibid., p. 376.

42. Goujon, "Vignoble du Saône-et-Loire," p. 210.   •

43. Margadant, *French Peasants in Revolt,* pp. 57-58.

44. Ibid., pp. 58-60; *Statistique de la France. Resultats généraux de l'enquête décennale de 1862* (Strasbourg: 1870), pp. lxxxviii, 150.

45. See Ernest Labrousse, ed., *Aspects de la crise et de la dépression de l'économie française au milieu du XIXᵉ siècle, 1846-1851*, Bibliothèque de la Révolution de 1848, 19 (La Roche-sur-Yon: Imprimerie centrale de l'ouest, 1956); Vigier, *La Seconde République dans la région alpine*; Dupeux, *L'Histoire sociale et politique du Loir-et-Cher*.

46. See AN C 946, 954, 960, 969.

47. Cited in Margadant, *French Peasants in Revolt*, p. 58.

48. Ibid., p. 80; AN C 954.

49. Margadant, *French Peasants in Revolt*, p. 64.

50. Gimel, *Division de la propriété*.

51. M. Gimel, "La Répartition de la propriété foncière dans le département de l'Yonne," *Annuaire historique de l'Yonne* (1865), p. 18. In the Yonne between one-half and two-thirds of the new *cotes* of one hectare or less represented purchases by farmers from bordering communes.

52. Levêque, "La Bourgogne," vol. 6, pp. 117-119.

53. Corbin, *Archaïsme et modernité*, 1:607-614.

54. Agulhon, "L'Agriculture et la société rurale," pp. 193-196. See also Price, "Labor Shortage"; Agulhon et al., *France rurale*, p. 139.

55. Agulhon et al., *France rurale*, p. 139.

56. Philippe Vigier, *Essai sur la répartition de la propriété foncière dans la région alpine* (Paris: S.E.V.P.E.N., 1963) p. 206. Beyond purely speculative purchases, bourgeois investors did buy vineyards in certain regions. See Raymond Dugrand, *Villes et campagnes en Bas-Languedoc* (Paris: Presses Universitaires de France, 1963).

57. Agulhon et al., *France rurale*, p. 114.

58. Ibid.

59. Ibid.

60. Ibid.; Vigier, *La Seconde République dans la région alpine*, 2:60-62; Levêque, "La Bourgogne," pp. 578-583; Christianne Marcilhacy, "Les Caractères de la crise sociale et politique de 1846 à 1852 das le département du Loiret," *Revue d'histoire moderne et contemporaine*, 6 (1959), 13. Ted Margadant, in *French Peasants in Revolt* (pp. 94-96), downplays the importance of peasant indebtedness during the July Monarchy and Second Republic on the basis of samples drawn from notarial records of loans. It is no doubt true, as Margadant argues, that the number and amounts of loans contracted before notaries was not excessive during this period. But the problem, as Pierre Levêque ("La Bourgogne," pp. 581-583) points out, is that most loans to peasant

cultivators were not contracted formally before a notary. Thus neither short-term usurious loans nor the common practice of third-party payment of promisory notes left written records. Levêque discovered these irregular transactions in the accounts of contemporary observers. Government officials, clergymen, travelers, and others described a fierce traffic in promisory notes in which a moneylender would advance the funds a peasant needed to pay off his notes. In this way, the peasant's *official* debt was replaced by an unrecorded unofficial debt, invariably at a higher rate of interest.

61. Philippe Vigier, "Le Paysan dans *Le Peuple* de Michelet," in *Michelet et "Le Peuple"* (Nanterre: University of Nanterre, 1975), p. 19: "Cet endettement rend le paysan beaucoup plus vulnérable à la conjoncture, et met fin à l'autonomie paysanne face à la société englobante."

62. Levêque, "La Bourgogne," pp. 290-291.

63. Goujon, "Vignoble du Saône-et-Loire," pp. 218-220.

64. Albert Soboul, *Paysans, sans-culottes et Jacobins* (Paris: Librairie Clavreuil, 1966).

65. *Statistique de la France. Territoire et population: Recensement de 1851* (Paris: 1855).

66. Any meaningful distinction between large and small industry—that is, between "Industry" and "Artisanat"—must be based on size of firm, not, as in the 1851 census, on the kind of goods produced. Use of the latter criterion meant that all textile manufacturers, for example, were placed under large industry, even though some—especially those who produced silk or linen cloth—employed no more than five workers.

67. I am indebted to William Reddy for pointing this out.

68. Crouzet, "French Economic Growth"; Crouzet, "Encore la croissance économique"; Lévy-Leboyer, Processus d'industrialisation, p. 296.

69. Crouzet, "French Economic Growth," p. 177. See also Braudel and Labrousse, eds., *Histoire économique et sociale*, 3:344. The question of why French basic industry got off to a slow and late start forms the basis of one of the oldest debates in French economic history. The position of the economic historians cited in this chapter, a position solidly grounded in an analysis of "factors of production," seems more useful than either David Landes's argument for the lack of "entrepreneurial spirit" in French businessmen or W. W. Rostow's insistence that successful industrialization requires a clearly identifiable "take-off" point. See David S. Landes, "French Business and the Business-

men: A Social and Cultural Analysis," in E. M. Earle, ed., *Modern France* (Princeton: Princeton University Press, 1951); Landes, *The Unbound Prometheus* (Cambridge: Cambridge University Press, 1969); Landes, "Social Attitudes, Entrepreneurship and Economic Development," *Explorations in Entrepreneurial History*, 6 (May 1954), 245-272; W. W. Rostow, *The Stages of Economic Growth* (Cambridge: Cambridge University Press, 1960; Rostow, *The Process of Economic Growth* (Oxford: Oxford University Press, 1962).

70. Lévy-Leboyer, "Croissance économique, p. 800.

71. Markovitch, "Revenu," p. 86; Christopher H. Johnson, "Economic Change and Artisan Discontent: The Tailors' History, 1800-1848," Price, ed., *Revolution and Reaction*, p. 87; Johnson, *Utopian Communism in France: Cabet and the Icarians, 1839-1851* (Ithaca: Cornell University Press, 1974), p. 158; Lévy-Leboyer, "Processus d'industrialisation," p. 287.

72. Crouzet, "Encore la croissance économique," p. 276. Industrial growth slowed to 1.6% per year in the second half of the century.

73. Pierre Ansart, *La Naissance de l'anarchisme* (Paris: Presses Universitaires de France, 1970), p. 66; Markovitch, "Revenu," p. 88.

74. Since population grew just 20% between 1815 and 1848, the 75% increase in industrial output could not have been the result simply of a growth in the work force. Even if the entire increase in population translated into an equivalent growth in the labor force—which was not the case—the sheer rise in the number of workers (productivity remaining the same) would have accounted for only a quarter of the growth in industrial production.

75. Johnson, "Economic Change," pp. 87-89; Georges Dupeux, *La Société française, 1789-1970* (Paris: A. Colin, 1964), pp. 125, 146.

76. Markovitch, "Revenu," p. 86.

77. Johnson, "Economic Change," p. 109.

78. Dupeux, *Société française*, p. 146. Real wages and prices fell steadily between 1817 and 1850. The decline in real wages was between 10 and 20%, depending upon the industry.

79. Johnson, "Economic Change."

80. Ibid.

81. Jeanne Gaillard, *Paris, la ville, 1852-1870* (Lille-Paris: Honoré Champion, 1976), p. 451; Paul Combe, "Thiers et la vallée industrielle de la Durolle," *Annales de géographie*, 31 (1922), 361-362.

82. Gaillard, *Paris*, p. 563.

83. Robert J. Bezucha, *The Lyon Uprising of 1834: Social and Political Conflict in the Early July Monarchy* (Cambridge, Mass.: Harvard

University Press, 1974), pp. 36-44; Ansart, *Naissance de l'anarchisme*, p. 156.

84. Mary Lynn McDougall, "After the Insurrections: The Workers' Movement in Lyon, 1834-1852" (Ph.D. diss., Columbia University, 1974); Ansart, *Naissance de l'anarchisme*, p. 147. Journeymen silk weavers joined their masters in massive demonstrations in favor of a *tarif*, or fixed minimum price for woven cloth, during the 1840s; Bezucha, *Lyon Uprising*, pp. 44-47 and passim.

85. Margadant, *French Peasants in Revolt*, pp. 80-81.

86. Ibid., p. 86; Jean-Claude Martinet, *Clamecy et ses flotteurs de la Monarchie de Juillet à l'insurrection des "Mariannes," 1830-1851* (La Charité-sur-Loire: Editions Delayance, 1975).

87. Martinet, *Clamecy et ses flotteurs*, pp. 36-58, 114.

88. Ibid.

89. Gaillard, *Paris*, p. 451; Johnson, "Economic Change," p. 87.

90. J. Vidalenc, *Le Département de l'Eure sous la Monarchie Constitutionelle* (Paris: M. Rivière, 1952), p. 683; P. Guillaume, "La Situation économique et sociale du département de la Loire d'après l'enquête sur le travail . . . du mai 1848," *Congrès national des sociétés savantes, actes, séction d'histoire moderne*, 86 (1961), 446.

91. AN C 946.

92. AN C 969.

93. AN C 969.

94. *Le Peuple souverain* (Auxerre), no. 7, 14 April 1848: "Profession de foi de l'ouvrier typographe Rousseau."

CHAPTER II. POLITICAL OPPOSITION AND POPULIST RELIGION

1. H. Malo, *Thiers* (Paris: Payot, 1922); William L. Langer, *Political and Social Upheaval* (New York: Harper and Row, 1969), pp. 520-527; A. Jardin and A. J. Tudesq, *La France des notables*, Nouvelle histoire de la France contemporaine, vol. 6 (Paris: Editions du Seuil, 1973), pp. 95-97.

2. Gérard Cholvy, "Expressions et évolution du sentiment religieux populaire dans la France du XIXe siècle au temps de la Restauration Catholique (1801-60)," in *Actes du 99e congrès national des sociétés savantes* (Paris: Bibliothèque Nationale, 1976), vol. 1, pp. 289-320; Agulhon, *La République au village*, p. 158.

3. Cholvy, "Expressions," pp. 302-303; Yves-Marie Hilaire, *Une Chrétienté au XIXe siècle? La Vie religieuse des populations du diocèse*

d'Arras 1840-1914 (Villeneuve-d'Ascq: University of Lille III, 1977), p. 63.

4. D. O. Evans, *Social Romanticism in France* (Oxford: Clarendon Press, 1951), p. 29.

5. Cited in ibid., p. 41.

6. Henri de Saint-Simon, *Le Nouveau Christianisme*, ed. H. Desroche (Paris: Editions du Seuil, 1969), p. 153.

7. It is by no means easy to discern the lines that divided democrats, republicans, socialists, and communists during the 1840s. Fourierists and Saint-Simonians tended to claim indifference to the quest for republican government and democratic institutions, but communists and other "socialists" believed in at least the temporary necessity of both. Cabet, founder of Icarian communism, showed allegiance to republicanism and to democratic political procedure. Louis Blanc considered himself at once a republican, a democrat, and a socialist, as did Pierre Leroux. For democratic parliamentarians and journalists like Ledru-Rollin and Garnier-Pagès, democracy and republicanism were synonymous. Often in accord on short-term objectives, the various groups differed over long-term goals. Radical politicians like Ledru-Rollin viewed democracy as an end in itself and subordinated the social question to the quest for such political reforms as expanded suffrage and freedom of the press. Cabet, on the other hand, saw democracy simply as the means by which to achieve his communitarian society. What united the two men in opposition to Fourierists and Saint-Simonians was their common belief that the Republic was a necessary precondition to all meaningful change. See M. Cuvillier, *Hommes et idéologies de 1840* (Paris: M. Rivière, 1956); Johnson, *Utopian Communism*; Georges Weill, *Histoire du parti républicain en France, 1814-1870* (Paris: Alcan, 1928); Paul Bastid, *Doctrines et institutions politiques de la Seconde République*, 2 vols. (Paris: Hachette, 1945), vol. 1.

8. Pierre Leroux, *Du Christianisme et de son origine démocratique* (Paris: 1848), p. 12.

9. Pierre Leroux, *Démocratie et Christianisme* (Paris: 1848), pp. 119-120.

10. Ibid., pp. 28ff. Leroux was not the only thinker of the period to identify Christianity with the revolutionary tradition. Alphonse Esquiros, in his *L'Evangile du peuple* (1841), wrote a history of Jesus in which the Christian messiah resembles closely a social revolutionary of '93. This book cost Esquiros eight months in prison. See also his *Histoire des Montagnards* (1845), p. 2: "La Révolution a été le bras

de Dieu, l'Evangile armé." Similarly, P. Buchez, in his *Historie parlementaire de la Révolution Française* (1834-1838), claimed that the popular sovereignty of 1793 was "Catholic in demanding that each be subject to all; it is Catholic in having a clear apprehension of the past, of the present and of the future; it is Catholic in recognizing a common nature in all mankind; . . . and finally it is Catholic in *proceeding directly from the influence of the Church*" (emphasis added). Cited by J. Droz, "Religious Aspects of the Revolutions of 1848 in Europe," in E. M. Acomb and M. Brown ed., *French Society and Culture Since the Old Regime* (New York: Holt, Rinehart and Winston, 1966).

11. *La Démocratie pacifique*, 2 November, 26 December 1843; Jacques Viard, "Michelet, disciple de Pierre Leroux," in *Michelet et "Le Peuple*," p. 5.

12. *La Démocratie pacifique*, 2 November 1843.

13. Ibid.

14. Johnson, *Utopian Communism*, p. 89; Georges Renard, "Cabet et les précurseurs de la Révolution de 1848," *La Révolution de 1848* (hereafter *1848*), 28 (1931), 183.

15. Johnson, *Utopian Communism*, pp. 100, 174.

16. Weill, *Histoire du parti républicain*, p. 242.

17. François-André Isambert, *Christianisme et classe ouvrière* (Paris: Casterman, 1961), p. 226.

18. F. Engels, *The New World and Gazette of the Rational Society*, 4 November 1843. Cited in Jean Bruhat, "Anti-clericalisme et mouvement ouvrier avant 1914," in François Bédarida and Jean Maitron, eds., *Christianisme et le monde ouvrier* (Paris: Editions ouvrières, 1975), p. 82 (my translation).

19. A. Spitzer, *Old Hatreds and New Hopes: The French Carbonari against the French Restoration* (Cambridge, Mass.: Harvard University Press, 1971); J. B. Duroselle, *Les Débuts du catholicisme social en France, 1822-1870* (Paris: Presses Universitaires de France, 1951), pp. 81-82.

20. Cited in Duroselle, *Débuts du catholicisme social*, p. 82.

21. Ibid., p. 83.

22. Ibid., p. 94.

23. *L'Atelier*, August 1841; Duroselle, *Débuts du catholicisme social*, p. 117; Armand Cuvillier, "L'Idéologie de 1848," *Revue philosophique*, 138 (October-December 1848), 418-419.

24. *L'Atelier*, April 1840, October 1844; Isambert, *Christianisme et classe ouvrière*, p. 223.

25. *L'Atelier*, 30 November 1842, quoted in Isambert, *Christianisme et classe ouvrière*, pp. 221, 226.

26. Ibid.

27. Saint-Simon, *Nouveau Christianisme*, p. 151.

28. Subtitled *Rédigé par une réunion de députés, de publicistes et de journalistes* (Paris: 1842). Referring to the *Dictionnaire* as the bible of moderate republicanism, Paul Bastid said, "Les publicistes démocrates s'y réferont religieusement" (Bastid, *Doctrines et institutions politiques*, 1:41). See also de Luna, *The French Republic under Cavaignac*, pp. 25-26.

29. *Dictionnaire politique*, p. 223.

30. Ibid., pp. 113-115.

31. See Leo Loubère, *Louis Blanc: His Life and His Contribution to the Rise of French Jacobin Socialism* (Evanston: Northwestern University Press, 1961).

32. Weill, *Histoire du parti républicain*, p. 242n.

33. Louis Blanc, *Histoire de dix ans*, cited in Isambert, *Christianisme et classe ouvrière*, pp. 164-165.

34. Ibid.

35. Georges Duveau, "Protestantisme et prolétariat en France au milieu du XIXᵉ siècle," *Revue d'histoire et de philosophie religieuses*, 31 (1951), 417-422. See also Weill, *Histoire de parti républicain*, p. 241.

36. Joseph Benoît, *Confessions d'un prolétaire* (Paris: Maspero, 1968), p. 59.

37. Duveau, "Protestantisme," pp. 417-421.

38. Nadaud, *Mémoires de Léonard*, ed. Agulhon, pp. 141, 325, 337.

39. Armand Cuvillier, *Un Journal d'ouvriers: "L'Atelier," 1840-1850* (Paris: Editions ouvrières, 1954), p. 177.

40. Johnson, *Utopian Communism*, p. 126; Georges Duveau, "L'Ouvrier de Quarante-huit," *Revue socialiste*, 17 (January-February 1948), 78. According to Duveau, the workers "ont plus de confiance dans ces bourgeois [social theorists] que dans leurs camarades qui se passent eux-mêmes en leaders et en théoriciens."

41. Duveau, "L'Ouvrier," p. 78.

42. See the proceedings of the conference on "Les Intermédiaires culturels," held at Aix-en-Provence, 16-18 June 1978 under the direction of Michel Vovelle.

43. Duveau, "L'Ouvrier," p. 78; Johnson, *Utopian Communism*, p. 149.

44. Johnson, *Utopian Communism*, p. 119.

45. René Guise, "Le Roman-feuilleton et la vulgarisation des idées politiques et sociales sous la Monarchie de Juillet," in *Romantisme et politique* (Paris: A. Colin, 1969), pp. 321-327.

46. Claude Pichois, "Les Cabinets de lecture à Paris durant la première moitié du XIXe siècle," *Annales: Economies, Sociétés, Civilisations*, 14 (1959), 521-534; Pierre Chaunu, "Eugène Sue, Témoin de son temps," *Annales: Economies, Sociétés, Civilisations*, 3 (1948), 302-303; Pierre Brochon, *Le Livre du colportage* (Paris: Gründ, 1954), p. 73; Archives Départementales, Yonne (hereafter ADY), 69T2-27, prefect to Minister of the Interior, 30 March 1825.

47. Maurice Agulhon, "Le Problème de la culture populaire en France autour de 1848," *Romantisme* 9 (1975), 55-56.

48. Ibid., p. 55.

49. Gérard Cholvy, "Biterrois et Narbonnais. Mutations économiques et évolution des mentalités à l'époque contemporaine," in Cholvy, ed., *Economie et société en Languedoc-Roussillon de 1789 à nos jours* (Montpellier: Faculté des lettres et sciences humaines de l'Université de Montpellier, 1978), p. 439: "Une troupe de colporteurs y [Béziers] repandait alors en [1834] à profusion les *Paroles d'un croyant.*" Langer, *Political and Social Upheaval*, p. 217.

50. F. de Lamennais, *Paroles d'un croyant* (Paris: Edition populaire, 1835), pp. 90-93.

51. Lamennais, *Livre du peuple* (Paris: 1838), p. 59.

52. Ibid., p. 39.

53. Gérard Cholvy, "Le Catholicisme populaire en France au 19e siècle," in B. Plongeron and R. Pannet, eds., *Le Christianisme populaire* (Paris: Centurion, 1976), p. 207; Duveau, "L'Ouvrier," p. 75; Brochon, *Colportage*, pp. 87-93; Augustin Dubois, *Les Anciens livres de colportage en Sologne* (Romorantin: Girard, 1938).

54. Cited in Cholvy, "Catholicisme populaire," p. 201.

55. Duveau, "Protestantisme," p. 417.

56. As Louis Chevalier has argued in *Classes dangereuses et classes laborieuses* (Paris: Plon, 1958).

57. Johnson, *Utopian Communism*, p. 206. Flaubert's Dussardier in *Sentimental Education* is a perfect example of the morally upright worker.

58. Paul Droulers, "Catholicisme et mouvement ouvrier au 19e siècle," in Bédarida and Maitron, eds., *Christianisme et le monde ouvrier*, p. 47.

59. Bruhat, "Anti-clericalisme," p. 82; Isambert, *Christianisme et classe ouvrière*, p. 232.

60. There is no recent full-length study of nineteenth-century working-class songwriters and their milieu. More than anyone else, Pierre Brochon has contributed to the awareness of these songs through his

excellent collection, *La Chanson française,* in two volumes: *Beranger et son temps* and *Le Pamphlet du pauvre* (1834-1851) (Paris: Editions sociales, 1954-1957). Brochon has also admirably fulfilled the task of compiling the life's work of Eugène Pottier, author of the "Internationale": Pottier, *Oeuvres complètes* (Paris: Maspero, 1966). For a hagiographic account of Pottier's life and work, see Maurice Dommanget, *Eugène Pottier* (Paris: Etudes et documentation internationales, 1971). The Bibliothèque Nationale (hereafter BN) has a huge collection of individual songsheets, often ill-printed and complete with drawings and caricatures. Many of these have never been published, and many are shelved under the BN call number Y^e 7185 (in folio). For other collections of nineteenth-century songs, see Pierre Brochon's bibliography in *Pamphlet du pauvre,* pp. 20-21.

61. Brochon, *Pamphlet du pauvre;* Dommanget, *Pottier,* p. 34.

62. See Edgar Leon Newman, "Sounds in the Desert: The Socialist Worker-Poets of the Bourgeois Monarchy, 1836-1848," in *Proceedings of the Third Annual Meeting of the Western Society for French History* (Austin: 1976), pp. 269-299. Thirty of the 39 worker-poets Newman studied were "strongly Christian," and most of the rest expressed some Christian message.

63. Cited in ibid., p. 271.

64. Ibid.

65. Ibid., p. 272.

66. Brochon, *Pamphlet du pauvre,* p. 39.

67. Ibid., pp. 96, 143.

68. Pierre Dupont, *Chants et chansons* (Paris: 1851).

69. Jean Delumeau, "Christianisation et déchristianisation, XVe-XVIIIe siècles," in *Etudes européennes. Mélanges offerts à Victor L. Tapié* (Paris: Publications de la Sorbonne, 1973), pp. 53-59; Delumeau, "Au sujet de la déchristianisation," *Revue d'histoire moderne et contemporaine,* 22 (January-March 1975), 111-131; Gabriel Le Bras, "Déchristianisation: Mot fallacieux," *Social Compas,* 10 (1963), 445-452; Le Bras, *Etudes de sociologie religieuse,* 2 vols. (Paris: Presses Universitaires de France, 1955-1956). Cf. Keith Thomas, *Religion and the Decline of Magic* (London: Weidenfeld and Nicholson, 1971), especially chaps. 6, 9, 21, 22.

70. Michel Vovelle, *Piété baroque et déchristianisation en Provence au XVIIIe siècle* (Paris: Editions du Seuil, 1973). In an exemplary study, Vovelle analyzes the content of some 16,000 wills as a means of measuring religious commitment during the eighteenth century. Observing a sharp decline in religious language, in requests for elaborate funeral

processions, and in gifts to the Church, Vovelle concludes that de-christianization did indeed occur in eighteenth-century Provence. The sharpest decline in the religious commitments of those wealthy enough to leave wills occurred after 1750.

71. Phillip T. Hoffman, "The Counter-Reformation and Rural Religion," unpublished paper presented to the Society for French Historical Studies, Bloomington, Indiana, March 1981.

72. Gérard Cholvy, "Réalités de la religion populaire dans la France contemporaine," in Bernard Plongeron, ed., *La Religion populaire dans l'occident chrétien* (Paris: Bibliothèque Beauchesne, 1976), pp. 155-156; André Latreille and René Rémond, *Histoire du catholicisme français* vol. 3 (Paris: Editions Spec, 1962), pp. 255-256.

73. Cholvy, "Réalités," pp. 155-156.

74. Cholvy, "Expressions," pp. 302-303; Hilaire, *Une Chrétienté,* p. 63.

75. Yves-Marie Hilaire, "Notes sur la religion populaire au XIXᵉ siècle," in *La Religion populaire* (Paris: Editions du Centre national de la recherche scientifique, 1979), p. 195: "L'éffacement de l'enseignement religieux traditionnel entraîne une résurgence d'une religiosité populaire pagane-chrétienne particulièrement sensible dans les régions ou l'encadrement ecclésiastique est le plus déficient."

76. Gérard Cholvy, "Un Saint populaire? La lente renaissance du culte de Saint-Roch dans le diocèse de Montpellier durant la première moitié du XIXᵉ siècle," in Cholvy, ed., *Béziers et le Biterrois* (Montpellier: Faculté des lettres de Montpellier, 1971), pp. 364-365.

77. Ibid.; M.-V. Le Meur, "Le Culte des saints dans le diocèse de Blois aux environs de 1840," *Cahiers de l'Institut d'histoire de la presse et de l'opinion,* 2 (1974), 23.

78. Le Meur, "Culte des saints," pp. 8-22.

79. Weber, *Peasants into Frenchmen.*

80. Cholvy, "Expressions," pp. 305, 320; Yves-Marie Hilaire, "La Pratique religieuse en France de 1815 à 1878," *L'Information historique,* 24, no. 2 (1963). Cholvy noted increased church attendance after 1830 in French Flanders, Metz, Besançon, Belley, Versailles, Angers, Nantes, Toulouse, Nîmes, Montpellier, and in the regions of Alsace and the Massif Central. He points out, moreover, that parents resumed sending their children to catechism classes and that the Agricultural and Industrial Survey of 1848 indicated that most French youths attended Sunday mass regularly until the First Communion.

81. Cholvy, "Expressions," pp. 319-320. Ultramontane priests tended to accept popular violations of doctrinal orthodoxy, whereas Gallicans,

influenced by Enlightenment strictures against irrationalism, sought
to impose purely Catholic ritual and belief.

82. Corbin, *Archaïsme et modernité*, p. 185.

83. C. Marcilhacy, *Le Diocèse d'Orléans au milieu du XIXe siècle* (Paris: Sirey, 1964), p. 370; my emphasis.

84. Archives Départementales, Basses-Alpes (hereafter ADBA), 50VV art. 7, canton Javie; emphasis in original.

85. Ibid., canton Barcelonnette.

86. Cholvy, "Réalités," p. 156.

87. Archives Départementales, Côte-d'Or (hereafter ADCD), IIV65* canton Dijon Nord.

88. ADBA 50VV art. 7, canton Noyers.

89. Ibid., canton Valonne.

90. Ibid., canton Sisteron.

91. Ibid., curé of Gaubert, canton Digne.

92. Marcilhacy, *Diocèse d'Orléans*, pp. 309-317.

93. Cited in René Luneau, "Monde rural et christianisation," *Archives des sciences sociales des religions*, 43, no. 1 (1977), 45.

94. ADBA 50VV art. 7, canton Barcelonnette.

95. Levêque, "La Bourgogne," p. 715; ADCD IIV 65*.

96. Cholvy, "Expressions," p. 308; Daniel Fabre and Jacques Lacroix, *La Vie quotidienne des paysans du Languedoc au XIXe siècle* (Paris: Hachette, 1973), p. 361; Luneau, "Monde rural," p. 41; ADBA 50VV art. 7.

97. Marcilhacy, *Diocèse d'Orléans*, pp. 309-317.

98. First published in 1904, Guillaumin's factual account of the life of a sharecropper named Tiennon is one of the classic descriptions of nineteenth-century rural France. See also Cholvy, "Expressions," p. 319.

99. Levêque, "La Bourgogne," p. 715.

100. Frédéric Mistral, *Mes origines: Mémoires et récits* (Paris: Plon, 1906), pp. 61-76.

101. Cholvy, "Expressions," p. 297.

102. ADBA 50VV art. 7, all cantons.

103. Ibid.

104. ADY V Mⁱⁱ7, 1832; Cholvy, "Saint populaire," p. 365.

105. ADCD IIV 65*.

106. Ibid. This source, a religious *enquête*, indicates that belief in the *maux des saints* was widespread in eastern Burgundy.

107. ADBA 50VV art. 7, canton Riez.

108. Ibid., curé of Barral, canton Digne.

109. Levêque, "La Bourgogne," pp. 720-723.
110. Agulhon, *La République au village*, p. 177.
111. ADBA 50VV art. 7, canton Mézel; emphasis mine.
112. Ibid., canton Les Mées.
113. Ibid., canton Digne.
114. Ibid., canton Moustier.
115. ADBA 6V¹, police chief of Digne to prefect, 15 Sept. 1848.
116. See for example, AN BB¹⁸ 983, 1127, 1185, 1197, 1216, 1321.
117. Cholvy, "Expressions," pp. 308-309; Hilaire, *Une Chrétienté*, p. 70.
118. AN BB¹⁸ 1127, royal prosecutor, Nancy, to Minister of Justice, 19 June 1825.
119. Michel Bée, "La révolte des confréries de charité de l'Eure en 1842-3," *Annales de Normandie*, 24, no. 1 (1974), 89-115.
120. Ibid., p. 98; emphasis mine.
121. Ibid., p. 115.
122. Agulhon, *La République au village*, p. 181.
123. Ibid., p. 182.
124. Weber, *Peasants into Frenchmen*, p. 342.
125. See the pioneering studies of popular literature and its diffusion by Geneviève Bollème: "Littérature populaire et littérature de colportage au XVIIIᵉ siècle," in François Furet, ed., *Livre et société* (Paris: Mouton, 1965) pp. 61-92; *La Bibliothèque bleue. Littérature populaire en France du XVIIᵉ au XIXᵉ siècles* (Paris: Julliard, 1971); *Les Almanachs populaires aux XVIIᵉ et XVIIIᵉ siècles* (Paris: Mouton, 1971).
126. Robert Darnton, "In Search of Enlightenment," *Journal of Modern History*, 43 (1971), 113-131.
127. Cholvy, "Expressions," pp. 308-309.
128. Bollème, "Littérature populaire," p. 66.
129. Ibid.; Bollème, *Bibliothèque bleue*, p. 16.
130. Brochon, *Colportage*, p. 96.
131. Dubois, *Livres de colportage en Sologne*, p. 19.
132. Brochon, *Colportage*, pp. 87-88; Albert J. George, "The Romantic Revolution and the Industrial Revolution in France," in James Friguglietti and Emet Kennedy, eds., *The Shaping of Modern France* (New York: Macmillan, 1969), pp. 240-248; Agulhon, "Culture populaire," p. 54.
133. Brochon, *Colportage*, pp. 88, 97; George, "Romantic Revolution and Industrial Revolution," p. 240.
134. Weber, *Peasants into Frenchmen*, pp. 456-457.
135. ADY VI M¹2 16, 5 Feb. 1833.

136. Agulhon, "La Culture populaire autour de 1848" (unpublished paper, Davis Center of Princeton University, 1974), pp. 35-36.

137. Cited in Cholvy, "Expressions," pp. 305-306.

138. Bollème, "Littérature populaire," p. 77.

139. Brochon, *Colportage*, p. 46; Bollème, "Littérature populaire," p. 78. Dubois, *Livres de colportage en Sologne*, p. 20: "Le peuple savait par coeur toutes les chansons des colporteurs, tellement il les avait entendues de fois, et il apprenait ainsi les grands faits de notre histoire, les actions des hommes illustrés, les noms marquants de *l'Ancien* et du *Nouveau Testament*."

140. Bollème, "Littérature populaire," p. 77.

141. Benoît Malon, "Fragment de mémoires," *Revue socialiste*, 45 (January-July 1907), 318-319.

142. Cholvy, "Réalités," p. 164; Brochon, *Colportage*, p. 56; Latreille et Rémond, *Catholicisme français*, pp. 255-256.

143. Bollème, "Littérature populaire," pp. 77-80.

144. Ibid., p. 78.

Chapter III. The Montagnard Party

1. Agulhon, *Les Quarante-huitards*, pp. 11, 23.

2. Quoted in Peter McPhee, "The Crisis of Radical Republicanism," *Historical Studies*, 16 (April 1974–October 1975), 72. See also Agulhon, *Les Quarante-huitards*, pp. 169-176, for a penetrating analysis of the dilemma that the June Days posed for the republican left.

3. Nadaud, *Mémoires de Léonard*, ed. Agulhon. See the editor's important introduction and p. 343.

4. Agulhon, *Les Quarante-huitards*, pp. 169-176.

5. AN AB^{xix} 683, Ledru-Rollin's speech before the Banquet du Châtelet aux Champs-Elysées, 22 Sept. 1848.

6. Bastid, *Doctrines et institutions politiques*, 1:63.

7. BN Cabinet des Estampes, Vinck collection of lithographs. Cabet's speech before the banquet of 22 Sept. 1848.

8. *La République*, 19 Oct. 1848.

9. Ibid.

10. Ibid.

11. Gabriel Mortillet, "La Propagande, c'est la Révolution," Paris 1848, AN AB ^{xix} 680; and "La Solidarité républicaine, Association pour le développement des droits et des intérêts de la démocratie" (statutes of the organization), Paris 1848, BN LB 54 1461.

12. Ibid.

13. Mortillet, "La Propagande."

14. Peter Amann, *Revolution and Mass Democracy: The Paris Club Movement in 1848* (Princeton: Princeton University Press, 1975).

15. Archives de la Préfecture de Police (hereafter APP) AA 432, police report, "Propagande démocratique et sociale" 2 March 1849.

16. BN LB 55 2202, prospectus of "La Propagande démocratique et sociale européenne," Paris 1848.

17. Ibid.

18. Mortillet, "La Propagande," p. 35.

19. APP AA 432, report, 25 Feb. 1849.

20. APP AA 432, 2 March 1849.

21. AN BB[18] 1449, Minister of Interior to Minister of Justice, 10 Feb. 1849: "[La Propagande est] en un mot, une affaire bien organisée et sur des bases solides." See also APP AA 432, report of 25 Feb. 1849.

22. AN BB[18] 1449, Minister of Interior to Minister of Justice, 10 Feb. 1849; APP AA 432, report 25 Feb. 1849.

23. APP AA 432, "Note sur la Propagande de 1849."

24. A law of 2 Jan. 1849 overhauled the French postal system and established a uniform nationwide postage for letters. See also Brochon, *Colportage*, pp. 87-88.

25. APP AA 432, 2 March 1849: "Cette organisation est la plus habile et la plus dangereuse de toutes les combinaisons de l'esprit révolutionnaire; elle deviendra, si elle ne l'est déjà devenue, une véritable puissance dans l'Etat. La presse sans cautionnement est plus que remplacée; elle est dépassée par les petits livres de la Propagande démocratique et sociale européenne."

26. AD Bouches-du-Rhône, 6 M 344, Minister of Interior to prefects, circular, 15 Nov. 1851.

27. APP AA 432, 2 March 1849; preceding quotation same reference.

28. Ibid. La Propagande démocratique et sociale européenne clearly resembles the propaganda network that Cabet organized during the July Monarchy, and it is not unlikely that Mortillet and Ballard used the Icarian experience as their model. See Johnson, *Utopian Communism.*

29. APP AA 432.

30. BN LB 55 2202. At the end of July 1851 La Propagande was in the black for 552 francs, 39 centimes. The original stockholders included the following Representatives of the People: Michel (de Bourges), Eugène Sue, V. Schoelcher, Greppo, Perdiguier, Arago (Emmanuel), Emile de Girardin, J. Miot, and Pelletier. In addition, there were five socialist writers, one socialist schoolteacher, an ex-president of the

Conclave socialiste, an ex-president of the Commission de secours pour les familles de détenus politiques, the director of *La Feuille du peuple*, the editorial secretary of the same paper, the former editor of the *Tribune des peuples*, a painter, a printer, a doctor, an accountant, two foreign political refugees, and one property owner.

31. AN BB[18] 1494, dossier on police surveillance of the press; BN LB 55 2202, the stockholders' report, July 1851.

32. Marcel Dessal, *Un Révolutionnaire jacobin: Charles Delescluze, 1809-1871* (Paris: M. Rivière, 1952), pp. 94-95; J. Maitron et al., *Dictionnaire biographique du mouvement ouvrier français, 1789-1864*, 3 vols. (Paris: Éditions ouvrières, 1964-1966).

33. Archives Historiques du Département de la Guerre (hereafter AHDG) F[1] 40, document entitled "Bulletin de la Solidarité." On 23 Jan. 1849 La Solidarité owed Ledru-Rollin Fr 5,000; it was the organization's only major outstanding debt. See also Agulhon, *1848*; Levêque, "La Bourgogne," p. 1303.

34. *Gazette des tribunaux*, 11 April 1850.

35. Dessal, *Un Révolutionnaire jacobin*; Maitron et al., *Dictionnaire*.

36. *La Voix du peuple* (hereafter *VP*), 13 Nov. 1848.

37. BN LB 54 1461, La Solidarité républicaine's statutes, art. 19.

38. BN LB 54 1461, La Solidarité républicaine's statutes; *VP*, 13 Nov. 1848.

39. *Gazette des tribunaux*, 11 April 1850.

40. BN LB 55 2803, Haute Cour de Versailles.

41. See Gabriel Perreux, *La Propagande républicaine au début de la Monarchie de Juillet* (Paris: Hachette, 1930). La Société des droits de l'homme made a valiant effort to organize in the provinces between 1832 and 1834, but the slowness of transportation and the unreliability of the postal system presented insurmountable obstacles to this early attempt to establish a nationwide organization. La Solidarité républicaine nonetheless learned from its predecessor's experiences.

42. AHDG F[1] 40, prefect of police, 12 Jan. 1849.

43. BN LB 54 1461, La Solidarité républicaine's statutes, art. 23.

44. Ibid., art. 22.

45. AHDG F[1] 40, report from the prefect of police, 12 Jan. 1849.

46. AHDG F[1] 40, report submitted to the Minister of War, January 1849; AN BB[30] 394, "Etat de poursuites dirigées contre La Solidarité républicaine."

47. AN BB[18] 1472, Viot to Pilette, secretary general of La Solidarité républicaine, Paris; though undated, this letter was clearly written in

early February 1849. See also ibid., Viot to Joly (Representative of People), 11 Jan. 1849.

48. AN BB[18] 1472, procureur général, Montpellier, to Minister of Justice, 25 Feb. 1849 and 14 March 1849.

49. Dupeux, *L'Histoire sociale et politique du Loir-et-Cher*, pp. 345-385.

50. Ibid., p. 345. Members included a doctor, an ex-notary, a book dealer, a merchant, a grocer, and a cobbler.

51. AN BB[18] 1472, commissaire de police, Blois, to procureur général, Orléans, January 1849.

52. Levêque, "La Bourgogne," p. 1303; AN BB[30] 400, dossier Carion.

53. Levêque, "La Bourgogne," p. 1303; AN BB[30] 394, "Etat de poursuites. . . . "

54. Levêque, "La Bourgogne," p. 1304; AN BB[18] 1474a.

55. O. Tixier, "Les Procès politiques dans l'Indre-et-Loire," *La Révolution de 1848*, 1 (1904), 194-200.

56. AN BB[30] 394, "Etat de poursuites dirigées contre les sociétés affiliées de la solidarité républicaine"; ADY III M[1] 134, "Dossier de la solidarité républicaine," subprefect, Sens, to prefect, Yonne, 5 Feb. 1849; also AN BB[18] 1472, gendarmerie, Dijon, to procureur général, Dijon, 8 April 1849. Cabet's propaganda efforts had politicized Niort long before the Revolution of 1848. See Johnson, *Utopian Communism*, pp. 197-202.

57. Levêque, "La Bourgogne," p. 1303.

58. AHDG F[1] 40. There were four arrestees for whom no profession was listed.

59. Ibid., "Bulletin de la Solidarité," 25 Jan. 1849.

60. AHDG F[1] 40; AN BB[30] 394; Dessal, *Un Révolutionnaire jacobin*, pp. 119-120; AN BB[18] 1472, "Dossier de la Solidarité républicaine."

61. AN BB[18] 1472, procureur général, Aix, to Minister of Interior, 10 January 1849.

62. AN BB[18] 1472, Minister of Interior to prefects, circular, 10 Jan. 1849; AHDG F[1] 40, prefect of police, 10 Nov. 1848.

63. AHDG F[1] 40, "compte rendu" of meeting held at the home of Representative of the People Gambon on 15 Feb. 1849.

64. Levêque, "La Bourgogne," p. 1303.

65. See Margadant, *French Peasants in Revolt*.

66. See Levêque, "La Bourgogne," pp. 1303-1304.

67. Alvin Calman, *Ledru-Rollin and the Second Republic* (New York: Columbia University Press, 1922), p. 276; Dessal, *Un Révolutionnaire jacobin*, p. 108.

68. Calman, *Ledru-Rollin*, p. 276; Agulhon, *1848*, p. 22.

69. Félix Pyat, *Toast aux paysans* (Paris: 1849). See also, Alexandre Zévaès, "La Propagande socialiste dans la campagne en 1848," *1848* 31 (1934-1935), 80-82.

CHAPTER IV. THE IDEOLOGY OF THE DEMOC-SOCS

1. See Amann, *Revolution and Mass Democracy*. Amann analyzes in fascinating detail the work of the multitude of political clubs that sprang up in Paris during the spring of 1848. He devotes more attention to their organizational and electoral activity than to their ideology. In *Sentimental Education*, Flaubert mocks with merciless contempt the bizarre doctrines of the Parisian clubs. Gustave Flaubert, *Education Sentimentale* (Paris: Livre de Poche, 1972), pp. 352-361.

2. See for example Georges Renard, "L'Esprit de 1848," *Revue politique et parlementaire*, 63 (1910), 563-578.

3. See Frank Paul Bowman, *Le Christ romantique* (Geneva: Droz, 1973), p. 114.

4. Gabriel Mortillet, "Bases de la politique," 1849, in AN AB[xix] 680.

5. *VP*, 5 Nov. 1848; emphasis added.

6. Ibid., 3 Jan. 1849.

7. *La République*, 14 Nov. 1848.

8. *VP*, 18 Oct. 1848.

9. La Ligue sociale, in AN AB[xix] 680.

10. *La République*, 16 April 1849.

11. An B[18] 1488, procureur général, Rennes, 22 Nov. 1850 (copy of a letter from Poirier-Lacote, Montagnard leader of Rennes, to Jugaux, tailor).

12. Louis Blanc, *Le Catéchisme des socialistes* (Paris: 1849).

13. *La République*, 3 May 1849.

14. A. Roubaud, "Réorganisation sociale," April 1849, in AD Drôme, Tribunal Montelimar.

15. Pierre Pierrard, *1848 . . . les pauvres, l'évangile et la révolution* (Paris: Desclée, 1977), pp. 180-182; AN BB[18] 1470c. The procureur général of Nantes included a song entitled "Le Christ socialiste" in his report of 12 March 1850. Perot, a democ-soc schoolteacher, called Jesus "that great socialist who lived eighteen centuries ago," in *La Feuille du village*, 5 Jan. 1850.

16. Blanc, *Catéchisme*, p. 30; *La République*, 20 Oct. 1848.

17. *La République*, 22 Feb. 1849. For a nearly identical statement,

see Victor Meunier, "Jésus-Christ devant les conseils de guerre," extract from *La Démocratie pacifique*, 28 Aug. 1848.

18. *VP*, 27-28 Nov. 1848.

19. *La République*, 14 Nov. 1848, speech by Pilon-Vorbe before a reunion of ex-delegates to the Luxembourg Commission.

20. *VP*, 25 Oct. 1848.

21. Ibid., 15-16 Jan. 1849.

22. Merriman, *Agony of the Republic*, presents a blow-by-blow account of the repression suffered by Montagnard activists at all levels during the Second Republic.

23. *La République*, 3 May 1849.

24. Ibid.

25. Unfortunately for the movement, a few members went overboard in their self-identification with Jesus and the apostles. Félix Pyat, for example, developed a martyr complex as ridiculous as it was counterproductive. Exiled for his role in the abortive rebellion of 13 June 1849, the Montagnard parliamentarian justified this pathetic and ruinous action as a means of expiating his guilt over France's crimes against the Roman Republic in 1849: "This suicide of the Mountain," declared Pyat, "will be its best work. . . . We buried ourselves alive in the tomb of the Roman Republic as expiatory victims who sacrificed ourselves in order to absolve the present, protect the future, and make up for this crime [against liberty] . . ." (AN BB[18] 1470c, procureur général, Toulouse, to Minister of Justice, 23 Nov. 1849, copy of a letter entitled "Lettre de F. Pyat aux électeurs de la Seine, de la Nièvre, et du Cher," Lausanne, Switzerland, Nov. 1849).

26. Dr. A. Guépin, *Le Socialisme expliqué aux enfants du peuple* (Paris: 1851), p. 7.

27. Charles Renouvier, *Manuel républicain de l'homme et du citoyen* (Paris: 1848), p. 7.

28. *VP*, 11 Nov. 1848.

29. See, for example, Louis Langomazino in *VP*, 26 April 1849.

30. Quoted approvingly in *VP*, 22-23 April 1850.

31. *VP*, 20-21 Nov. 1848.

32. *VP*, 8 March, 18 July 1849.

33. *Le Républicain du Nord*, 3 Dec. 1849.

34. Raymond Huard, "La Défense du suffrage universel sous la Seconde République," *Annales du Midi*, 83 (1971), 330; Louis Blanc in *VP*, 25 April 1850; Laponneraye in *VP*, 1 June 1849.

35. Huard, "Défense du suffrage universel," p. 330.

36. Quoted in *VP*, 25 April 1850.

37. Laponneraye, in *VP*, 30 Oct. 1848.

38. *L'Union républicaine* (hereafter *UR*), 28 March 1849.

39. Greppo, "La République" (Paris: 1849), in AN AB^xix 680.

40. *VP*, 30 Oct. 1849. According to *Le Républicain du Nord*, 3 Dec. 1849, socialism is the doctrine of those who "want widespread social reforms." In an April 1849 toast to "mes frères des campagnes," Joigneaux argued that "socialists are all those who want reforms and improvement, who want something new that is more equitable than that which exists." For Joigneaux's toast, see Eugène Sue et al., *Le Républicain des campagnes* (Paris: 1851).

41. Guépin, *Socialisme expliqué aux enfants*, p. 9.

42. *Petit manuel républicain à l'usage des habitants des campagnes* (Macon: 1849), pp. 12-14.

43. *L'Atelier*, 7 Aug. 1848.

44. *La République*, 20 June 1849.

45. *La République du peuple* (Colmar), 25 Jan. 1850.

46. *Le Suffrage universel*, 15 Nov. 1851.

47. *La République*, 8 Oct. 1848.

48. *VP*, 4-5 June 1849.

49. *Le Républicain de Lyon*, 25 Feb. 1849.

50. *Le Peuple souverain*, 8 March 1849.

51. *UR*, 7 Aug. 1850.

52. Jeanne Gaillard, "La Question du crédit et les almanachs autour de 1850," *Etudes de la Bibliothèque de la Révolution de 1848*, 16 (1954), 82. Democ-soc spokesmen usually placed owners of the largest factories among the ranks of capitalists.

53. Ibid.

54. Pierrre-Léon Salin, "Réponse aux attaques de M. le Curé contre le socialisme et les socialistes," cited in Martinet, *Clamecy et ses flotteurs*, p. 128.

55. Martin Loulerie, "La Politique de Jean-Pierre" (Paris: 1849). Pamphlet issued by La Propagande démocratique et sociale européenne.

56. Ibid.

57. *Le Républicain des Ardennes*, 8 June 1850; emphasis in original.

58. Alphonse Esquiros, *Le Droit au travail, de son organisation par la réforme des institutions de crédit* (Blois: 1849), p. 14.

59. *Le Républicain du Gard*, 12 Oct. 1849; *UR*, 1 Feb. 1851.

60. *UR*, 2 Aug. 1851.

61. "Les Réflections d'un bon villageois" (Paris: 1849), in AN BB^18 1470b.

62. The merchant capitalists' dominant hold over manufacture and market agriculture has been demonstrated in Chapter I.

63. *Le Peuple* (Nevers), 30 Oct. 1850.

64. A. Laponneraye, "Catéchisme républicain," Paris, 1848, p. 3.

65. *La Révolution démocratique et sociale*, 26 Feb. 1849.

66. *L'Atelier*, 30 June 1850; *La République*, 24 Sept. 1848.

67. *UR*, 5 Nov. 1851.

68. *VP*, 20 Jan. 4-5 June 1849.

69. *L'Atelier*, 26 March 1848.

70. *La République*, 26 Dec. 1848. Cf. the quotation from *La Démocratie pacifique* in Chapter II, p. 40.

71. Bastid, *Doctrines et institutions politiques*, p. 63.

72. William H. Sewell Jr., "Property, Labor, and the Emergence of Socialism in France, 1789-1848," in John M. Merriman, ed., *Consciousness and Class Experience in Nineteenth-Century Europe* (New York: Holmes and Meier, 1980), pp. 48-49.

73. Ibid., p. 53.

74. Victor Considérant, *Théorie du droit de propriété et du droit au travail* (Paris: 1839), p. 35; Bastid, *Doctrines et institutions politiques*, p. 64.

75. See McPhee, "Crisis of Radical Republicanism."

76. Amann, *Revolution and Mass Democracy*; Rémi Gossez, *Les Ouvriers de Paris. L'Organisation, 1848-1851* (La Roche-sur-Yon: Bibliothèque de la Révolution de 1848, 1967).

77. Bastid, *Doctrines et institutions politiques*, pp. 63-64.

78. Esquiros, *Le Droit au travail*, p. 18.

79. "Déclaration au peuple," in AHDG F¹ 40.

80. Ibid.: "Far from seeking to abolish private property, we want to extend it, generalize it, and make it accessible to everyone. . . ."

81. Esquiros, *Le Droit au travail*, p. 32.

82. Considérant, *Théorie du droit de propriété*.

83. Esquiros, *Le Droit au travail*, pp. 14-15, 25.

84. *L'Atelier*, July 1850.

85. "Déclaration au peuple."

86. *UR*, 28 March 1849. For similar statements, see *VP*, 27 Jan., 28 Nov. 1849; *Le Républicain des Ardennes*, 8 June 1850. *La Feuille du village*, 25 Oct. 1849, urged that "the state be banker to the peasant by accepting his property as collateral for loans at 2 or 2.5 percent." See also Gaillard, "La Question du crédit," and Esquiros, *Le Droit au travail*, p. 32.

87. See *VP*, 11-12 April 1849; *La Feuille du village*, 25 Oct. 1849. See J. Dagnan, *Le Gers sous la Seconde République* (Auch: Imprimerie

Brevetée, 1928), p. 211, for the program of the Montagnard paper *L'Egalité*.

88. Nationalizations and major tax reforms figured prominently in the democ-soc campaign platform for the highly important election of 1849. In codifying much of the left's ideology, the platform's fifteen points amounted to nothing less than a succinct plan for political and economic democracy:

1. Energetic defense of republican institutions and of direct universal suffrage.
2. Subordination of executive power to the National Assembly.
3. Complete liberty of the press and association.
4. The droit au travail.
5. Free and obligatory education.
6. Extensive legal reform, especially the establishment of free legal services and the abolition of the death penalty.
7. A democratic army and the abolition of military conscription.
8. A vast system of "democratic credit."
9. Nationalization of insurance, banking, railroads, canals, all means of communication and mines.
10. Abolition of usury.
11. Abolition of all indirect taxes.
12. An "equitable distribution of taxes."
13. Government encouragement of industrial and agricultural development.
14. Creation of a national system of bazaars and *comptoirs communaux*.
15. Government encouragement of agricultural and industrial associations.

The platform bore the title "Manifest de la Montagne." It was published in *VP*, 12 April 1849.

89. Renard, "L'Esprit de 1848"; Gaillard, "La Question du crédit," p. 87.

90. See Proudhon's *Le Peuple* for 1848; Bernard Moss, *The Origins of the French Labor Movement* (Berkeley and Los Angeles: University of California Press, 1976), pp. 6-8, 44, 207.

91. George Duveau, "Les Idéologies de 1848," in Charles Moulin, ed., *Le Livre du Centenaire* (Paris: Editions atlas, 1948), p. 193. Duveau, one of the only historians to take the ideology of 1848 seriously, remarked, "The historic failure of 1848 does not prove that the ideologues of this period were simply dreamers who spun abstract and chimeric theories. They made mistakes, but their principal error was to overestimate the speed of historical change. With a penetration and

a lucidity that were often admirable, they discovered and analyzed the contradictions in the midst of which the capitalist system operated. Fascinated by their own discoveries, they expected the rapid downfall of a system which caused such ferocious and bitter competition."

92. Moss, *French Labor Movement*, p. 44; Bernard Schnapper, "Les Sociétés ouvrières de production pendant la Seconde République," *Revue d'histoire économique et sociale*, 43 (1965), 163-168; Johnson, "Economic Change." There were an estimated 800 producers' cooperatives in the provinces.

93. Vigier, *La Seconde République dans la région alpine*, vol. 2, pt. 4, chaps. 2, 3; Levêque, "La Bourgogne," p. 1168; *La Feuille du village*.

94. *L'Atelier*, 30 June 1850; Moss, "Parisian Producers' Associations: The Socialism of Skilled Workers," in Price, ed., *Revolution and Reaction*, p. 83.

95. See, for example, July 1850.

96. Cuvillier, "L'Idéologie de 1848," pp. 423-425.

97. Cited in ibid., p. 423.

98. Ibid.

99. Gabriel Mortillet, "Droit au travail" (Paris: 1849), in AN AB[xix] 680.

100. For nearly identical descriptions of this system of bazaars, see *UR*, 1 Feb. 1851; *L'Atelier*, 30 June 1850. See also "Le Conseil central aux électeurs républicains-démocrates-socialistes," Nov. 1848, in AN AB[xix] 680.

101. Jean Dubois, *Le Vocabulaire politique et social en France de 1869 à 1872* (Paris: Librairie Larousse, 1962), p. 83.

CHAPTER V. RURAL COMMUNICATION

1. See *La République au village*, esp. pt. 1, chaps. 4-6, for Agulhon's pioneering analysis of the relationship between existing village culture and new political propaganda during the July Monarchy.

2. See Chapter III for a similar point concerning the ability of La Propagande démocratique et sociale européenne, a commercial operation, to escape government repression.

3. See Chapter III, pp. 81-83.

4. AN BB[18] 1470c, procureur général, Rennes.

5. An BB[18] 1470c, procureur général, Riom, 24 Feb. and 12 Aug. 1849.

6. AN BB[18] 1470c, procureur général, Rennes, 11 May, 5 Aug., 15 Oct. 1849.

7. Michelet to Beranger, 16 June 1848, in Agulhon, "Le Problème de la culture populaire," p. 61. Shortly before the explosion of working-class anger and frustration in June 1848, Michelet argued for the establishment of an elaborate network of propaganda designed to politicize the masses and thus to prevent them from succumbing to a mindless Bonapartism. In order to spread the ideals of democracy, Michelet proposed public reading societies in which the best reader would read aloud a (republican) bulletin to all the others, colorfully illustrated billboards with short messages printed in large letters, and a carefully organized system of colportage. There is no evidence that leaders of the démocrate-socialiste left explicitly followed Michelet's advice, but perhaps, as a result of his profound sensitivity to popular culture, he anticipated many of the methods of propaganda diffusion soon to be adopted by the Montagnards.

8. Charles Nisard, "Essai sur le colportage de librairie," *Journal de la société de la morale chrétienne*, 5 no. 1 (Paris: 1855), 49-50. Nisard, a high functionary of the Second Empire, sought to use colportage in the service of goals substantially different from those of Michelet. For Nisard, colportage was the means by which to inculcate obedience and conservative values. It is noteworthy nonetheless that both saw colportage as the key to altering the mentality of the masses and that both sought to create an organized and purposeful means of doing that.

9. Benoît, *Confessions d'un prolétaire*, cited in Agulhon, "Le Problème de la culture populaire," p. 61.

10. Agulhon, "Le Problème de la culture populaire," pp. 61-62.

11. ADY 71 T 1, "Police de colportage," 1815-1892.

12. AN BB[30] 380, procureur général, Metz, 8 Jan. 1850.

13. AN BB[30] 374, procureur général, Bourges, 1 March 1850.

14. AN BB[30] 368, procureur général, Besançon, Jan. 1850.

15. AN BB[30] 368, procureur général, Bordeaux, Jan. 1850.

16. AN BB[30] 368, procureur général, Toulouse, 4 Jan. 1850.

17. AN BB[18] 1449, procureur général, Paris, to Minister of Justice, 5 Jan. 1850. The tribunal of Le Mans in the Sarthe made a similar ruling in September 1850.

18. I owe this information to Noel Laveau, who is preparing his doctorat d'état on early-nineteenth-century insurance companies.

19. AD Nièvre, Series U, Sociétés Secrètes, Cosne (hereafter SSC), dossier Gueneau.

20. AN BB[30] 393, procureur général, Montpellier, 29 April 1851.

21. AN BB[18] 1488. See also Marcel Dessal, "Le Complot de Lyon et la résistance au coup d'état dans les départements du Sud-Est," *1848*, 189 (1951), 83-96.

22. AN BB[18] 1481, procureur général, Dijon, 29 Nov. 1849. The procureur's pleasure in receiving this information did not prevent him from recommending punishment for Millet, the postal busybody. Millet was sentenced to eight days in jail and a 25-franc fine.

23. ADY III M[1] 126, subprefect, Avallon, 1 Oct. 1850; subprefect, Tonnerre, 20 July 1850.

24. AN BB[30] 388, procureur général, Toulouse, 4 Jan. 1850.

25. AN BB[30] 383, procureur général, Paris, 15 Jan. 1851; ADY III M[1] 133, 22 Oct. 1848.

26. AD Nièvre, SSC, dossier Sabainne.

27. AN BB[30] 374, procureur général, Bourges, 30 Nov. 1849; AN F[14] 1070, prefect, Cher, to Minister of Public Works, 21 June 1849.

28. AN F[14] 1070, Minister of Interior to Minister of Public Works, 6 July 1849.

29. AN BB[18] 1474, procureur général, Rouen, to Minister of Justice, 15 Jan. 1850.

30. AHDG, Justice Militaire (hereafter JM) 259 (Yonne), police chief, Joigny, to subprefect, 19 April 1851.

31. Ibid., 22 April 1851.

32. ADY III M[1] 145, prefect of police, Paris, to prefect, Yonne, 11 April 1851.

33. Gazette des tribunaux, 18 Aug. 1850. The Cour de Cassation ruled that "la loi de 1849 n'a eu pour but de réprimer et d'interdire que le colportage et la distribution faite directement et personnellement par les porteurs de l'écrit, mais qu'elle n'a pas entendu réglementer la distribution par la voie de la poste qui est régie par des lois spéciales."

34. AN BB[18] 1529, Minister of Interior to Minister of Justice, 12 Feb. 1851.

35. La Feuille du village, 25 Oct. 1849.

36. AN BB[30] 383, procureur général, Paris, 17 April 1850. See also Roger McGraw, "Pierre Joigneaux and Socialist Propaganda in the French Countryside, 1849-1851," French Historical Studies, 10 (Fall 1978), 599-640.

37. AN BB[18] 1449, Minister of Interior to Minister of Justice, 18 Nov. 1849.

38. AN BB[30] 392[B], procureur général, Douai, 6 May 1851.

39. AN BB[30] 383, procureur général, Paris, 1 June 1850. See also AD Nièvre, SSC, dossier 029; ADY III M[1] 145, prefect to subprefect, Auxerre, 27 April 1850.

40. AN BB[30] 383, procureur général, Paris, 27 Feb. 1850.

41. ADY III M[1] 145, subprefect, Auxerre, to prefect, 30 Sept. 1850.

42. AN BB[18] 1449, procureur général, Grenoble, 4 Feb. 1850.

43. AN BB[30] 400, dossier Tisserandot.

44. ADY III M[1] 145, Minister of Interior to prefect, Yonne, 30 Oct. 1850; AN BB[30] 327, procureur général, Grenoble, 29 Oct. 1850.

45. On the role of provincial social groups in the formation and leadership of Montagnard secret societies, see Margadant, *French Peasants in Revolt*, chaps. 6-8.

46. Roger Price, *The French Second Republic: A Social History* (London: Batsford, 1972), pp. 291-295; AN F[7] 2588-2595; AN BB[30] 423. See also Nadaud, *Mémoires de Léonard*, p. 369, for the key role of doctors as local democ-soc propagandists.

47. AD Nièvre, SSC, dossier Basset.

48. AN BB[30] 402, dossier Lachamp.

49. Léon Guyon, *Un Médecin de campagne d'autrefois. Notes et souvenirs, 1795-1865* (Le Mans: A. de Saint Denis, 1902).

50. Ibid., p. 56.

51. Ibid., p. 69.

52. Ibid., p. 58.

53. See AN BB[30] 396, procureur général, Rouen, 3 Feb. 1852; AN BB[18] 1449, procureur général, Douai, 1 May 1850.

54. AN BB[30] 374, procureur général, Bourges, 30 Nov. 1849.

55. AN BB[30] 394, procureur général, Montpellier, 18 July 1852.

56. AN BB[18] 1449, Minister of Interior to Minister of Justice, 6 Aug. 1850.

57. AN BB[18] 1449, procureur général, Limoges, to Minister of Justice, 26 Feb. 1850.

58. AN BB[18] 1449, Erlarassain to Laruelle, 8 Feb. 1850.

59. AN BB[18] 1449, Dussoubes to Laruelle, 8 Feb. 1850.

60. AHDG JM 259, police chief, Joigny, to subprefect, 29 Sept. 1851.

61. AHDG JM 228, dossier Lefebvre, letter dated 5 May 1849.

62. Raymond Huard, "La Pré-histoire des partis" (Thèse de doctorat d'état, Université de Paris IV, 1977), pp. 465-475; Louis Chevalier, "Les Fondements économiques et sociaux de l'histoire politique de la région parisienne" (Thèse de doctorat d'état, Université de Paris, Sorbonne, 1950), p. 425; Levêque, "La Bourgogne," pp. 1323-45. See also Nadaud, *Mémoires de Léonard*, pp. 366-369, for a portrait of the artisans' role in spreading democ-soc propaganda among the peasantry.

63. AD Nièvre, SCC, dossier 031.

64. Ibid.

65. AD Aix 14-U 53, Sociétés secrètes, Béziers, 22 Feb. 1851. For

an excellent analysis of Relin and the Montagnard movement in Béziers, see Margadant, *French Peasants in Revolt*, pp. 127-130.

66. AN BB[18] 1449, procureur of the Republic, Valence, to procureur général, Grenoble, 27 Sept. 1850.

67. AN BB[18] 1470c, Pierre Joigneaux, "Les Cabarets dans nos campagnes." John Merriman presents a similar portrait of the café's political role in provincial France; see *Agony of the Republic*, pp. 97-101.

68. See Chapter VI for more on the importance of village cafés and chambrées to the democ-soc press.

69. AN BB[30] 383, procureur général, Paris, 16 May 1851.

70. ADY III M[1] 145, police chief, Toucy, to prefect, 30 Sept. 1850.

71. Prefect, Gers, 22 Jan. 1850, quoted in Dagnan, *Gers sous la Seconde République*, pp. 408-409.

72. AN BB[18] 1470c, Joigneaux, "Les Cabarets."

73. See Emile Guillaumin, *La Vie d'un simple* (Paris: Editions Stock, 1943), pp. 51-60, for a touching account of a young boy left out in the cold for hours while his father squandered family resources in the village café; compare Balzac's *Les Paysans* for a portrait of the social independence that rural cafés could help to foster.

74. AN BB[18] 1481, dossier, "Police des cabarets."

75. AN BB[18] 1481, procureur général, Nancy, 1 Feb. 1850.

76. AN BB[18] 1481, procureur général, Lyon, 11 Jan. 1850.

77. AN BB[18], 11 Jan. 1850.

78. See Chapter IV and Appendix.

79. AD Bouches-du-Rhône, 6M 344, Minister of Interior to prefect, 14 Nov. 1849.

80. Ibid.

81. Abbé Bernard, "Bibliothèque catholique et populaire" (Paris: 1849); emphasis added.

82. The BN's collection of song sheets is catalogued under the *cote* Y[e] 7185 and Y[e] 34927. Most song sheets cost 5 centimes or 2 francs, 50 centimes per hundred.

83. Bollème, *Bibliothèque bleue*, pp. 17-18. According to A. Dubois, *Livres de colportage en Sologne*, p. 23: "Almanacs were nothing more than a compendium of pictures and sorts of hieroglyphics designed for those who could not read. All of the almanacs' information was provided by conventional signs . . . that indicate holidays, workdays . . . good days to take medicine, to cut hair, to trim a beard, and even to beat one's wife." See also AN BB[30] 392[B], procureur général, Bordeaux, 8 June 1851: "Among the masses . . . one finds an enormous faith in that which is printed."

84. *La Voix du peuple ou les républicaines de 1848. Recueil des chants populaires démocratiques et sociaux* (Paris à la librairie de Durand, 32 rue de Rambuteau, 1848 and 1849). A large percentage of the individual song sheets that circulated in the countryside were published by Durand and included in the two anthologies he published under the title *La Voix du peuple*. Compare these anthologies with the individual song sheets collected in BN folios Y^e 969, Y^e 34927, and Y^e 7185. Durand envisaged his song sheets as well as his two anthologies as works of democ-soc propaganda. In the preface to the 1848 anthology Durand wrote: "In order to make it [the anthology] accessible to people at all levels of income, we have priced our volume as low as possible. If the public shows widespread interest in our collection, we will feel encouraged to publish a new one each year."

85. Pierre Joigneaux, *Souvenirs historiques*, 2 vols. (Paris: 1871), 2:65.

86. Brochon, *Pamphlet du pauvre*, pp. 76-77.

87. All lines from "Le Chant du vote" (Paris: 1850); price, 10 centimes.

88. *DBMOF*, 2:504.

89. Brochon, *Pamphlet du pauvre*, p. 90.

90. Ibid., p. 88.

91. Ibid., p. 80.

92. Ibid., p. 69.

93. Ibid., pp. 62-63.

94. BN Y^e 7185 (444).

95. BN Y^e 7185 (462).

96. BN Y^e 7185 (364).

97. *La Voix du peuple*, 1848, pp. 187-191.

98. Ibid., 1849, p. 7.

99. BN Y^e 7185 (440).

100. *La Voix du peuple*, 1849, p. 29.

101. Ibid., p. 45. Eugène Baillet's ode to Raspail similarly identifies a martyred democ-soc leader with Jesus; see ibid., p. 47.

102. Ibid., pp. 42-43.

CHAPTER VI. PROVINCIAL PRESS AND SECRET SOCIETIES

1. See Merriman, *Agony of the Republic*, chap. 3.

2. See Amann, *Revolution and Mass Democracy*, for a superb analysis of the Parisian club movement.

3. AN BB^{18} 1449, procureur général, Besançon, to Minister of Justice,

5 Sept. 1849. This carton contains a number of copies of electoral proclamations posted in various communes.

4. Ibid.

5. See ADY III M¹ 133; Levêque, "La Bourgogne," pp. 1307-1322.

6. This paragraph follows Agulhon, La République au village, pp, 207-284.

7. M. Agulhon, "La Diffusion d'un journal montagnard. Le Démocrate du Var sous la Deuxième République," Provence historique, 10 (1960), 11-27.

8. AN BB³⁰ 386, procureur général, Riom, 14 May 1849.

9. Ibid.

10. Quoted in Agulhon, "Diffusion," p. 15.

11. Dagnan, Gers sous la Seconde République, pp. 160-164; Paul Leuilliot, La Presse et l'histoire. Notes sur la presse en Alsace (Paris: Sirey, 1965), p. 12.

12. AD Nièvre, SSC, dossier Laurent. Alfred Terrain, a wheelwright arrested for rebellion in the Yonne, painted a similar portrait of the press's influence on his behavior: "The times I discussed politics were when I read the newspapers. I subscribed to the Union républicaine about a month ago. That newspaper and others are the cause of all this [i.e., the insurrection and ensuing repression]. I am certain that if I had never known them, I would not have done what I did" (AHDG JM 258, dossier Terrain). Merriman quotes from the same document in his discussion of the Montagnard press; Agony of the Republic, pp. 25-26.

13. L'Eclaireur républicain, 3 March 1849. For a similar statement see L'Union républicaine, quoted in Claude Lévy, "Un journal 'rouge' sous la Seconde République. L'Union républicaine," Annales de Bourgogne, 31 (July-September 1961), 155.

14. UR, 7 March 1849.

15. Lévy, "Un journal 'rouge,' " p. 150.

16. AN BB³⁰ 380, procureur général, Montpellier, 11 April 1850.

17. AD Hérault 39M 132, police chief, Bédarieux, to procureur général, 29 Dec 1849. On a trip to Bédarieux, Auriol stayed with an ouvrier tanneur.

18. AN BB³⁰ 380, procureur général, Montpellier, 22 Jan. 1850.

19. AN B¹⁸ 1470b, procureur général, Aix, 16 Jan. 1850.

20. Agulhon, "Diffusion," pp. 23-24. See also Agulhon Une Ville ouvrière au temps du socialisme utopique. Toulon de 1815 à 1851 (Paris: Mouton, 1970).

21. AD Hérault 39M 132, subprefect, Béziers, to prefect, 27 Oct.

1850. The confiscated letter was written by two democ-soc Representatives of the People, Brives and Savoy, and dated 21 Oct. 1850.
Brives represented the Hérault.

22. Agulhon, "Diffusion," p. 24.

23. Ibid., pp. 16-17.

24. Ibid.

25. AD Bouches-du-Rhône (Dépôt Aix), 12-U/2, mayor of Gardanne
to procureur général, 2 April 1849. See Chapter V for more details on
the role of cafés in democ-soc propaganda.

26. AD Hérault 39M 132, police chief, Floreniac, to prefect, 19 Jan.
1850; AN BB[30] 380, procureur général, Paris, 16 May 1851.

27. AN BB[18] 1449, Minister of Justice to Minister of Interior, 11
April 1850.

28. See Merriman, *Agony of the Republic*, for details of antirepub-
lican repression.

29. Agulhon, "Diffusion," p. 26.

30. See Merriman's *Agony of the Republic*, chaps. 3-4, for an il-
luminating analysis not only of the government's systematic repression
of democ-soc newspapers and voluntary organizations but also of the
nature and importance of Montagnard press and propaganda.

31. AN BB[18] 1494, procureur général, Aix, to Minister of the Interior,
6 Jan. 1850.

32. AN BB[18] 1470[b], procureur général, Lyon, 21 Oct. 1849. AN
carton BB[18] 1470[b] is filled with documents showing evidence of significant conflicts within the French bureaucracy over the means by
which to proceed with the repression of the left. Lyon's procureur
général believed that the law provided only slim justification for pros-
ecuting joint-stock journalistic enterprises, but the Minister of the
Interior and members of his prefectoral corps disagreed. The latter
group felt much less bound by legal scruples than did the nation's
procureurs. This divergence over the importance of maintaining a sem-
blance of legality in the midst of the government's repressive crusade
against the republican left often created serious conflict within the state
bureaucracy between judicial officials and members of the prefectoral
corps. Such disagreements probably served to mitigate anti-Monta-
gnard repression and provided the opposition with a number of loop-
holes through which it could operate—at least for a time—with im-
punity.

33. AN BB[18] 1470c, procureur of the Republic, Lyon, to procureur
général, Lyon, 27 April 1850. See AN BB[30] 388, procureur général,

Toulouse, 22 July 1850, for an attempt to establish a similar journalistic-commercial venture in Toulouse.

34. See AN BB[18] 1470b, procureur général, Aix, to Minister of Justice, 9 and 17 Jan. 1850, for the government's fear of *La Voix du peuple*.

35. A nearly complete collection of *La Voix du peuple* can be found at the Bibliothèque Nationale, Versailles annex. On Charles Poumicon, see AD Bouches-du-Rhône (Dépôt Aix) 14-U/19 and *DBMOF*, 3:248. On H. Bondilh, see *DBMOF*, 1:258.

36. Laponneraye's lead article in the 23 Feb. 1849 issue of *La Voix du peuple* stated: "In view of the coming election, it is primarily to the rural workers, that is, to the peasantry, that our friends must address themselves. The peasants form the vast majority of the electorate, and as they have recently demonstrated, they can decide the election. . . . We must show them three things: their poverty, their numbers, and the pacific but invincible force that universal suffrage gives them. . . . The peasants must understand that suffrage is not something to be complacent about, but that it is a matter of conviction and personal interest."

37. On Langomazino, see Vigier, *La Seconde République dans la région alpine*, 2:187-190, 196-197, 219-220, 423-426; Agulhon, *La République au village*, p. 316; *DBMOF* 2:524.

38. Vigier, *La Seconde République dans la région alpine* 2:186-208.

39. Dessal, "Le Complot de Lyon."

40. AD Var 4M 19/1 Brignoles, judge of the Tribunal de Première Instance, Marseille, to procureur of the Republic, Draguignan. 15 Jan. 1852; AN BB[18] 1470b, procureur général, Aix, 16 Jan. 1850.

41. AD Var 4M 19/1 Brignoles. I am indebted to Ted Margadant for making me aware of this document.

42. Ibid.

43. Ibid.

44. AD Aix 14-U/19.

45. AN C 967A.

46. AD Aix 14-U/19.

47. Ibid.

48. AD Aix 12-U/2, mayor of Gardanne to procureur général, Aix, 26 April 1849.

49. See notes 37 and 38.

50. Agulhon, "Diffusion," p. 17.

51. AD Aix 14-U/19, 22 Oct. 1851.

52. AD Aix 14-U/19, Arnaud to *VP*, 28 June 1851.

53. AD Aix 14-U/19. See, for example, Oliver to *VP*, 1 Nov. 1851, and numerous other letters from the spring and fall of 1851.

54. AD Aix 14-U/19, 19 Oct. 1851.

55. AD Aix 14-U/19, Oliver to *VP*, 1 Nov. 1851.

56. AD Aix 14-U/19. See, for example, Relin to *VP*, prison of Aix, 16 May 1851, and Biard to *VP*, prison of Martignes, 22 Oct. 1851.

57. AD Aix 14-U/19, proprietor of the Café d'Europe to *VP*, Aix, 10 May 1851.

58. AD Aix 14-U/19, Pomme to *VP*, 1 Nov. 1851; Dubois to *VP*, 2 Nov. 1851.

59. AD Aix 14-U/19, Millaud to *VP*, St. Rémy (Bouches-du-Rhône), 1 Oct. 1851.

60. AD Aix 14-U/19. See for example, Michel to *VP*, 18 Oct. 1851; Minard to *VP*, 9 Nov. 1851; Aetrard to *VP*, 28 July 1851.

61. AD Aix 14-U/19, Aetrard to *VP*, 28 July 1851; Barthelemy to *VP*, 23 Oct. 1851.

62. AD Aix 14-U/19, Cafetier of St.-Chamas to *VP*, 29 Oct. 1851.

63. AD Aix 14-U/19, Biard to *VP*, 22 Oct. 1851.

64. Thanks to Ted W. Margadant's excellent study, the Second Republic's secret societies have emerged from their historical shrouds. For a sophisticated analysis of the nature and membership of these societies, see Margadant, *French Peasants in Revolt*, chaps. 6-8. See also Vigier, *La Seconde République dans la région alpine* 2:307-337; Huard, "La Pré-histoire des partis," pp. 318-340; Price, *French Second Republic*, chap. 7; Agulhon, *La République au village*, pp. 376-470.

65. AD Hérault 39M 159, especially dossier Thibeyrenc; AD Var 4M 19/1; AHDG JM 251-260 (Yonne).

66. Huard, "La Pré-histoire des partis," pp. 335-336: "La société [secrète] est essentiellement un instrument pour parvenir à la réalisation d'un programme déjà existant."

67. Margadant, *French Peasants in Revolt*, pp. 115-117.

68. AN BB^{30} 396.

69. See Maurice Agulhon, *Pénitents et francs-maçons de l'ancienne Provence* (Paris: Fayard, 1968), pt. 1.

70. AD Var 4M 19/1, dossier Bonnet.

71. See for example, AN BB^{18} 1488, testimony of M. Lombard; AD Var 4M 19/1, commune of Artignosc; AD Nièvre, SSC, dossiers Allary and Bouge.

72. AD Var 4M 19/1.

73. AD Var 4M 19/1, dossiers 011, 012; Vigier, *La Seconde République dans la région alpine*, 2:263-264.

74. AD Nièvre, SSC, dossier Bourdeau.

75. AD Nièvre, dossier Jacq; AN BB[30] 393, procureur général, Montpellier, 1 June 1851.

76. AD Var 4M 19/1.

77. AD Nièvre, SSC, dossier Pichot.

78. AD Var 4M 19/1, dossier 013.

79. Margadant, *French Peasants in Revolt*, chap. 4.

80. See the interrogations of prisoners in AHDG JM 251-260 for the Yonne; AD Nièvre, SSC; and AD Hérault 39M 146-158.

81. AHDG JM 256.

82. AHDG JM 237.

83. See AD Nièvre, SSC, dossier Berry-Coubret.

84. AD Nièvre, SSC, dossiers, Desassure, Clément, Malville.

85. AD Nièvre, SSC, dossier Aubertin.

86. AD Nièvre, SSC, dossier Delacroix.

87. AD Hérault, 39M 146.

88. AD Hérault 39M 146, dossier Bousquet.

89. AD Hérault 39M 159.

90. AD Hérault 39M 153.

91. Ibid.

92. AHDG JM 258.

93. Ibid.

94. AD Nièvre SSC.

95. AD Hérault 39M 144.

96. Ibid.

97. AHDG JM 257, dossier Libercier.

98. ADY III M[1] 145, subprefect, Joigny, 24 Nov. 1851. Report based on the testimony of a society member named Perrin, who, intimidated by the police, broke down and talked.

99. AD Var 4M 19/1, dossier Fabre; AHDG JM 259, dossier Rhodez.

100. AD Hérault 39M 151, dossier Arnaud; AN BB[30] 393, procureur général, Montpellier, 4 Sept. 1851.

101. The avocat-général at Auch, cited in Dagnan, *Gers sous la Seconde République*, p. 441; AN BB[30] 396, procureur général, Orléans, 30 Dec. 1851.

102. AHDG JM 258, dossier Bonnerat.

103. AD Var 4M 19/1, dossier 004; AN BB[30] 396, procureur général, Lyon, "Rapport général, Evénements de Décembre 1851"; AN BB[30] 394, prefect, Var, 5 Dec. 1850; Martinet, *Clamecy et ses flotteurs*, p. 120.

104. AN BB[30] 393, procureur général, Montpellier, 1 June 1851.

105. See for example Dagnan, *Gers sous la Seconde République*, p. 469.

106. See AN BB³⁰ 400-402; AHDG JM passim; AD Var 4M 19/1 passim.

CHAPTER VII. COMMITMENT TO DEMOC-SOC DOCTRINE

1. *L'Ami de la religion*, March 1848, cited in Isambert, *Christianisme et classe ouvrière*, p. 171.

2. Pierrard, *1848*, pp. 31-33.

3. Cited in Isambert, *Christianisme et classe ouvrière*, p. 172; emphasis added.

4. Maurice Tournier, "Le Vocabulaire des pétitions ouvrières de 1848," in Régine Robin, ed., *Histoire et linguistique* (Paris: A. Colin, 1974), pp. 261-303. Obviously, attempts to base analyses of political meaning on word counting must not be taken too far. Nonetheless, it is notable that, when compared with the discourse of Robespierre, Hébert, L. Blanc, G. Sand, Lamartine, Hugo, Blanqui, Barbès, and *L'Atelier*, the language of the Luxembourg Commission registered a significant correlation (.38) only with the latter source.

5. *L'Atelier*, May 1850, p. 530.

6. Ibid.

7. Ibid.

8. Ibid. Maurice Agulhon, who cites the same description, makes no mention of the lithograph's religious allusions; Agulhon, *Marianne au combat* (Paris: Flammarion, 1979), p. 135.

9. See A. Corbon, *Le Secret du peuple de Paris* (Paris: 1865), p. 303. Better than most of his contemporaries, Corbon understood the role that religiosity played in workers' commitment to the democratic and social republic. He referred to the democ-socs as the "Eglise de la révolution" and stressed the importance of their desire for earthly redemption.

10. AD Hérault 39M 132.

11. AN BB³⁰ 380, procureur général, Montpellier, 29 Nov. 1850.

12. AN BB³⁰ 391, procureur général, Grenoble, 4 Jan. 1851; AN BB³⁰ 380, procureur général, Montpellier, 7 Aug. 1851.

13. AD Bouches-du-Rhône (Aix) 12-U/8, procureur de la République to procureur général, 2 Sept. 1851.

14. A. Van Gennep, *Manuel de folklore français contemporain* (Paris: Picard, 1947), vol. 1, pt. 3, p. 881.

15. Ibid., pp. 962-995.

16. Van Gennep views the carnival as lacking sacred qualities and as being unrelated to the cult of saints. But the fact that the drowning of saints resembled that of the carnival dummy suggests the possibility of a link between the two customs. Could the carnival dummy have represented a saint whose ritual sacrifice would pacify the divine forces that were angered by human actions? See Van Gennep, *Manuel de folklore français*, and above, Chapter II, pp. 61.

17. *Gazette des tribunaux*, 11 April 1852.

18. AN BB[30] 392, procureur général, Paris, 17 March 1851.

19. R. Germond, "La Mascarade séditieuse de Mauzé," *Bulletin de la société historique et scientifique des Deux-Sèvres*, 11 (1961), 551-555. For another analysis of the same event, see Robert Bezucha, "Masks of Revolution: A Study of Popular Culture during the Second Republic," in Price, ed., *Revolution and Reaction*, pp. 247-249.

20. ADY III M¹ 142, mayor of St. Florentin to prefect, 8 Feb. 1849.

21. Ibid.

22. Bezucha, "Masks of Revolution."

23. Rémi Gossez, "La Résistance à l'impôt: Les Quarante-cinq centimes," *1848*, 15 (1953), 89-131; Raymond Huard, "Montagne rouge et montagne blanche en Languedoc-Roussillon sous la Seconde République," in *Droite et gauche de 1789 à nos jours* (Montpellier: Centre d'histoire contemporaine du Languedoc, 1975), pp. 139-160.

24. See Chapter II, pp. 65-66.

25. AN BB[30] 393, procureur général, Rennes, 23 July 1851.

26. Emile Zola, *La Fortune des Rougon* (Paris: Garnier-Flammarion, 1969), p. 71.

27. AD Nièvre, SSC, dossier Buisson.

28. AN BB[30] 423, dossier, région du centre.

29. See Margadant, *French Peasants in Revolt*, chaps. 10-11.

30. Vigier, *La Seconde République dans la région alpine*, 2:333.

31. C. Bellanger et al., *Histoire de la presse française*, vol. 2 (Paris: Presses Universitaires de France, 1969), p. 247.

32. F.-J. Fortin, *Souvenirs*, 2 vols, (Auxerre: 1865), 1:383.

33. AD Nièvre, SSC, dossier Pascault.

34. Cited in Bezucha, "Masks of Revolution," p. 238.

35. Rémi, "La Marianne dans les campagnes," *Almanach administrative historique et statistique de l'Yonne*, 1881, p. 25.

36. AHDG JM 195, dossier Joigneaux, Philippe Bouché to Joigneaux, 4 May 1851. Bouché was from Bienville in the Haute Marne.

37. AN C 969.

38. Ibid.

39. On Joigneaux and socialist entraide, see Agulhon, "Le Problème de la culture populaire," p. 61.

40. *Le Républicain démocrate*, 18 May, 24 July 1851, cited in Levêque, "La Bourgogne," pp. 1168-1169.

41. AD Bouches-du-Rhône (Aix) 14U/19, Mastroul to *VP*, 10 November 1851. This letter is just one of many in this dossier showing examples of democ-soc entraide.

42. AN BB[30] 380, procureur général, Montpellier, June 1850; Huard, "La Pré-histoire des partis," p. 435.

43. Corbin, *Archaïsme et modernité*, pp. 829-830.

44. Bouillon, "Les Démocrates-socialistes," pp. 70, 78.

45. Gordon Wright, *France in Modern Times* (Chicago: Rand McNally, 1974), p. 53.

46. Bouillon, "Les Démocrates-socialistes," p. 70.

47. See Huard, "Défense du suffrage universel," pp. 331-336, for a discussion of the importance lower-class Frenchmen attached to universal suffrage.

48. Ibid. pp. 330-333.

49. Cited in Vigier, *La Seconde République dans la région alpine*, 2:334.

50. Ibid., pp. 334-335.

51. Ibid.

52. Eugen Weber and others have argued that 1851 represented just one more *jacquerie* in rural France's violence-punctuated history. See Weber's *Peasants into Frenchmen*. For views that dispute Weber's position, see Maurice Agulhon, "La Résistance au coup d'état en Provence. Esquisse d'historiographie," *Revue d'histoire moderne et contemporaine*, 22 (1974), 18-26; Tilly, "How Protest Modernized in France"; Margadant, *French Peasants in Revolt*, chap. 11.

53. AD Hérault 39M 159, dossier Thibeyrenc. This section owes much to Margadant's important work on the insurrection of 1851. In *French Peasants in Revolt*, chaps. 10-11, Margadant discusses the rebels' unwillingness to fight against regular army troops. Insurrectionaries tended to employ force only when they faced no more than token opposition.

54. AHDG JM 258, dossier Broit.

55. AHDG JM 255, dossier Patasson. For further examples of this sort of decorum, see Margadant, *French Peasants in Revolt*, chap. 11.

56. AD Hérault 39M 151, dossier Gouron.

57. AD Hérault 39M 159, dossier Thibeyrenc.

58. AHDG JM 255, dossier Breton.

Chapter VIII. The Démocrate-socialiste Legacy

1. Corbin, *Archaïsme et modernité*. Volume 2 of Corbin's study is subtitled "La Naissance d'une tradition de gauche."

2. Bouillon, "Les Démocrates-socialistes," p. 82; François Goguel, *Géographie des élections françaises de 1870 à 1951* (Paris: A. Colin, 1951), pp. 53-87.

3. *Le Monde*, 20 March 1978; Bouillon, "Les Démocrates-socialistes," p. 82; Goguel, *Géographie des élections*, pp. 53-87.

4. Bouillon, "Les Démocrates-socialistes," p. 82; Goguel, *Géographie des élections*, pp. 53-87.

5. Levêque, "La Bourgogne," p. 1617.

6. Huard, "La Pré-histoire des partis," p. 535.

7. Moss, *French Labor Movement*.

8. AN BB[18] 1470c, procureur général, Toulouse, to Minister of Justice, 23 Nov. 1849, contains a copy of Félix Pyat's "Lettre de F. Pyat aux électeurs de la Seine, de la Nièvre et du Cher," Lausanne, Nov. 1849.

9. Ibid.

10. Ibid.

11. A. Thuillier, *Economie et société nivernaises*, p. 179.

12. *UR*, 27 Sept. 1851.

13. *La Voix des travailleurs* (Carmaux), 1 Dec. 1889, cited in Joan Scott, *The Glassworkers of Carmaux* (Cambridge, Mass.: Harvard University Press, 1974), p. 126.

14. Jean Jaurès, *La Question religieuse et le socialisme*, ed. Michel Launay (Paris: Editions de Minuit, 1959), pp. 30-31; emphasis added.

15. Michelle Perrot, "Les Guesdistes: Controverse sur l'introduction du Marxisme en France," *Annales: Economies, Sociétés, Civilisations*, 22 (May-June 1967), 710.

16. Ibid.

17. Scott, *Glassworkers of Carmaux*, pp. 129-130.

18. Ibid., p. 137.

19. Ibid.

20. Jean Jaurès, "La République et le socialisme," speech to the Chamber of Deputies, 21 Nov. 1893, quoted in Michelle Perrot and Annie Kriegel, *Le Socialisme français et le pouvoir* (Paris: EDI, 1966), p. 59.

21. Jean Jaurès, "Le Socialisme français" (1898), quoted in ibid., p. 60.

22. Perrot and Kriegel, *Socialisme français et le pouvoir*, p. 60.

23. Ibid.

24. Jaurès, "La République et le socialisme."

25. Ibid.

26. Ibid.

27. *Le Socialiste*, 26 Aug. 1893, quoted in Perrot and Kriegel, *Socialisme français et le pouvoir*, p. 51; emphasis added.

28. Leslie Derfler, "Reformism and Jules Guesde," *International Review of Social History*, 12 (1968), 70.

29. *Le Socialiste*, 19 Feb. 1898, quoted in Perrot and Kriegel, *Socialisme français et le pouvoir*, p. 51.

30. 6 March 1892, quoted in Georges Rougeron, "Les Débuts de la presse ouvrière en Allier (1885-1900)," *Notre Bourbonnais*, 210 (1979), 234.

31. Ibid., pp. 236-237.

32. Claude Willard, *Le Mouvement socialiste en France, 1893-1905: Les Guesdistes* (Paris: Editions sociales, 1965), p. 303.

33. Ibid., p. 310.

34. Tony Judt, *Socialism in Provence, 1871-1914* (Cambridge: Cambridge University Press, 1979), p. 231.

35. Ibid., pp. 229-230.

36. *VP*, 11-12 April 1849.

37. Jolyon Howorth, "Vaillent, la République et le socialisme en 1900," *Bulletin de la société d'études jaurésiennes*, 50 (July-September 1973), 13.

38. Michel Winock, "Les Allemanistes," *Bulletin de la société d'études jaurésiennes*, 50 (1973), 20-26.

39. Yves Lequin, "Classe ouvrière et idéologie dans la région lyonnaise à la fin du XIXᵉ siècle," *Mouvement social*, 69 (October-Decmeber 1969), 16-17.

40. Gérard Delfau, "Socialisme et Marxisme en France au tournant du siècle (1880-1905)," *Nouvelle revue socialiste*, 8 (1975), 33; Perrot, "Les Guesdistes," p. 705.

41. Quoted in Bernard Moss, *French Labor Movement*, p. 116.

42. Willard, *Mouvement socialiste*, pp. 554-555.

43. Quoted in Perrot, "Les Guesdistes," p. 705.

44. Ibid., pp. 707-709.

45. Ibid., p. 709.

46. Ibid. See also Moss, *French Labor Movement*, pp. 85, 116.

BIBLIOGRAPHY

Primary Sources

Archives Nationales

AB^{xix} 680-683	Printed documents, pamphlets, brochures, etc.
BB¹⁸ 961-1515	General correspondence of the Criminal Division of the Ministry of Justice
1449	Colportage
1470a, b, c,	Surveillance of the press
1472	Secret societies
1474	Clubs and associations
1481	Cafés and cabarets
1488	The "Complot de Lyon"
1494	Surveillance of the press
BB³⁰ 333-424	Papers and reports of the Ministry of Justice
358-366	Letters from the procureurs généraux
370-388	Monthly reports from the procureurs généraux, Nov. 1849–Feb. 1852
391-397	Political affairs, Nov. 1850–Jan. 1852
398-402	Records of the Mixed Commissions on the insurrection of December 1851
C 944-969	Agricultural and Industrial Survey of 1848
946	Department of the Aude
954	Department of the Hérault
960	Department of the Nièvre
969	Department of the Yonne
F⁷ 2583-2595	Master registers of the Mixed Commissions
F¹⁴ 1070	Correspondence, Ministry of Public Works
F²⁰ 765	Impôts foncières

Archives of the Ministry of War (Vincennes)

F¹ 40	General correspondence
Justice Militaire	Dossiers of prisoners and suspects in the insurrection of December 1851
JM 195	Dossiers, Paris

JM 228   Interrogations of prisoners from the Aube
JM 250-59   Interrogations of prisoners from the Yonne

Archives of the Prefecture of Police (Paris)

AA 432   Surveillance of secret societies in Paris, 1849

Archives Départementales

Basses-Alpes (now called Alpes de Haute Provence)
    50VV article 7 Enquête religieuse, 1840-1841
    6V¹   Prefectoral correspondence, 1848-1850
Bouches-du-Rhône
    6M 344   Correspondence, prefect
    12U/2 (Aix)   Dossiers on *Le Peuple*
    14U/19 (Aix)   Dossiers on *Le Peuple*
    14U/53 (Aix)   Secret societies, Béziers
Côte-d'Or
    IIV 65*   Enquête religieuse, 1838
Drôme
    M 1297, 1346   Police and prefectoral reports
    12U 34   Tribunal of Montelimar
Hérault
    34M 132   Correspondence of police officials
    34M 144-160   Interrogations of suspects tried by the Military
                    Commissions at Béziers
Nièvre
    Series U   Secret societies, arrondissement of Cosne
Var
    4M 19-21   Interrogations of suspects in insurrectionary
                    movement of December 1851
Yonne
    V Mⁱⁱ 7   Correspondence of police officials, 1832
    VI Mⁱ2 16   Correspondence of police officials, 1833
    III M¹ 125-145 Official correspondence of prefects, subprefects,
                    mayors, and police chiefs
    69T¹ 27   Press
    71T¹   Surveillance of colportage, 1815-1892

Bibliothèque Nationale

    LB 55 2202 Prospectus of La Propagande démocratique et sociale
                européenne, Paris, 1848
    LB 54 1461 "La Solidarité républicaine. Association pour le
                développement des droits et des intérêts de la
                démocratie," Paris, 1848

LB 55 2803 Haute Cour de Versailles. Trial of members of La
             Solidarité républicaine
Y^e 7185   Political songs of the Second Republic
Cabinet des Estampes. Collection de Vinck

Diocesan Archives

Archives, Evêché de Digne (Alpes de Haute Provence)
    5E 2
Archives, Evêché de Valence (Drôme)
    Papers of Monseigneur Chatrousse

Newspapers

Paris
    L'Atelier
    La Démocratie pacifique
    La Feuille du village
    Gazette des tribunaux
    Le Peuple
    La Réforme
    La République
    La Révolution démocratique et sociale

Departments
    Le Peuple (Nevers)
    Le Peuple souverain (Auxerre)
    Le Républicain de Lyon
    Le Républicain du Gard
    Le Républicain du Nord
    La République du peuple (Colmar)
    Le Suffrage universel (Montpellier)
    L'Union républicaine
    La Voix du peuple (Marseille)

Statistics

Bulletin de statistique et législation comparés
    Vol. 12 (1882), pp. 321-325: La Répartition des cotes foncières.
    Vol. 13 (1883), pp. 576-609: La Nouvelle évaluation du revenu
    foncier des propriétés non bâties.
*Statistique de la France. Territoire et population: Recensement de
1851.* Paris: 1855.

Statistique de la France. Resultats généraux de l'enquête décennale, 1862. Strasbourg: 1870.

Statistique de la France: Recensement professionnel de 1866. Paris: 1872.

Memoirs and Works by Contemporaries

Benoît, Joseph. *Confessions d'un prolétaire*. Paris: Maspero, 1968.

Blanc, Louis. *Le Catéchisme des socialistes*. Paris: 1849.

———. *Histoire de dix ans*. Paris: 1844.

Considérant, Victor. *Théorie du droit de propriété et du droit au travail*. Paris: 1839.

Corbon, A. *Le Secret du peuple de Paris*. Paris: 1865.

Delafond, O. *Progrès agricole et amélioration du gros bétail de la Nièvre*. Paris: 1849.

Durand, Claude. *La Voix du peuple ou les républicaines de 1848. Recueil de chants démocratiques et sociaux*. Paris: 1848-1849.

Esquiros, Alphonse. *Le Droit au travail, de son organisation par la réforme des institutions de crédit*. Blois: 1849.

Flaubert, Gustave. *Education sentimentale*. Paris: Livre de Poche, 1972.

Guépin, Dr. A. *Le Socialisme expliqué aux enfants du peuple*. Paris: 1851.

Joigneaux, Pierre. "Letters d'un paysan aux cultivateurs." Paris: 1849.

Lammenais, F. de. *Livre du peuple*. Paris: 1838.

———. *Paroles d'un croyant*. Paris: Edition populaire, 1835.

Leroux, Pierre. *Démocratie et Christianisme*. Paris: 1848.

———. *Du Christianisme et de son origine démocratique*. Paris: 1848.

Marx, Karl. *The Eighteenth Brumaire of Louis Bonaparte*. New York: International Publishers, 1972.

Malon, Benoît. "Fragment de mémoires." *Revue socialiste*, 45 (January-July 1907), 318-319.

Mortillet, Gabriel. "Bases de la politique." Paris: 1849.

———. "La Propagande, c'est la Révolution." Paris: 1848.

Nadaud, Martin. *Mémoires de Léonard*. Edited by M. Agulhon. Paris: Hachette, 1976.

Nisard, Charles, "Essai sur le colportage de librairie." *Journal de la société de la morale chrétienne*, 5 (1855).

Perdiguier, Agricol. *Mémoires d'un compagnon*. Paris: Maspero, 1977.

Pottier, Eugène. *Oeuvres complètes*. Edited by Pierre Brochon. Paris: Maspero, 1966.

Pyat, Félix. "Toast aux paysans." Paris: 1849.

Renouvier, Charles. *Manuel républicain de l'homme et du citoyen.* Paris: 1848.

Saint-Simon, Henri de. *Le Nouveau Christianisme.* Edited by H. Desroche. Paris: Editions du Seuil, 1969.

Sue, Eugène, et al. *Le Républicain des campagnes.* Paris: 1851.

Ténot, Eugène. *La Province en décembre 1851. Etude historique sur le coup d'état.* Paris: 1868.

————. *Le Suffrage universel et les paysans.* Paris: 1865.

Zola, Emile. *La Fortune des Rougon.* Paris: Garnier-Flammarion, 1969.

SECONDARY SOURCES

Agulhon, Maurice. "L'Agriculture et la société rurale du Var dans la première moitié du XIXᵉ siècle." In *Etudes d'histoire Provençale.* Paris: Oprhrys, 1971.

————. "La Diffusion d'un journal montagnard. *Le Démocrate du Var* sous la Deuxième République." *Provence historique,* 10 (1960), 11-27.

————. *1848 ou l'apprentissage de la république, 1848-1852.* Nouvelle histoire de la France contemporaine, 8. Paris: Editions du Seuil, 1973.

————, et al. *Histoire de la France rurale.* Vol. 3. Paris: Editions du Seuil, 1976.

————. "Il y a cent ans, la victoire de la gauche." *L'Histoire,* 2 (June 1978).

————. *Marianne au combat.* Paris: Flammarion, 1979.

————. *Pénitents et francs-maçons de l'ancienne Provence.* Paris: Fayard, 1968.

————. "Le Problème de la culture populaire en France autour de 1848." *Romantisme,* 9 (1975), 50-64.

————. *Les Quarante-huitards.* Collection Archives. Paris: Editions Gallimard/Juillard, 1975.

————. *La République au village.* Paris: Plon, 1970.

————. "La Résistance au coup d'état en Provence. Esquisse d'historiographie." *Revue d'histoire moderne et contemporaine,* 21 (1974), 18-26.

————. *Une Ville ouvrière au temps du socialisme utopique. Toulon de 1815 à 1851.* Paris: Mouton, 1970.

Amann, Peter. "The Changing Outlines of 1848." *American Historical Review,* 68 (1963), 938-953.

Amann, Peter. *Revolution and Mass Democracy: The Paris Club Movement in 1848*. Princeton: Princeton University Press, 1975.

Ansart, Pierre. *La Naissance de l'anarchisme*. Paris: Presses Universitaires de France, 1970.

Armengaud, André. *Les Populations de l'Est aquitain au début de l'époque contemporaine (vers 1848-vers 1871)*. Paris: Mouton, 1961.

Atlas historique de la France contemporaine, 1800-1965. Collection U. Série "Histoire contemporaine." Paris: A. Colin, 1966.

Baker, Robert P. "Socialism in the Nord, 1880-1914." *International Review of Social History*, 12 (1967), 357-389.

Balent, André. "La Fédération socialiste des Pyrénées Orientales de juillet 1895 à mai 1898." *Massana*, 28 (1975), 356-369.

————. "La Fondation de la fédération socialiste des Pyrénées Orientales (1895)." *Massana*, 25 (1975), 62-85.

Barral, P. *Le Département de l'Isère sous la Troisième République*. Paris: A. Colin, 1962.

Bastid, Paul. *Doctrines et institutions politiques de la Seconde République*. 2 vols. Paris: Hachette, 1945.

Bée, Michel. "La Révolte des confréries de charité de l'Eure en 1842-1843." *Annales de Normandie*, 24, no. 1 (1974), 89-115.

Bellanger, C., et al. *Histoire de la presse française*. Vol. 2. Paris: Presses Universitaires de France, 1969.

Bezucha, Robert J. *The Lyon Uprising of 1834. Social and Political Conflict in the Early July Monarchy*. Cambridge, Mass.: Harvard University Press, 1974.

————. "Masks of Revolution: A Study of Popular Culture during the Second Republic." In Roger Price, ed., *Revolution and Reaction: 1848 and the Second French Republic*, pp. 236-253. New York: Barnes and Noble, 1975.

Bollème, Geneviève. *Les Almanachs populaires aux XVIIe et XVIIIe siècles*. Paris: Mouton, 1971.

————. *La Bibliothèque Bleue. Littérature populaire en France du XVIIe au XIXe siècle*. Collection Archives. Paris: Juilliard, 1971.

————. "Littérature populaire et littérature de colportage au XVIIIe siècle." In François Furet, ed., *Livre et société*, pp. 61-92. Paris: Mouton, 1965.

Bouillon, Jacques. "Les Démocrates-socialistes aux élections de 1849." *Revue française de sciences politiques*, 6 (1956), 71-95.

Bowman, Frank Paul. *Le Christ romantique*. Geneva: Droz, 1973.

Braudel, Fernand, and Labrousse, Ernest, eds. *Histoire économique et sociale de la France.* 3 vols. Paris: Presses Universitaires de France, 1968-1976.

Brochon, Pierre. *La Chanson française,* vol. 2: *Le Pamphlet du pauvre (1834-1851).* Paris: Editions sociales, 1957.

————. *Le Livre du colportage.* Paris: Gründ, 1954.

Burke, Peter. *Popular Culture in Early Modern Europe.* New York: Harper and Row, 1978.

Calman, Alvin. *Ledru-Rollin and the Second French Repulbic.* New York: Columbia University Press, 1922.

Chaunu, Pierre. "Eugène Sue, Témoin de son temps." *Annales: Economies, Sociétés, Civilisations,* 3 (1948), 302-303.

Chevalier, Louis. "Les Fondements économiques et sociaux de l'histoire politique de la région parisienne, 1848-1851." Thèse de doctorat, Université de Paris, 1950.

Cholvy, Gérard. "Biterrois et Narbonnais. Mutations économiques et évolution des mentalités à l'époque contemporaine." In Cholvy, ed., *Economie et société en Languedoc-Roussillon de 1789 à nos jours,* pp. 415-444. Montpellier: Faculté des lettres et sciences humaines de l'Université de Montpellier, 1978.

————. "Le Catholicisme populaire en France au 19e siècle." In B. Plongeron and R. Pannet, eds., *Le Christianisme populaire.* Paris: Centurion, 1976.

————. "Expressions et évolution du sentiment religieux populaire dans la France du XIXe siècle au temps de la Restauration Catholique (1801-60)." In *Actes du 99e Congrès national des sociétés savantes,* pp. 289-320. Paris: Bibliothèque Nationale, 1976.

————. "Réalités de la religion populaire dans la France contemporaine." In Bernard Plongeron, ed., *La Religion populaire dans l'occident chrétien.* Paris: Bibliothèque Beauchesne, 1976.

————. "Un Saint populaire? La Lente renaissance du culte de Saint-Roch dans le diocèse de Montpellier durant la première moitié du XIXe siècle." In Cholvy, ed., *Béziers et le Biterrois.* Montpellier: Faculté des lettres de Montpellier, 1971.

Clapham, J. H. *The Economic Development of France and Germany, 1815-1914.* Cambridge: Cambridge University Press, 1936.

Clark, Timothy J. *Image of the People.* Greenwich, Conn.: New York Graphic Society Ltd., 1973.

Collins, E.J.T. "Labor Supply and Demand in European Agriculture, 1800-1880." In E. L. Jones and J. J. Woolf, eds., *Agrarian Change and Economic Development.* London: Methuen, 1969.

Collins, Irene. *The Government and the Newspaper Press in France, 1814-1881.* London: Oxford University Press, 1959.

Corbin, Alain. *Archaïsme et modernité en Limousin au XIXᵉ siècle 1845-1880.* 2 vols. Paris: Rivière, 1975.

Crouzet, François. "Encore la croissance économique française au XIXᵉ siècle." *Revue du Nord,* 62 (1972), 271-288.

————. "French Economic Growth in the Nineteenth Century Reconsidered." *History,* 59 (1974), 167-179.

Cuvillier, Armand. *Hommes et idéologies de 1840.* Paris: M. Rivière 1956.

————. "L'Idéologie de 1848." *Revue philosophique,* 138 (October-December 1848), 409-426.

————. *Un Journal d'ouvriers: "L'Atelier," 1840-1850.* Paris: Editions ouvrières, 1954.

Dagnan, J. *Le Gers sous la Seconde République.* Auch: Imprimerie Brevetée, 1928.

Darmon, J. J. *Le Colportage de librairie en France sous le Second Empire.* Paris: Plon, 1972.

Delfau, Gerard. "Socialisme et Marxisme en France au tournant du siècle (1880-1905)." *Nouvelle revue socialiste,* 8 (1975), 31-37.

Delumeau, Jean. "Christianisation et déchristianisation, XVᵉ-XVIIIᵉ siècles." In *Etudes européennes, Mélanges offerts à Victor L. Tapié,* pp. 53-59. Paris: Publications de la Sorbonne, 1973.

————. "Au sujet de la déchristianisation." *Revue d'histoire moderne et contemporaine,* 22 (January-March 1975), 111-131.

De Luna, Frederick A. *The French Republic Under Cavaignac 1848.* Princeton: Princeton University Press, 1969.

Derruau-Bonniol, Simone. "Le Socialisme dans l'Allier de 1848 à 1914." *Cahiers d'histoire,* 2 (1957), 115-161.

Dessal, Marcel. "Le Complot de Lyon et la résistance au coup d'état dans les départements du Sud-Est." *1848,* no. 189 (1951), 83-96.

————. *Un Révolutionnaire jacobin: Charles Delescluze, 1809-1871.* Paris: M. Rivière, 1952.

Dictionnaire politique et parlementaire, Rédigé par une réunion de députés, de publicistes et de journalistes. Paris: 1842.

Dommanget, Maurice. *Eugène Pottier.* Paris: Etudes et documentation internationales, 1971.

Droulers, Paul. "Catholicisme et mouvement ouvrier au 19ᵉ siècle." In François Bédarida and Jean Maitron, eds., *Christianisme et le monde ouvrier.* Paris: Editions ouvrières, 1975.

Droz, J. "Religious Aspects of the Revolutions of 1848 in Europe." In E. M. Acomb and M. Brown, eds., *French Society and Culture Since the Old Regime.* New York: Holt, Rinehart and Winston, 1966.

Dubois, Augustin. *Les Anciens livres de colportage en Sologne*. Romorantin: Girard, 1938.

Dubois, Jean. *Le Vocabulaire politique et sociale en France de 1869 à 1872*. Paris: Librairie Larousse, 1962.

Dupeux, Georges. *Aspects de l'histoire sociale et politique du Loir-et-Cher, 1848-1914*. Paris: Mouton, 1962.

————. *La Société française, 1789-1970*. Paris: A. Colin, 1964.

Duroselle, J. B. *Les Débuts du catholicisme social en France, 1822-1870*. Paris: Presses Universitaires de France, 1951.

Duveau, George. "Les Idéologies de 1848." In Charles Moulin, ed., *Le Livre du Centenaire*. Paris: Editions atlas, 1948.

————. "L'Ouvrier de Quarante-huit." *Revue Socialiste*, 17 (January-February 1948), 191-200.

————. "Protestantisme et prolétariat en France au milieu du XIXᵉ siècle." *Revue d'histoire et de philosophie religieuses*, 31 (1951), 417-428.

Evans, D. O. *Social Romanticism in France*. Oxford: Clarendon Press, 1951.

Fabre, Daniel, and Lacroix, Jacques. *La Vie quotidienne des paysans du Languedoc au XIXᵉ siècle*. Paris: Hachette, 1973.

Gaillard, Jeanne. "La Question du crédit et les almanachs autour de 1850." *Etudes de la Bibliothèque de la Révolution de 1848*, 16 (1954), 79-87.

————. *Paris, la Ville, 1852-1870*. Lille-Paris: Honoré Champion, 1976.

Gimel, M. *La Division de la propriété*. Nancy: 1883.

————. "La Répartition de la propriété foncière dans le département de l'Yonne." *Annuaire historique de l'Yonne* (1865), pp. 1-122.

Ginzburg, Carlo. *The Cheese and the Worms*. New York: Penguin Books, 1982.

Gossez, Rémi. "Presse parisienne à destination des ouvriers, 1848-1851." In Jacques Godechot, ed., *La Presse ouvrière 1819-1850*, pp. 123-188. Société d'histoire de la Révolution de 1848. Bures-sur-Yvette: Essons, 1966.

————. "La Résistance à l'impôt: Les Quarante-cinq centimes." *Etudes, Bibliothèque de la Révolution de 1848*, 15 (1953), 89-131.

Goujon, Pierre. "Le Vignoble du Saône-et-Loire au XIXᵉ siècle (1815-1870)." Doctorat du 3ᵉ Cycle, Université de Lyon, 1968.

Grantham, George W. "Scale and Organization in French Farming, 1840-1880." In William N. Parker and Eric L. Jones., eds., *European Peasants and their Markets*, pp. 293-326. Princeton: Princeton University Press, 1975.

Guillaume, P. "La Situation économique et sociale du département de la Loire d'après l'enquête sur le travail . . . du mai 1848." *Congrès national des sociétés savantes, actes, section d'histoire*, 86 (1961), 429-450.

Guillaumin, Emile, *La Vie d'un simple*. Paris: Editions Stock, 1943.

Guise, René. "Le Roman-feuilleton et la vulgarisation des idées politiques et sociales sous la Monarchie de Juillet." In *Romantisme et politique*, pp. 317-327. Paris: A. Colin, 1969.

Guyon, Léon. *Un Médecin de campagne d'autrefois. Notes et souvenirs, 1795-1865*. Le Mans: A. de Saint Denis, 1902.

Hilaire, Yves-Marie. *Une Chrétienté au XIXe siècle? La Vie religieuse des populations du diocèse d'Arras 1840-1914*. Villeneuve-d'Ascq: Université de Lille III, 1977.

———. "La Pratique religieuse en France de 1815 à 1878." *L'Information historique*, 24, no. 2 (1963), 57-69.

———. "Notes sur la religion populaire au XIXe siècle." In *La Religion populaire*, pp. 193-198. Paris: Editions du Centre national de la recherche scientifique, 1979.

Howorth, Jolyon. "Vaillant, la République et le socialisme en 1900." *Bulletin de la société d'études jaurésiennes*, 50 (July-September 1973), 11-20.

Huard, Raymond. "La Défense du suffrage universel sous la Seconde République." *Annales du Midi*, 83 (1971), 331-336.

———. "Montagne rouge et montagne blanche en Languedoc-Roussillon sous la Seconde République." In *Droite et gauche de 1789 à nos jours*, pp. 139-160. Montpellier: Centre d'histoire contemporaine du Languedoc, 1975.

———. "La Pré-histoire des partis. Le Parti républicain et l'opinion républicaine dans le Gard, 1848-1881." Thèse de Doctorat, Université de Paris IV, 1977.

Isambert, F. A. *Christianisme et classe ouvrière*. Paris: Casterman, 1961.

Jardin, A., and Tudesq, A. J. *La France des notables*. Nouvelle histoire de la France contemporaine, vols. 6, 7. Paris: Editions du Seuil, 1973.

Jaurès, Jean. *La Question religieuse et le socialisme*. Edited by Michel Launay. Paris: Editions de Minuit, 1959.

Johnson, Christopher H. "Economic Change and Artisan Discontent: The Tailors' History, 1800-1848." In Price, ed., *Revolution and Reaction*, pp. 87-114.

———. "Some Recent French Village Studies." *Peasant Studies Newsletter*, (2 October 1973), 9-16.

————. *Utopian Communism in France: Cabet and the Icarians, 1839-1851*. Ithaca: Cornell University Press, 1974.

Judt, Tony. *Socialism in Provence, 1871-1914*. Cambridge: Cambridge University Press, 1979.

Kayser, Jacques. *Les Grandes batailles du radicalisme*. Paris: Rivière, 1962.

Labrousse, Ernest, ed. Aspects de la crise et de la dépression de l'économie française au milieu du XIXe siècle, 1846-1851. Bibliothèque de la Révolution de 1848, no 19. La-Roche-sur-Yon: Imprimerie centrale de l'ouest, 1956.

Langer, William L. *Political and Social Upheaval*. New York: Harper and Row, 1969.

Latreille, André, and Rémond, René. *Historie du catholicisme français*. Vol. 3. Paris: Editions spes 1962.

Le Bras, Gabriel. "Déchristianisation: Mot fallacieux." *Social Compas*, 10 (1963), 445-452.

————. *Etudes de sociologie religieuse*. 2 vols. Paris: Presses Universitaires de France, 1955-1956.

Le Meur, M.-V. "Le Culte des saints dans le diocèse de Blois aux environs de 1840." *Cahiers de l'Institut d'histoire de la presse et de l'opinion*, 2 (1974), 8-23.

Lequin, Yves. "Classe ouvrière et idéologie dans la région lyonnaise à la fin du XIXe siècle." *Mouvement social*, 69 (October-December 1969), 3-20.

Leuilliot, Paul. "En Marge d'une thèse. La Seconde République et le socialisme rural." *Annales: Economies, Sociétés, Civilisations*, 19 (September-October 1964), 973-978.

————. *La Presse et l'histoire: Notes sur la presse en Alsace*. Paris: Sirey, 1965.

Levêque, Pierre. "La Bourgogne, 1830-1851." Doctorat d'Etat, Université de Paris, IV, 1977.

Lévy, Claude. "Un Journal 'rouge' sous la Seconde République. *L'Union républicaine*." *Annales de Bourgogne*, 31 (July-September 1951), 145-159.

————. "Notes sur les fondements sociaux de l'insurrection du décembre 1851 en province." *Information historique*, 16 (1954), 142-145.

Lévy-Leboyer, Maurice. "La Croissance économique en France au XIXe siècle." *Annales: Economies, Sociétés, Civilisations*, 23 (December 1968), 788-807.

————. "Le Processus d'industrialisation. Le cas de l'Angleterre et de la France." *Revue historique*, 239 (1968), 281-298.

Loubère, Leo. "The Emergence of the Extreme Left in Lower Languedoc, 1848-1851: Social and Economic Factors in Politics." *American Historical Review*, 73 (1968), 1019-1051.

———. *Louis Blanc: His Life and His Contribution to the Rise of French Jacobin Socialism*. Evanston: Northwestern University Press, 1961.

Luneau, René. "Monde rural et christianisation." *Archives des sciences sociales des religions*, 43, no 1. (1977), 39-52.

McPhee, Peter. "The Crisis of Radical Republicanism." *Historical Studies*, 16 (April 1974-October 1975), 71-88.

———. "Popular Culture, Symbolism and Rural Radicalism in Nineteenth-Century France." *Journal of Peasant Studies*, 6 (1979), 238-253.

Mcgraw, Roger. "Pierre Joigneaux and Socialist Propaganda in the French Countryside, 1849-1851." *French Historical Studies*, 10 (Fall 1978), 599-640.

Maitron, J., et al. *Dictionnaire biographique du mouvement ouvrier français*. 3 vols. Paris: Editions ouvrières, 1964-1966.

Malo, H. *Thiers*. Paris: Payot, 1922.

Marcilhacy, Christianne. "Les Caractères de la crise sociale et politique de 1846 à 1852 das le département du Loiret." *Revue d'histoire moderne et contemporaine* 6 (1959), 5-59.

———. *Le diocèse d'Orléans au milieu du XIXe siècle*. Paris: Sirey, 1964.

Margadant, Ted. W. *French Peasants in Revolt: The Insurrection of 1851*. Princeton: Princeton University Press, 1979.

———. "Peasant Protest in the Second Republic." *Journal of Interdisciplinary History*, 5, no. 1 (Summer 1974), 119-130.

Markovitch, T. J. "L'Industrie française de 1789 à 1964. Conclusions générales." *Cahiers de l'Institut de science économique appliqué*, series AF, no. 7 (November 1966).

———. "Le Revenu industriel et artisanal sous la Monarchie de Juillet et le Second Empire." *Economies et sociétés*, no. 4 (April 1967).

———. "La Révolution industrielle: Le cas de France." *Revue d'histoire économique et sociale*, 52 (1974), 115-125.

Martinet, Jean-Claude. *Clamecy et ses flotteurs de la Monarchie de Juillet à l'insurrection des "Mariannes," 1830-1851*. La Charite-sur-Loire: Editions Delayance, 1975.

Merriman, John M. *The Agony of the Republic*. New Haven: Yale University Press, 1978.

Moodie, Thomas. "The Reorientation of French Socialism in 1888-90." *International Review of Social History*, 12 (1967), 357-389.

Moss, Bernard. *The Origins of the French Labor Movement.* Berkeley: University of California Press, 1976.

――――. "Parisian Producers Associations: The Socialism of Skilled Workers." In Price, ed., *Revolution and Reaction,* pp. 73-86.

Newell, William H. "The Agricultural Revolution in Nineteenth-Century France." *Journal of Economic History,* 33 (December 1973), 697-731.

――――. "The Agricultural Revolution in France, an Exchange." *Journal of Economic History,* 36 (1976), 436-438.

Newman, Edgar Leon. "Sounds in the Desert: The Socialist Worker-Poets of the Bourgeois Monarchy, 1836-1848." In *Proceedings of the Third Annual Meeting of the Western Society for French History,* pp. 269-299. Austin, Tex., 1976.

O'Brian, Patrick, and Keyder, Caglar. *Economic Growth in Britain and France, 1780-1914.* London: George Allen and Unwin, 1978.

Perreux, Gabriel. *La Propagande républicaine au début de la Monarchie de Juillet.* Paris: Hachette, 1930.

Perrot, Michelle. "Les Guesdistes. Controverse sur l'introduction du Marxisme en France." *Annales: Economies, Sociétés, Civilisations,* 22 (May-June 1967), 701-710.

――――, and Kriegel, Annie. *Le socialisme français et le pouvoir.* Paris: EDI, 1966.

Pichois, Claude. "Les Cabinets de lecture à Paris durant la première moitié du XIXe siècle." *Annales: Economies, Sociétés, Civilisations,* 14 (1959), 521-534.

Pierrard, Pierre. *1848 . . . les pauvres, l'évangile et la révolution.* Paris: Desclée, 1977.

Pouthas, Charles. *La Population française pendant la première moitié du XIXe siècle.* Paris: Presses Universitaires de France, 1956.

Price, Roger. *The French Second Republic: A Social History.* London: Batsford, 1972.

――――. "The Onset of Labor Shortage in Nineteenth-Century French Agriculture." *Economic History Review,* ser. 2, 38 (1975), 260-279.

――――, ed. *Revolution and Reaction: 1848 and the Second French Republic.* New York: Barnes and Noble, 1975.

Religions et traditions populaires. Paris: Musée des arts et traditions populaires, 1979.

Rémi. "La Marianne dans les campagnes." *Almanach administrative historique et statistique de l'Yonne* (1881), pp. 16-48.

Renard, Georges. "Cabet et les précurseurs de la Révolution de 1848." *La Révolution de 1848,* 28 (1931), 181-192.

Renard, Georges. "L'Esprit de 1848." *Revue politique et parlementaire*, 63 (1910), 563-578.

──────. *La République de 1848.* Vol. 9 of *Histoire socialiste*, ed. Jean Jaurès. Paris: Rouff, 1906.

Rigaudias-Weiss, H. *Les Enquêtes ouvrières en France entre 1830 et 1848.* Paris: Presses Universitaires de France, 1936.

Rougeron, Georges. "Les Débuts de la presse ouvrière en Allier (1885-1900)." *Notre Bourbonnais*, 210 (1979), 232-242.

Schnerb, R. *Ledru-Rollin.* Paris: Presses Universitaires de France, 1948.

Scott, Joan. *The Glassworkers of Carmaux.* Cambridge, Mass.: Harvard University Press, 1974.

Sewell, William H., Jr. "La Classe ouvrière de Marseille sous la Seconde République: Structure sociale et comportement politique." *Le Mouvement social*, 76 (July-September, 1971), 27-65.

──────. "Property, Labor, and the Emergence of Socialism in France, 1789-1848." In John Merriman, ed., *Consciousness and Class Experience in Nineteenth-Century Europe.* New York: Holmes and Meier, 1980.

──────. "The Structure of the Working Class of Marseille in the Middle of the Nineteenth Century." Ph.D. diss., University of California, Berkely, 1971.

──────. "Social Change and the Rise of Working-Class Politics in Nineteenth-Century Marseille." *Past & Present*, 65 (November 1974), 75-109.

──────. *Work and Revolution in France. The Language of Labor from the Old Regime to 1848.* Cambridge: Cambridge University Press, 1980.

Spitzer, A. *Old Hatreds and New Hopes: The French Carbonari against the French Restoration.* Cambridge, Mass.: Harvard University Press, 1971.

Soboul, Albert. *Paysans, sans-culottes et Jacobins.* Paris: Librairie Clavreuil, 1966.

Tchernoff, I. *Associations et sociétés secrètes sous la IIe République.* Paris: Alcan, 1905.

──────. *Le Parti républicain sous la Monarchie de Juillet.* Paris: Pedone, 1901.

──────. *Le Parti républicain au coup d'état et sous le Second Empire.* Paris: Pedone, 1906.

Thuillier, André. *Economie et société nivernaises au début du XIXe siècle.* Paris: Mouton, 1974.

Thuillier, Guy. *Aspects de l'économie nivernaise au XIXe siècle.* Paris: A. Colin, 1966.

Tipps, Dean C. "Modernization and the Comparative Study of Societies." *Comparative Studies in Society and History*, 15 (1973), 199-229.

Tilly, Charles. "How Protest Modernized in France, 1845-1855." In W. Aydelotte, ed., *The Dimensions of Quantitative Research in History*, pp. 192-255. Princeton: Princeton University Press, 1972.

Tilly, Charles, and Lees, Lynn. "The People of June." In Price, ed., *Revolution and Reaction*.

Tixier, O. "Les Procès politiques dans l'Indre-et-Loire." *1848*, 1 (1904), 194-200.

Tournier, Maurice. "Le Vocabulaire des pétitions ouvrières de 1848." In Régine Robin, ed., *Histoire et linguistique*, pp. 261-303. Paris: A. Colin, 1974.

Toutain, J. "La Population de la France, 1700 à 1959." *Cahiers de l'Institut de science économique appliqué*, series AF, no. 3 (January 1963).

———. *La Production de l'agriculture française, 1700-1958*. Vols. 1-2 of *Histoire quantitative de la France*. Paris: L'Institut de science économique appliqué, 1961.

Tudesq, André-Jean. *L'Election présidentielle de Louis-Napoléon Bonaparte*. Paris: A. Colin, 1965.

———. *Les Grands notables en France (1840-1849)*. 2 vols. Paris: Presses Universitaires de France, 1964.

Van Gennep, A. *Manuel de folklore français contemporain*. Paris: Picard, 1947.

Vigier, Philippe. "Elections municipales et prise de conscience politique sous la Monarchie de Juillet." In C.-H. Pouthas, ed., *La France au XIXᵉ siècle*. Paris: Université de Paris, Sorbonne, 1973.

———. *Essai sur la répartition de la propriété foncière dans la région alpine*. Paris: S.E.V.P.E.N., 1963.

———. "Le Paysan dans *Le Peuple* de Michelet." In *Michelet et "Le Peuple*," pp. 14-17. Nanterre: Université de Nanterre, 1975.

———. "Un Quart de siècle de recherches historiques sur la Province." *Annales historiques de la Révolution Française*, 47 (1975), 622-645.

———. *La Seconde République*. Collection "Que sais-je?" Paris: Presses Universitaires de France, 1967.

———. *La Seconde République dans la région alpine*. 2 vols. Paris: Presses Universitaires de France, 1963.

Vovelle, Michel. *Piété baroque et déchristianisation en Provence au XVIIIᵉ siècle*. Paris: Editions du Seuil, 1973.

Weill, Georges. *Histoire du parti républicain en France, 1814-1870.* Paris: Alcan, 1928.

————. "Les Journaux ouvriers à Paris (1830-1870)." *Revue d'histoire moderne et contemporaine,* 9 (October 1907-February 1908), 89-103.

Weber, Eugen. Peasants into Frenchmen: The Modernization of Rural France, 1870-1914. Stanford: Stanford University Press, 1976.

Willard, Claude. *Le Mouvement socialiste en France, 1893-1905. Les Guesdistes.* Paris: Editions sociales, 1965.

Winock, Michel. "Les Allemanistes." *Bulletin de la société d'études jaurésiennes,* 50 (1973), 20-26.

Zévaès, Alexandre. "La Propagande socialiste dans la campagne en 1848." *1848,* 31 (1934-1935), 75-94.

INDEX

Library of Congress Cataloging in Publication Data

Berenson, Edward, 1949-
Populist religion and left-wing politics in France, 1830-1852.
Bibliography: p.   Includes index.
1. France—Politics and government—1830-1848.
2. France—Politics and government—1848-1852.
3. France—Church history—19th century.
4. Church and state—France—History—19th century.
5. Socialism—France—History—19th century. I. Title.
DC266.5.B47 1984   944.07   83-42548
ISBN 0-691-05396-0